*Everyone has Superman or Wonder Woman lurking
within; those who can tap into that power will
leap tall barriers and think
faster than a speeding
bullet*

The Superman Syndrome—The Magic of Myth in The Pursuit of Power

THE SUPERMAN SYNDROME—THE MAGIC OF MYTH IN THE PURSUIT OF POWER

The Positive Mental Moxie of Myth for Personal Growth

Gene N. Landrum, Ph.D.

iUniverse, Inc.

New York Lincoln Shanghai

The Superman Syndrome—The Magic of Myth in The Pursuit of Power
The Positive Mental Moxie of Myth for Personal Growth

iUniverse books may be ordered through booksellers or by contacting:

iUniverse
2021 Pine Lake Road, Suite 100
Lincoln, NE 68512
www.iuniverse.com
1-800-Authors (1-800-288-4677)

ISBN-13: 978-0-595-34697-4 (pbk)
ISBN-13: 978-0-595-79442-3 (ebk)
ISBN-10: 0-595-34697-9 (pbk)
ISBN-10: 0-595-79442-4 (ebk)

Printed in the United States of America

For

The World's Wannabes

Who

Were programmed to Cant-Be

but

Have opted for the path of Can-Be

By adopting a myth to emulate

Tattoo a Superman image on your psyche and pretend you can fly through walls and sometimes you just might!

Contents

▼

List of Illustrations

List of Tables

INTRODUCTION
MYTH — THE PANACEA OF POWER

▼

What Makes Us, Breaks Us—Making Fantasy the Fuel to the Top

Tattoo an S on your psyche to become empowered!

"All of our images are masks and each of us is a mythological representation of our inner truth. Our jobs are merely symbols of a larger mythological meaning in our lives"
Joseph Campbell to Bill Moyer, *The Power of Myth*

Supermen are those individuals who have been transformed. They have experienced a metamorphosis from underdog into top dog and the transformation is more metaphysical than physical. Such individuals are able to emulate a hero to remake themselves into a greater being. Mythical-hero-mentoring takes them beyond mortal limitations. They are able to let go of the real to enter a more surreal world. The trek takes them from normal to supernormal, from average to special. Few people are willing or capable of such a transformation. And that is why so few people become rich and powerful or alter paradigms.

This work is about those unique and intrepid souls who were so inclined. Such a transition took place when Sophie Vonholt-Zerbgst, a German teenager with uterine urges, used her iron will to become Catherine the Great. Another epiphany was the transformation of Russian defector Alissa Rosenbaum. Allisa made herself into American Ayn Rand to write the great philosophic epic novel *Atlas Shrugged* that created a whole new philosophy known as Objectivism. In a different way, but equally as effective, Buckminster Fuller walked to Lake Michigan to end it all. And out of his agony came a revelation: it wasn't externalities but internal thinking that caused his traumas. And out of those ashes came a Renaissance inventor and visionary. These intrepid warriors stepped into a metaphorical phone booth and emerged as a greater force than when they entered. The lesson here is that one can't hang with the beagles and expect to fly with the eagles. Those who can don the Spider-Man persona as Peter Parker and leave the vagaries of mediocrity in their wake are special. Don that S or lighting bolt on your psyche and life's roadblocks are minimized but more importantly the limits to the top are mitigated as well.

The bold dude who believes he can leap tall buildings and run faster than a speeding bullet has a better chance of becoming a man of steel than others. He enters a mythical world of the surreal that supercedes the real. Imagination is his license to superstardom. Tattoo "Superman" on your psyche and the world is far easier to conquer whatever your business or career path. And that trip to the top is far more fun. Sounds far out but fantasy was the fuel used by many of the world's visionaries to conquer their inner fears. That big red S on their imaginative chest transformed them from also-rans into special beings. Is such a trip non-traditional? Sure is! Is it counter to what we have learned in school? Absolutely! But read on to find the secret of how others used hero-mentoring to empower themselves. How they refused to buy into life's no's.

Joseph Campbell offered sage insight into what makes us tick when he told Bill Moyer, "Myths are models for understanding your life. All myths create heroes out of those who heed them." He implored everyone to adopt a myth to slay the inhibiting dragons that have been conditioned in each of us. For the average person to follow Campbell's profound advice is difficult. Why? They have been taught to conform to tradition. To not rock boats and to draw within the lines. That is antithetic to greatness. That is the road to mediocrity. Well-meaning parents, teachers, and bosses insist on drawing within the lines and following convention. Whose convention? Theirs! They want everyone to see the world through their filter but their filter is traditional and average. The eminent of the world are willing to be ridiculed for being different and board the train known as Possibility. That road is not popular but leads to super success. So leave Conventional City and climb aboard the train to Possibility where Superman and Wonder Woman live. Innovative geniuses live in magic land and love the magical land of fantasy.

Fantasies permit imaginative dreams to be fulfilled. That is what this book is about. The message, often stated in metaphor, is to imprint Superman on your soul and ride him to your personal Utopia. Adopt a fantasy hero or superstar and wrap yourself in his cape and fly ride that horse to your dream. Fantasies are a means of offsetting those cynics who don't get you or prefer to see you fail. They destroy any chance at creativity. We are all programmed to conform at an early age but we can rise above that conditioning by being what we are not. This is not always easy to do; family and friends will think you have lost it or are smoking some funny cigarettes. You are getting high. But the high is internalized imagery of being more than could otherwise be possible. Refuse to be placed in that box of mediocrity by using a myth to go beyond the real into the surreal. Paint Superman on your psyche and dare anyone to knock him off.

The Superman Syndrome—Transformed & Empowered

What is a Superman Syndrome? It is a series of common behaviors that permit an otherwise normal individual to rise above normality to alter paradigms. What makes a myth key to transforming oneself? To begin most people have been programmed in school and at home to conform and to grow up and leave their imaginative ways to the children. They are told to go to work and become a slave to traditional ways and to live life in the slow lane. The world's visionaries have not been so molded or have altered that mold to fit their needs. They have a strong sense of self often born of a willingness to be different. When that is coupled with a mythical mentor that is larger-than-life, the possibilities open up vast opportunities. Most people are unwilling to play in such an arcane arena. But those who can emulate a hero are destined to be more than they thought possible.

That is what this book is about. It might seem far-fetched but the genius of Frank Lloyd Wright was imbued in him by a deluded mother. His mother raised this high school dropout to believe that he was the reincarnation of the mythical Welsh God Taliesin. Was he? Of course not! But the delusion armed him with such a strong belief in his ability that he felt he could design buildings as he saw them: married to the environment not to some tradition-bound criteria. Such thinking led the *New York Times* to refer to him as an "architectural anarchist" and "Frank Lloyd Wrong." Wright became the protagonist model for Ayn Rand's *Fountainhead* hero Howard Roark. Without his delusional self-belief it is highly unlikely he would have been able to produce the elegant masterpieces *Fallingwater* and the *Guggenheim Museum*.

Mythical mentoring is about Clark Kent stepping into a phone booth and emerging as Superman, Bruce Wayne entering the Batcave and coming out as Batman, Billy Batson yelling "Shazam"—a magical Egyptian word and changing from a submissive boy into a man's man replete with lightning bolt on chest. In a similar transformation Peter Parker changes into a mystical costume to save the weak and disenfranchised. These stories border on mysticism but have a long history of reality parallels in reality. Allisa Rosenbaum boarded a ship in Europe and landed in America. To sound like an American she stole a name from her Remington-Rand typewriter and became the daunting Ayn Rand creating superheroes like Howard Roark and John Galt. Through them she founded the philosophy of Objectivism that emerged from a raging psyche dedicated to destroying Communism. Rand admitted later in life to being a "hero worshipper" and committed to "writing psycho-epistemology to get Russia out of my system." When asked by the media Rand admitted the heroine Dagny Taggert from *Atlas Shrugged* "is me."

Equally as eerie is the transition from loser to winner of the British writer Ian Fleming. This irresponsible son of a notable family was actually a loser, a man who could not keep a job and who failed miserably at every single career path he embarked on. Then one day he stepped on that airplane heading for Golden Eye in Jamaica and experienced a mythical metamorphosis that resulted in the protagonist James Bond as his alter ego. It was not a coincidence that 007 did all the things that Fleming feared. From that moment Fleming was transformed and each winter spent eight weeks at Golden Eye writing a James Bond spy novel. And as they say, the rest is history. Bond would become the #1 movie hero in history. The irony is that his creator was a blatant loser who had to have an epiphany to become a winner.

Lance Armstrong took a similar transitional path from a man who could not finish the Tour de France to a man who could not be defeated. The path was strange indeed. Testicular, lung, and brain cancer led physicians to predict his demise. World-renowned cancer experts in Houston told him they could preserve his life but the cost would be his ability to walk—and ride a bike. The price was far too great. Lance opted for a far more dangerous treatment in Indiana that would transform him from a loser into a five-time winner of the Tour de France. It took his transition into a *Superman Syndrome* to pull off.

Many paradoxes will be drawn in this work because such incongruities are lost on most people. Most people think they should take the job that pays the most. That is ludicrous. They should only take the job they love passionately. If they do the money will come. In business or life we always get the behavior we pay for. When you pay yourself with only financial rewards that is all you get. Sounds weird! But it is true. Psychologist John Diamond called such a "psycho-biological harmony." Psychologist Mihaly Csikszentmihalyi researched the causal factors of genius and found, "A person who is fully differentiated and integrated becomes a complex individual—one with the best chance at leading a happy, vital and meaningful life." The idea is to be what you are but also what you are not as in as in mythical magic.

Power emanates from within. Until we understand this we can't modify it. That makes true power paradoxical. Drawing within the lines just doesn't get it done. One must have the courage and moxie to draw outside the lines to be innovative. Friedrich Nietzsche was enamored of what made a Great Man and concluded it was a Superman (Overman) in his Will-to-Power thesis. It led him to say:

"The Great Man is colder, harder, less hesitating, and without fear of opinion; he lacks the virtues that accompany respect and respectability, and altogether everything that is the virtue of the herd. There is a solitude within him that is inaccessible to praise or blame."

Fantasy opportunities are the fuel that makes some men great and shocks the also-rans. Research at Princeton University on ESP and telekinesis led to researchers saying, "Archetypal or mythical images trigger the unconscious thus producing the strongest psychokinetic effects" (McTaggart, *The Field*, 2001, p. 134). What does all this mean? Those who can escape the real can truly find the surreal. Those who permit their imaginations to run rampant are better equipped to be in touch with the arcane or with others of a similar bent. This research sends a message that it is okay to dream and allow our passions to run amuck. Those who intend to be in touch with the future must resist becoming too grounded.

Cut off Your Head to Get in Touch with Your Body

Research has shown that the harder we try the less success we experience. Sounds really goofy! Walk up to a par five on the golf course and you invariable try to hit the longest drive of your life. What you do is hit the shortest drive of your life because you were attempting the opposite. The mind gets in the way of the body in this illustration. The genesis of this thinking began with Victor Frankl's work on Logotherapy in which he concocted the concept of Paradoxical Intention. While working as a German psychiatrist after World War II Frankl discovered that male impotence was mostly in the head, not the body. The harder men tried to have an erection the less chance they had. When they stopped trying they could. It was the ultimate paradox. In his landmark work *In Search of Meaning* Frankl (1959) wrote:

"Don't aim for success—the more you aim at it and make it a target, the more you're going to miss it. For success like happiness cannot be pursued; it must ensue as the unintended side-effect of one's personal dedication to a course greater than oneself"

Another paradox in the trek through life is stupidity. Stupid people seldom are aware of their stupidity. Even weirder is that the fact we often don't know that we are stupid can be a good thing. The salesperson that is too stupid to know where not to go is often the most successful. They walk in doors they shouldn't and walk out with huge deals. During those halcyon days when I was developing the first Chuck E. Cheese restaurant prototype I was too stupid to know that I should not have a rat mascot in a restaurant or activities counter to an eating environment. Due to my ignorance I installed a ball-crawl for small children in the 1970s prototype, to the chagrin of the restaurant personnel. Small children were peeing in the balls and the manager was furious. They thought these things were stupid but the kids loved the whole gee-whiz mysticism of the place.

The Path to Empowerment Is Paved with Myth & Paradox

What Makes Us, Breaks Us

Paradox One To be more than you are you must be what you are not—tapping into your opposite permits you to be
[Synthesization] more than you could otherwise be. Validation: Joseph Campbell & Coco Chanel

Paradox Two Acting as if you are in the poorhouse is what permits you to buy a penthouse—trying to get rich only
[Money as Goal] ensures you won't since it programs you for all the wrong decisions. Validation: Bucky Fuller & Oprah Winfrey

Paradox Three Chasing happiness is contra to finding it— happiness ensues as the by-product of optimum functioning in
[Happiness Anomaly] the moment. Validation: Maria Montessori & Dr. Seuss

Paradox Four Ignore conventional wisdom—it comes from experts who have such a psychological
[Ignore Experts] investment in what is they can't see what might be. Validation: Albert Einstein & Golda Meier

Paradox Five Romance cannot be found by trying, only by being—stop chasing love and it will bite you big time;
[Love Is Blind] enjoy the titillating journeys into the surreal. Validation: Carl Jung & Madonna

Paradox Six There is always someone stronger so stop worshipping strength and attack weaknesses—
[Attack Weakness] find strength in mythical allure. Validation: Maya Angelou & Jack Nicholson

Paradox Seven Superstars are smart enough to act stupid; they never know too much for their own good—
[Dumb Is Smart] mythical masters escape into the vagaries of the wild to learn. Validation: Bertrand Russell and Margaret Mead

Paradox Eight Titans are maniacs on a mission—they are hyper to a fault and outrun mistakes; speed is panacea of
[Icons Are Quick] eminence and energizes and empowers. Validation: Helena Rubinstein & Picasso

Paradox Nine Breakdown leads to breakthrough just as crisis leads to creativity— the bottom fuels the trip to the top;
[Pain & Change] trauma is a path to power. Validation: Ayn Rand & Lance Armstrong

Paradox Ten Supermen use insecurity to energize and overachieve—the fear of failure is highly motivational;
[Fight Fear] the fear of failing leads to success. Validation: Thomas Edison & George Bernard Shaw

Paradox Eleven It takes an abnormal oddball to creatively destroy what is—normal people are normally successful;
[Divergence Works] Abnormality leads to innovative creations. Validation: Nikola Tesla & Isadora Duncan

Paradox Twelve Positive energy empowers and leads to consummate progress by those who refuse to hang with losers—
[Positive Energy Works] positive energy permeates the life and work of supermen. Validation: Frank Lloyd Wright & Amelia Earhart

Paradox Thirteen Power is an external manifestation of an internal sense of self and positive energy—
[Will Power Wins] power is a surreal journey. Validation: Catherine the Great & Napoleon Bonaparte

What is important in any new venture is satisfying the needs and wants of the customers not the employees. Doing the verboten was wild and exciting for the young patrons even though it was considered insanity to those steeped in traditional methods for operating a restaurant. The CEO of Holiday Inn told me, "Gene, you can't have a rat delivering pizzas in a restaurant. Rats are antithetic to all that food is about." But it was the rat that made the place unique as Chuck danced with the birthday child who was ecstatic with joy. The paradoxes above are aimed at validating this simple truth.

Mythical Mentoring as Fuel for Success

In my research on greatness it has became blatantly obvious that early programming has cast most people into what they can and cannot do and they are unable to move out of the prognosis of mediocrity. But by adopting a mythical hero they can remove those inner limits by becoming what they are not. Even if deluded, if you think you are messianic—as Napoleon, Hitler, and Frank Lloyd Wright did—you are far more likely to overcome limits to achievement.

Research has shown that many geniuses have been voracious readers. This was true of Thomas Edison, Madam Curie, Henry Ford, Nikola Tesla, and Bill Gates. For them the protagonist in their readings often became surrogate hero-mentors that permitted them to function way outside convention. When one buys into a fantasy it is easy to emulate the hero of that fantasy, be it Superman, Batman, or a human like Alexander the Great. Walt Disney chose fairy tales as his whimsical fantasies and it led to Disneyland. Such escapes into mythical vistas have been responsible for many of the world's great innovations. Without the escape into an ethereal Land of Oz, dreams often stagnate on wannabe vines.

Mythical mentors fuel success beyond what might otherwise have happened. Two towering men in history offered insight into this—Carl Jung and Joseph Campbell. Both Jung and Campbell spent much of their life in that ethereal land of what if and make-believe. Jung wrote of what he found in the Archetypes saying, "All our concepts are mythological images. All our impulses are instincts." Campbell evolved this into a more definitive system of success via myth saying, "Myths make heroes out of those who heed them. Myths are imprinted Archetypes."

A myth permits a person to tread in arenas that the herd resists. Fantasy escapes into mystical vistas like fairy tales. Spiderman or Wonder Woman titillates and motivates. Such fantasy-mentors can be transformational for a kid locked into societal reality. Early programming into what is possible and what is not can prove incapacitating. By escaping into a make-believe world the imagination is permitted to explore life's what ifs? Internalizing the limits of others paralyzes creativity in children and adults. Those limits find their way into the head and the heart and stymie innovation. Until those limits are dispelled or replaced eminence is difficult or impossible. This was never said in a more profound way than Jung's aphorism, "It is not Goethe who creates *Faust,* but *Faust* who creates Goethe. *Faust* is but a symbol."Campbell took this even further: "Images of myths are reflections of the inner being; A myth is a life-shaping image."

In my doctoral work *The Innovator Personality* (1991) I first discovered that the world's preeminent visionaries tend to use mythical mentors to arm them for the tough trek to alter the world. Protagonists from books, mostly mythical heroes like Attila the Hun and Alexander the Great, inspired Ted Turner to go beyond the norm in his quest to be great. While attending military school he became enamored of the heroic deeds of these men plus the World War II hero General George Patton. Turner's creation of CNN was only possible due to early ethereal escapes into the minds and moves of his heroic mentors. It is no accident that his Atlanta office had a sign above the door proclaiming it as The War Room. Fred Smith of Federal Express fame and Steve Jobs of Apple had a similar propensity; Jobs traveled to India to seek out Maharishi Yogi in a quest for enlightenment. Even more telling was Berry Gordy, the founder of Motown, whose epiphany at age eight altered his life. "When Joe Louis won the World's Heavyweight Championship" Gordy wrote of his transformation saying, "For me Joe Louis was the greatest hero in the universe. In that moment a fire started deep inside me, a burning desire to be special, to win, to be somebody" (Landrum 1997 p. 173).

It would appear that all power is intrinsic, not extrinsic. To excel, find a fantasy to chase and chase it like a sixteen-year-old on Viagra. That is precisely what this book on the paradoxes of power is about. These paradoxes are delineated in each chapter with examples of a male and female who escaped the vagaries of their reality to make their mark with help from a mythical-mentor. How does one reprogram oneself to live outside convention? How to get rid of all those "No's", "Don'ts," and the *not possible's!* that rob us of the creative bent. Those who tattoo

"Superman" on their psyche or "Peter Pan" on their souls are far better equipped to overcome the vagaries of the trek to Neverland.

The Logical Paradox

Political leaders since the beginning of socialization of the masses have used logical fear to maintain order. They used force or mystical ghosts to frighten the less educated into conforming. In such a world it was important to follow the leader and play by their rules or pay a dear price for your dalliances. These devious rulers were the types who poisoned Socrates for trying to teach young Athenians to think on their own. Later scholars would criticize Leonardo da Vinci for not having indexed his incredible *Notebooks*. What lunacy! How provincial is that? The sad commentary of life and progress is putting everyone in a box, a box of mediocrity, in the hopes of creating order. Well, there is only one order, especially in a dynamic world of change, and that is chaotic insight that doesn't come from rules or budgets. Budgets are great tools, but they are only tools and those who would like to keep us in line say, "You can't do that since it isn't in the budget." But what if you could triple returns or destroy the competition? To hell with the budget, which is not the most politically correct thing to say but it is the most valid in a chaotic world.

In the case of Leonardo, arguably the greatest mind who ever lived, a man of incredible imagination and vision, would he have followed those rules had they been in vogue at the time? He certainly wouldn't have painted the Mona Lisa since it was not budgeted this quarter. Today's educational institutions have a way of criticizing students' ingenious work for not having abided by the APA style.

Biographer Michael Gelb studied the creative process for his book *How to Think Like Leonardo* (1998) and wrote, "Mona Lisa is Leonardo's supreme expression of paradox." What was he saying? The face was the consummate dichotomy, both smiling and grimacing. And furthermore one side was smiling the other austere. The painting was real yet surreal. This most elegant of all paintings showed the mastery of a visionary who could show the paradox of good and evil, compassion and cruelty, seduction and innocence. Freud analyzed Leonard's imaginative style and childish work saying:

The great Leonardo remained like a child for the whole of his life. Even as an adult he continued to play, another reason he often appeared uncanny and incomprehensible to his contemporaries.

Supermen Often Lie Dormant Until Needed

A kind of kinesthetic karma coexists in the mind and body of superstars. It makes them uniquely powerful beyond the norm, permitting them to transcend physical, mental and emotional limits. They seem to be able to take themselves into a zone-like state of omnipotence. We have long known that muscle-memory is hard-wired into our physical neurology. That is why we can jump on a bicycle and ride it after years of never having ridden. This muscle-memory permits us to unconsciously react in the car to avoid an accident without thinking about the action. Scientists have recently discovered that there is a similar memory in the mind and memory just as it is in the muscles. They have labeled this "Mirror Neurons." We not only can remember how to ride that bike we also have recorded in our mental database mental and emotional imprints from past environmental influences. Social interactions of the past are recorded in our neurology that makes us behave in given ways. *Mirror neurons* are what some call "chemistry" or what causes certain spontaneous reactions to a given remark. ZMET—Zaltman Metaphor Elicitation Techniques testing at Harvard have validated why Coke lovers repeatedly choose Pepsi in blind tests. (U.S. & News Report, Feb. 28, 2005 p. 57). These brain scan tests have now shown why 95 percent of our behavior is unconscious.

Mirror Neurons—Muscle Memory for the Mind & Emotions

In March 2005 (PloS Biology) professor Iacoboni of UCLA said, "People seem to have specific neurons that code the 'why' of some action, predicting the behavior of others." In a 2005 meeting at the American Advancement of Science researchers said, "We do not just see an action," like hitting a golf ball out of a sand trap, "we also experience what it feels like to someone else." This internalizing or imprinting is attributed to the *mirror neurons* that "re-create the experience of others within ourselves." That is the essence of modeling behavior to learn the right way or wrong way to do something. It also offers some validity to those kids who tripped out on comic book heroes and have their actions and superhuman feats imprinted within. These kids often grow up to model what they remember and do so without knowing the reason behind their audacious behavior. Christian Keysers of the University of Groningen says, "we start to feel their actions and sensations in our own cortex as if we would be doing these actions and having those sensations." In other words, find a superstar who is eminent at their craft and mimic them and you will rise above the herd.

A Hierarchy of Power

I wrote a book on *Power & Success* (1995) in which I postulated power as an outward manifestation of an inner sense of one's destiny. The bottom line is that power evolves from within an individual's belief of what is possible or probable. Power does not come out of the barrel of a gun as Mao was famous for saying, but from the will of a man. Any baby validates this simple axiom: when it cries everyone jumps. Those who think that some force like Big Brother has power are sadly misinformed. Those in power do have the ability to approve or disapprove, hire and fire, and make life miserable for their adversaries. When the top dogs at the Ben Franklin chain told Sam Walton to stop dreaming of opening an oversized discount store and just go back to Bentonville and keep operating his 5 & 10 stores, they were merely exercising their power of the moment. Sam went back but started building the first Wal-Mart, which would ultimately destroy the powerful Ben Franklin chain. The same happened when IBM told Ross Perot to just forget his idea of leasing computer time and when Shaw told Jeff Bezos to forget about selling books on the Internet.

At the bottom of the power hierarchy illustrated below are the followers who have forfeited their dreams to power brokers who have convinced them that force is the ultimate power. Those who get stuck at this stage of power are those who have forfeited their power to those above them in the hierarchy. Courageous and optimistic types rise above such nihilism to achieve some semblance of success in their trek through life by gaining knowledge or money or both to rise up in the power game. Men like Bill Gates and women like Mother Teresa became empowered by their inner sense of self. The enlightened and peaceful like Jesus and Mahatma Gandhi were sustained by their wills. This book is about disowning the paradoxes that disembowel and permitting oneself to chase the brass rings of life through inner power.

The last chapter of this book will be about empowerment and the trek to that surrealistic state. In *Profiles of Power & Success* I developed a hierarchy that showed power emanating from the bottom where guns and muscles prevail up to a Nietzschean will-to-power at the top. The lower powers are all externally manifested; those at the top come from within a driven person. At the bottom the Darwinian alpha male reins supreme as king of the jungle. But it is axiomatic that what makes us can break us. There is always someone stronger and those that rely on muscles or guns will ultimately die of their limited vision. This is also true as you move up the hierarchy, as those with more money, title, or charm prevail at their respective levels. The top two agents of power in this hierarchy are *Charismatic Power* and *Will-to-Power*. When an individual possesses these powers, lower powers become possible. An ability to communicate effectively and go within to reach the mystical summits make one special. That was the power of Alexander the Great, Mahatma Gandhi, and Mother Theresa. This hierarchy is as follows:

Hierarchy of Power—Adopt a Superman Persona
Landrum's *Profiles of Power* (1996)

WILL
TO
POWER
(Passionate Intensity)
- - - - - - - - -
CHARISMATIC POWER
(Personal Magnetism)
- - - - - - - - - - -
TITULAR POWER
(Authority or Pedigrees)
- - - - - - - - - - - - .
KNOWLEDGE POWER
(Brains & Self-Efficacy)
- - - - - - - - - - - - - - -
FINANCIAL POWER (Mega Bucks Open Doors)
- - - - - - - - - - - - - - - -
PHYSICAL POWER (Force Is a Formidable Ally)

CHAPTER 1

▼

SUPERMEN SYNTHESIZE TO SUCCESS—ADAPTING TO NEEDS

Be what you're not to be more than you could otherwise be

"Images of myths are reflections of the inner being; a myth is a life-shaping image"
Joseph Campbell

"Truth is always approximate. Truth is a tendency"
Buckminster Fuller

"Reality is made up of circles, but we see straight lines"
Peter Senge, *The Fifth Discipline*

Want to be special? Then permit yourself to be special and to play in lands that the ordinary fear. To be a super performer it is imperative to don a cape and mental omnipotence and ride that horse where it takes you. Those individuals who can identify mentally and spiritually with a fantasy mentor can remove the human limits that have conditioned all of us for very human achievements. There are many examples of individuals who successfully deluded themselves and who refused to leave their childhood dreams of life in the Emerald City. Many supermen are featured in this work to show that one can only be more than is otherwise possible by being what one is not.

Individuals capable of escaping into the ethereal reverie of a larger-than-life hero are creating a support system that defies logic and diffuses adversaries. Without knowing it, NBA superstar Shaq O'Neill has risen above his great talents by being more than a huge presence. How? By those tattoos on his arm, the license plate and shower door where Superman is blatantly imprinted. That invincible caped marvel imbues Shaq with an ability to go beyond the physical into the ethereal. Those who think they are Superman may not be able to fly but their supposed delusion makes them special. The escape from earthly mortality removes self-imposed limits that are conditioned into all of us early in life. In the inimitable words of Joseph Campbell, "Myths make heroes out of those who heed them. Myths are imprinted Archetypes." Mimicking highly successful people or heroes out of comic books can be unconsciously motivational far beyond what most people realize. When Oprah was asked to anchor an evening news show at age nineteen she was so frightened she told herself to mimic her idol Barbara Walters. Walking out in front of those cameras she talked and walked like her heroine. It worked like magic.

Limits to Success Are Programmed Inhibitions

Self-actualization à la Abraham Maslow is about escaping self-imposed limits. To become more than we are we must become what we are not. A bit wacky but it is true. When we escape reality we are able to live a more surreal existence, which is what happened to Alexander the Great, Mother Teresa, Napoleon, and other eminent people. It is the secret of self-actualization. We are programmed for what we can, and what we can't do—by our parents, siblings, teachers, and preachers. All are well-meaning but cripple most people relative to great success. Most of the world lives within confined limits of what is prudent and conventional. But prudence and convention are not the fuel of greatness. The masses never permit themselves to go beyond prudent limits. Those internal limitations have been preprogrammed. They have been tattooed on psyches from an early age. Research has shown that all children have 100 percent of their creative potential, whatever that potential is, at age five. But at age seven half is gone according to studies by UCLA and the University of Georgia. Why? They have been programmed to conform, to sit in rows not unlike what was in vogue in a 1975 factory. They conform and lose their creative potential. By age forty they have but 1 percent left.

The internal limits that program people for mediocrity are both mental and emotional—the head and the heart. We have been indoctrinated to what to fear and what to avoid. We know way too much about what we should not pursue and what arenas are impossible. Until we permit ourselves to move beyond those limits we are destined to remain average. Fantasy-mentors can remove such limits. How? By releasing us from what is to the world of what can be for a superstar or Spiderman. Such fictitious functioning lets us dare to be different. Being different takes both guts and a strong ego, both the strength to challenge the conventional ways of the establishment and the self-esteem to believe we can go our own way and succeed. Remember the controversial statement by Arnold Schwarzenegger at the 2004 Republican convention? The intrepid California governor delighted the convention when he dared say, "Don't be economic girly-men," in reference to the state of the economy. That took a strong sense of self and a true risk-taking personality.

Individuals like Schwarzenegger are flexible enough to adapt and self-confident enough to say what they think no matter the consequences. If you're a brainy intellectual, à la Jack Nicholson, it is sometimes important to disarm others by playing the nerd or off-the-wall renegade on the screen. Loony tunes like Adolph Hitler or Jim Jones must characterize themselves as messianic saviors of the pack in order to gain power. Such people are mythical but have attacked their inner fears head on. Richard Branson of Virgin Atlantic Airlines is an example of such success. When Branson's firms ran out of cash he expanded instead of cutting back, which is the conventional wisdom. To escape from chaos create more chaos. The problem is often lost in the resolution. Branson's approach appears to be a bit foolhardy but it is the path to power for those with the intestinal fortitude to live life on the edge. As I tell my class, ***Tattoo Spider-Man on your psyche and attempt to fly across steep precipices and sometimes you just might make it.***

Synchronicities & Synthesis

The term *synchronicities* was coined by Carl Jung to describe those often weird or mystical experiences that are ascribed to coincidental occurrences. We have all thought of someone only to have the phone ring and find that person on the line. Even more disturbing is to dream of a friend dying and read the obituaries and find them listed. One such eerie event was well documented in the 1930s when the daughter of Will Rogers was appearing in a Broadway play about her father dying unexpectedly in a plane crash. During one performance Rogers died in an Alaskan air crash while filming a documentary with famous aviator Wiley Post. Even more incredulous were the words being typed in the back of the plane by a newspaper reporter covering the trip. The last word he had typed was *death*.

Carl Jung expressed the weird and illusory as internal imagery escaping the unconscious during moments of special awareness. "All our concepts are mythological images," he wrote. "All our impulses are instincts." Such mystical metaphors pervaded the work of Jung, who spent his life looking at the idiosyncrasies and nuances of personality. The psychotherapist was in touch with his inner being like few other men, even his mentor Freud. His uncanny sense of mysticism was often almost telekinetic, with quotes like "It is not Goethe who creates *Faust,* but *Faust* who creates Goethe. *Faust* is but a symbol" eerily exacting. Jung led the way in documenting the validity of hero-mentoring, which has permeated many of my books (including this one). And the concept is key to the success of many of the world's great visionaries. Napoleon was mesmerized by the august feats of his hero Alexander the Great and his hero-worship was instrumental in the Little Corsican's attack on Egypt. The battle made no political or economic sense to anyone but the man who fashioned himself the reincarnation of Alexander. In a similar manner the madman Hitler envisioned himself a Nietzschean *Superman,* as did Picasso. To some degree they were all deluded but their delusions were a catalyst to their success.

Synthesizing to Success—Be Real to Find the Surreal

By synthesizing all facets of the mind, body, and soul we are able to be what we are and what we are not. Sounds weird but it is true. If we are fearful and then become fearless we have eliminated an Achilles heel forever. If we are petrified of speaking in front of large groups but join Toastmasters and become fully proficient in front of groups we are far more than we would otherwise be. Fear of flying can destroy any ability to see the world. But taking flying lessons can neutralize such a fear and far more than could otherwise have been will be true. Why does this work? Attacking any weakness is the only way to live a normalized life. Neutralizing weakness always makes you better than your adversary since they now are unsure of how to attack you. The control freak who has mastered the ability to delegate important issues suddenly is a more self-assured and well-rounded leader.

Eminence is more about adapting and synthesizing than anything else. As soon as you can flip-flop between the real and surreal, strength and weakness, the quantitative and the qualitative, the world is no longer a mystery but an opportunity. When an individual becomes more centered emotionally and physically they are far less rigid and adaptable. Attacking fear eliminates fear. Until a person can be what they are not they will be incapable of being more than they are.

The real can lead to the surreal just as the surreal can lead to the real. This is lost on most grounded individuals. It was not lost on a visionary like Pablo Picasso. The Spanish artist painted way outside logic or conformity and it brought him much criticism in the early years as most people thought he was just deluded. He was! But the delusion was what led to him documenting the chaos of the twentieth century in art. Great artists, whether in the literary arts or the visual arts, are basically philosophers with a bent for projecting an image of the world from a different perspective. The metaphors of Picasso's Cubism and Surrealism were philosophical message about the nihilism of a chaotic world. In Guernica he would document the horrid destruction of his Spanish homeland by the Nazis. No matter what you think of Picasso's artwork he portrayed the arcane and the destructive nature of man for the sake of power. Picasso portrayed the tormented psyche of the most destructive century in the history of mankind.

Most people are way too grounded to be truly innovative. They conform out of fear of total rejection by society. Drawing within the lines led both Walt Disney and Dr. Seuss to drop out of art school. They were willing to thumb their nose at traditional ways but they are in the minority. Xenophobia permeates the lives and behavior of most people and that legislates against their being innovative. Most of the world is from Missouri—the Show Me State. They must be shown. The innovative are not so inclined. Visionary geniuses like Leonardo da Vinci, Carl Jung, Nikola Tesla, and Albert Einstein are stimulated by the unknown and foreign and fully capable of living and loving way outside reality. For them it is rational to be irrational. In other words, they pursue the surreal and out of that enigmatic state they find their reality. An ability to think irrationally allowed them to solve enigmatic problems. Such visionaries are not caught up with being wrong—they started out wrong. They concentrated on what might be and consequently broke new ground like few others in history.

Complimentary Forces à la Chinese Wisdom

The yin and yang are complementary poles of endless change that offer insight into the process of synthesizing. Many millennia ago the Chinese were thinking about the ephemeral nature of life and gender. Only those who can come to grips with vagaries of change can arm themselves to deal with it. Those lost in their own self-deprecating reality or fear will be destined to live a life of mediocrity. The yang focuses toward the center. The yin diffuses toward the periphery. The paradox is that an individual must become one with what they  are and what they are not. This is counterintuitive but is axiomatic for an optimal life. If you fear water you had better jump into the water. Only then will that fear get extinguished. If you fear the dark go sit in a dark room. If you fear flying take flying lessons or skydive. Any other approach leads to a life of frustration. The only way to have a climax or an erection is to stop trying. Stop worrying and get immersed in the moment and it all happens.

It was twenty-five hundred years ago that the Chinese first drew the symbol of the yin and yang to describe the perpetual circular logic of life. In their system all things were opposite poles and centering was a key to mastering in their system. For them the yin and yang formed one whole but were different as well as similar. In such a system there are no absolutes. They were right in suggesting the world is not black or white but grey. In their symbolic representation above, the yin-yang, the outer circle represents everything; the yin is feminine energy, the yang masculine energy; each is separated by a flowing line depicting the dualism of an ever-changing and cyclical nature. This image depicts a *Oneness* within and without, both manifest and unmanifest, insight and ingenuity. It is an agreement within a paradox of order that makes all things optimal.

The yin-yang is about hot and cold, love and hate, life and death, day and night, man and woman, and on and on. It tells us that there is no beauty in the absence of ugliness just as there is no pleasure in the absence of pain. Even death is but an absence of life. We cannot know what we are until we know what we are not. Sounds weird but it is the reality of what makes us tick. In the inimitable words of the philosopher John Stuart Mill, "Ask yourself whether you are happy, and you cease to be so." In the world of yin and yang everything is important yet nothing is important. To become whole it is important to embrace the polarities, to synthesize and see what you are not, to come full circle into what you are. Embracing opposite polarities is the secret to becoming whole. Lao-Tzu wrote, "Tao creates One," as if to show that to have peace and tranquility one must embrace havoc and strife. Chinese wisdom tells us there is always yang in any yin and yin in any yang. To optimize is to synthesize.

Psychological Synthesizing—Breakdown & Breakthrough

To be grounded is to be godly in traditional societies. Pay attention to the rules and dogmas and all things are good. But it is not so. Drawing outside the lines permits us to better understand the nature of life within the lines. Most of mankind is lost in their programmed life in the safe lane where problems are threats not opportunities. The truth is that problems are the opportunities. Those who get fired finally have the guts and opportunity to chase their own dreams. This was the case of Walt Disney, Bucky Fuller, and a myriad of others who would never have made their mark in the world had they not been terminated from their jobs. Had Soichiro Honda's parts factory not been bombed and destroyed he would never have considered entering the motorcycle business. Had Oprah not been fired as a news anchor for incompetence she would never have become a talk show host.

Until we break down we cannot break through. Sounds illogical, but it is the way of life in the fast lane. While stuck in reality we are ill prepared to see the possibilities. Tradition is laden with a mantra of No's! while opportunity is but a mantra of Why Not?s.

Carl Jung was spellbound by the role played by personality in man. His delving deep into the nature of what makes man tick led him to what he would label *syzygy*—that conjunction in the unconscious of the male and female. This inner place is where macho men go to find their feminine side and where femme fatales go to get in touch with their more masculine nature. This was the ultimate synthesis for Jung in balancing life and love. Jung wrote, "The psyche is a self-regulating system that maintains its equilibrium just as the body does. The anima in man is the archetype of life itself." For him that unconscious archetype was the driving force that makes us function effectively. In Jung's system woman is the yin—*eros* or *spirit*. Man is the yang for logos or reason. In his words, "The *animus* (masculine) in women corresponds to the paternal *Logos* just as the *anima* (feminine) corresponds to the *Eros* in man."

This intellectualizing is aimed at showing the importance of cerebral centering. John Diamond in his work on behavioral kinesiology wrote, "Life Energy is high when brain hemispheres are balanced, when they are in psycho-biological harmony" (*Life Energy*, John Diamond 1990, p. 84). He went on to say, "Life Energy is high when both hemispheres are active and symmetrical—cerebral balance. It is low when in what I call a state of the stress of physiological disequilibrium."

In *The Art of Seduction* (2001) Robert Greene encourages us to become the opposite of who we are to seduce effectively. Greene spoke of "the greatest Don Juan's" having "a touch of prettiness and femininity and the most attractive courtesans a masculine streak." This logic was a motivational influence for the Russians' dubbing Margaret Thatcher *The Iron Lady* since she didn't fit their idea of femininity. Such thinking was also present when Israeli Prime Minister David Ben Gurion said, "Golda Meier is the only man in my cabinet." The truth was she was the only woman. It was also at work in the Indian leader Mahatma Gandhi, whose biographer wrote:

> ***"Gandhi was a combination of the masculine and feminine; He had a man's steel strength of body and will, yet he was also sweetly gentle and softly tender" (Louis Fischer 195)***

The heyday of Hollywood took place during the Great Depression. The reason was that life was a horror story that became real and people escaped into the fantasy of Tinseltown's epic romances. When life is cheap fantasy runs rampant. When one in four people is unemployed there is a passionate need to escape the insidious real into a surreal world of possibilities. All through the Great Depression millions escaped into booze, comic books, and movies. It was no accident that this era produced such fantasies as Pinocchio, King Kong, Snow White, and the Wizard of Oz. When visiting a Shangri La or Utopia in the movies or television we have a respite from the problems of late mortgage payments or love gone awry. That is why the Great Depression brought us musical love stories never since seen or songs like *Old Man River* that just kept just rolling along without a worry in the world. When reality is too harsh we must find solace from that schizophrenic horror story and even if fleeting find an idyllic world of make-believe. Such is the pathway to peace even if it is in the Shangri La of the mind.

A Paradox of Behavior

The French Paradox—eating fat to lose fat—is nutritional irony that defies logic and mystifies the medical community. The French drink voracious amounts of wine and indulge themselves in carboholic pastry treats but remain trim. A 2004 study in New York discovered that in three groups—wine drinkers, hard-liquor drinkers, and nondrinkers—on the identical diet, wine drinkers lost the most weight. Wine makes life more amenable, especially in moderation. Recent studies show that one or two glasses a day are preferable to not drinking at all. An Arizona study reported people actually devour 20 times more chocolate than they admit. The object was to show that those who did not delude themselves were "four times more successful in losing weight" than the normal population (Protein Power p. 125).

Remaining a child appears to be preferable if one is interested in living a happy and innovative life. Freud wrote, "The great Leonardo remained like a child for the whole of his life. Even as an adult he continued to play." Einstein admitted that he had not had an original idea since his imaginative teens. "Picasso's lifelong ambition," according to biographer Todd Siler, was to "create like a child." The message here is that to remain creative it is imperative to chase wild imaginative dreams like in childhood. Adults are considered eccentric with they remain so inclined, as was the case with Dr. Seuss. In an interview late in life the creative medical genius Jonas Salk, inventor of the polio vaccine, said, "I'm 76 now and I still feel like a child, an adolescent, as if I still have lots to do."

Most people tend to rely on their strengths and avoid their weaknesses whether they are working or playing. Just watch weekend tennis players who continually run around their backhand to hit that safe forehand. What happens with such behavior? They get a stronger forehand and a still weaker backhand. Such behavior makes us better and better at what we are already good at and worse and worse at what we are bad at. The superstars tend to do the opposite. They hit so many backhands they become better at that than their forehands. And suddenly what does an adversary have to pick on? Author Anne Rice said it best, "I think all my writing is about a battle with my fears. I explore my worst fears and then take my protagonist right into awful that I myself am terrified by."

William Wrigley of chewing gum fame said, "A man's doubts and worries are his worst enemies." That has now been validated in the research labs of America. In 2004 Iowa State University researchers found, "People weight costs more than rewards when making important decisions" (Self-Fulfilling Prophecies, Dec. 2004 Psychological Science). Fear leads to risk avoidance and the negativity that prevails in most people when trying to test the waters. Attacking fear is the only way to dispel it, but most people permit the fear to dominate their minds and bodies. Visionaries never permit the negative to interfere with where they are headed as shown by the following quote from the eminent composer Igor Stravinsky, "I have learned as a composer chiefly through my mistakes and pursuits of false assumptions, not by my exposure to founts of wisdom and knowledge." Bertrand Russell said, "Wise people are full of doubts" and that is why they succeed. Psychiatrist Victor Frankl offered great insight into this thinking paradox when he said, "Fear brings about that for which we are afraid." In *The Story of Psychology* (1993 p. 547) Morton Hunt discussed the paradox of human behavior when gambling, writing, "When choosing between gains people are risk-averse. When choosing between losses, they are risk-seeking, and in both cases they are likely to make poor judgments."

Attack Fears & They Disappear

We are only as sick as our deepest fears!

Afraid of public speaking?

Join Toastmasters.

Afraid of water?

Take scuba lessons.

Afraid of flying?

Take flying lessons.

Afraid of numbers?

Major in economics.

Afraid of rejection by a mate?

Take a chance.

Syzygy—A Jungian Synthesis of Maleness and Femaleness

Carl Jung believed in the power of an Archetype, an unconscious power within a collective unconscious that drives us to be proactive, reactive, or inactive. He labeled this area the *syzygy*. There is much research validating Jung's thesis. Friends of President John F. Kennedy commented on his femininity despite a true macho mystique. Catherine the Great vacillated between extreme femininity—she spent $1.5 billion on paramours in 1990 dollar equivalents—and a highly dictatorial style that would have made most men look like wimps. Indian Guru Mahatma Gandhi was also prone to androgyny. The following quote by his biographer Louis Fischer, "Gandhi was a combination of the masculine and feminine. He looked very male and had a man's steel strength of body and will, yet he was also sweetly gentle and softly tender like a woman" (Fischer 1954, p. 129) offers insight into his dual nature.

General de Segur of Napoleon's Grand Army said of the Little Corsican, "In moments of sublime power, he no longer commands like a man, but seduces like a woman." Long before Jung spoke of this gender anomaly Sophocles had written, "When woman becomes the equal of man she becomes his superior." Psychologist Nathaniel Branden wrote, "Creative individuals have not only the strengths of their own gender but that of the other. They escape rigid gender role stereotyping tending to androgyny." More recently the University of Chicago psychologist Mihaly Csikszentmihalyi, while researching ninety-one of the most eminent geniuses in the twentieth century, found:

Creative individuals have not only the strengths of their own gender but that of the other. They escape rigid gender role stereotyping tending to androgyny.
(Csikszentmihalyi 1996, *Creativity*)

In *The Art of Seduction* Robert Greene wrote, "The greatest Don Juan's have had a touch of prettiness and femininity and the most attractive courtesans have had a masculine streak." Margaret Thatcher is an example; she ruled in England with an iron fist leading to her nickname The Iron Lady from the Russians. Even her friend and confidante Ronald Reagan told the media, "Thatcher's the best man in England."

Synthesizing to Success—Instrumental to Meeting All Challenges

The true path to the top in most disciplines is the ability to parlay your strengths while disarming your weaknesses. This is easier said than done. It is about centering yourself in what Jung called the syzygy. The table below depicts that arena where the real meets the surreal, the micro meets the macro, positives offset negatives, and the global and local synthesize to success.

SYNTHESIZING (flip-flopping) TO SUCCESS

S is for Synergy where the real meets the surreal, the micro and macro meet, positives offset negatives, and the global and local synthesize to success.

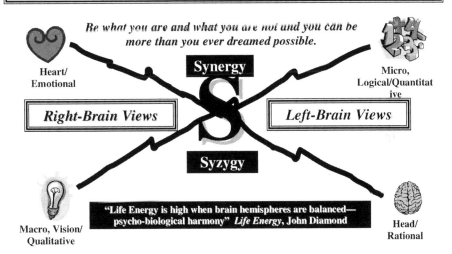

Be what you are and what you are not and you can be more than you ever dreamed possible.

Heart/
Emotional

Synergy

Micro,
Logical/Quantitat
ive

Right-Brain Views

Left-Brain Views

Syzygy

"Life Energy is high when brain hemispheres are balanced—psycho-biological harmony" *Life Energy*, John Diamond

Macro, Vision/
Qualitative

Head/
Rational

Gandhi offers insight into this in writing his first book, *Indian Home Rule* (1908), using both left and right hands in order to give it opposite expressions. In a similar manner Leonardo painted the *Last Supper* with both hands. He would begin painting with the left and when tiring would shift to the right and then back again as necessity demanded. Was he adaptable? You bet! Babe Ruth had a similar propensity. The Sultan of Swat often went bowling with teammates and after pummeling them left-handed started using his right hand and beat them that way as well.

A willingness to jump on the train to Hogwarts—violating tradition—permits an individual to tap into their inner wizardry far more than boarding the train to Main Street. Mythical pursuits can often lead to unbelievable opportunities and permit us to morph into more than we would otherwise be. Often a lightning bolt is the necessary catalyst to mysterious powers that give us the energy and resolve to break down barriers. Miracles turn out to be little other than a willingness to live outside the bounds of mere mortals. Mythical schools of magic reprogram the mind and heart permitting super-normality. Disneyland is a place where kids like to visit because it permits one to believe in magic again and suspend the rigors of reality. It is where we can remove the shackles of too many rules, too many policies, too much in-the-box routine. Mysticism works and few people confuse the map with the territory.

Power & Metaphorical Passion

Symbols and metaphors like flags, crests, totems, and emblems are the rallying call for the wannabes. They are magical motivators that imbue passion in those who need a greater cause to keep on playing the game of life. For eons leaders have used symbolic icons and religious dogma to keep their flocks in line. The Star of David is sacred in Judaism just as the cross is for Christianity. The City of Mecca has become the holy city for Islam, the Zen garden lotus leaf and dharma wheel central in Buddhism. For Hindus the gods Vishna, Krishna, Shiva, and Kali reign supreme.

Few symbols in history have had such an emotional appeal as symbols of a greater force than the Nazi Swastika. A quick glance at the flag can still cause inflammatory feelings that are both positive and negative. More than a half-century after it came to represent the blot on history by Third Reich in Germany the flag still has an inflammatory affect on people. During its heyday the flag caused citizens to stop and salute, become transfixed or break out in a cold sweat. Hitler took the symbol from an ancient Buddhist religion and altered it to inflame a nation as shown in this dialogue:

The swastika is an ancient religious symbol dating back 3000 years. Many historians believe it was a symbol of fire and sun. Up until the 20th century, it evolved as a highly auspicious talisman evoking thoughts of reverence, good fortune, and well being. In the Buddhist tradition of India, it is referred to as 'The Seal on Buddha's Heart'. In Japanese and Chinese Buddhism, a swastika often appears on the chest of past and modern images of Gautama Buddha; however, due to the continued consternation of Western tourists, many modern Asian artists have chosen to eliminate it as one of the 32 signs of a supreme being. The debate as to whether this ancient religious symbol can be restored to its rightful place in history tirelessly continues. How such an auspicious and truly noble symbol came to represent racial genocide and tyrannical oppression is perhaps one of the greatest paradoxes of world history.

Adolph Hitler was a loser who was trained by German intellectual Dietrich Eckart to become a mesmerizing guru. Eckart was a fan of the human-potential movement known as Thulism—a mystical society aligned for charismatic behavior and mind expansion. Hitler became his tool for espousing his ideas and to demonstrate that an otherwise lost cause like Hitler could become a motivational speaker and human-potential guru. It worked from the perspective of transforming an unemployed painter into a mesmerizing leader of a splinter group that became the National Socialist Party. Hitler was soon able to bring people to tears with compelling oratory. Hitler shrewdly decided to come up with a common rallying symbol of the Master Race cause—that was the swastika. The swastika depicted force and an idyllic power struggle between the power elite and the masses as rooted in the power philosophies of Arthur Schopenhauer and Frederick Nietzsche.

Hitler was an iconoclast, loner, and manic-depressive with obsessive-compulsive tendencies. He was intent on leading the Germanic people to victory over Europe's old-line power elite under the veil of the Third Reich. The swastika became his rallying call with its negativity pulled off by the crimson and black  background colors aimed at depicting socialism and passion. The white circle symbolized the struggle of the Aryan race to rise to its rightful place in history. Very adroitly Hitler reversed the swastika's right-handed orientation—peace and optimism in Buddhism—to a left-handed adversarial and negative connotation. It was a symbolic gesture that took white magic and turned it into black magic, optimism into nihilism. Hitler's demonic mind created a symbol of negative power and it worked.

In the twenty-first century avatars, symbolic teaching aids, are found in computer training programs. Avatars are now replacing people to conserve money in addition to making the process adventurous but real. Avatars can emulate and simulate real-world situations that humans could hardly achieve such as pizza-making or air conditioner or bridge repair. Often an audience can better relate to an icon hanging off a bridge than to an actor describing the process. These computer-generated surrogates can be any age, sex, race, or political persuasion to fit the needs of the work. Firms are opting for avatars to train because they never tire or take coffee breaks and they can be far more memorable. Psychologists have found they make the training more entertaining plus the productivity is controlled. They offer a personal touch without the cost and other vagaries of real people.

Being what you are not lets you be more than you are

Coco Chanel & Joseph Campbell validate the concept

Joseph Campbell was the father of modern mythology. He spent his whole life pursuing the mysteries of icons and their impact on how we function and are motivated. Campbell saw mythical characterizations as the catalysts for learning and growing. After a lifetime of studying the meaning of symbols for various cultures he wrote, "A myth is a model for understanding your life. Images are masks and a myth is a metaphor. Myths create heroes out of those who heed them." In his classic work on the subject, *Hero with a Thousand Faces,* he wrote:

Myths arise spontaneously from the psyche (the unconscious). For the symbols of mythology are not manufactured; they cannot be ordered, invented, or permanently suppressed. They are spontaneous productions of the psyche.

As a young child Campbell became enthralled by mythological heroes like Buffalo Bill, by Indian totems and cowboy symbolisms. At age five Campbell visited the New York City Museum of Natural History and according to his memoirs experienced an epiphany that dramatically altered the rest of his life. Later when his dad took him to see a Wild West Show at Madison Square Garden Buffalo Bill entranced him. Then a trip to the Natural Museum of History with American Indian lore hooked him, leading him to devour all the books in the library on Indians and icons. He would write, "I read and read since I lived next door to the public library, devouring volumes of *Bureau of American Ethnology.*" In his famous TV special with Bill Moyer on the Power of Myth he said:

"I fell in love with American Indians. I began to read American Indian myths, and it wasn't long before I found the same motifs in the American Indian stories that I was being taught by the nuns at school" (Bill Moyer, Power of Myth)

Campbell discovered Carl Jung's books on Archetypes and their influence on how we live and function in the world. It would ultimately influence Campbell to say, "Masks are imprinted Archetypes—Myths do not just refer to Archetypes but actually manifest them." Campbell's work has a living testimony for Americans who grew up idolizing the heroic deeds of Superman, Batman, Robin Hood, and James Bond. Testimony to the influence of such heroes, even mythical ones, is the place held by the famous 007 from the movies as he has since been proclaimed the #1 hero of all time in American movie folklore. This should not surprise most men who are transfixed by the daring Bond, who would go where mere mortals only dreamed. Bond became every man's idyllic hero with brazen moves in work and play.

Despite a Roman Catholic upbringing, Campbell, like many other visionaries, turned to Buddhism later in life. Religious icons and myths were central to the Campbell system of thought. A 2004 study at the Higher Education Research Institute at UCLA found there was "a link between faith and mental health." In this study of 3680 third-year college students investigator Alexander Astin reported, "Being religious or spiritual certainly seems to contribute to one's sense of psychological well-being" (USA Today Oct. 27, 2004 p. 7D). After a lifetime searching for the truth in myth at the age of fifty Campbell went to Japan and learned to read and write Japanese to better understand the nuances of Asian myths. Campbell is an example of gaining personal power by developing a power of thought over some life mystery. His words offer validation of this:

"Mythological figures...are not only symptoms of the unconscious (as indeed are all human thoughts and acts) but also controlled and intended statements of certain spiritual principles...all things and beings are the effects of a ubiquitous power out of which they arise, which supports and fills them during the period of their manifestations" (Hero p. 257)

The twentieth century's acknowledged female entrepreneurial genius was Coco Chanel, the French couture. Coco escaped from the horrid reality of a childhood as an orphan and rose to the pinnacle of Parisian power with her House of Chanel. Coco, like Campbell was a renegade visionary who refused to conform to societal rules, never marrying or bearing children as it was incompatible with her business. Coco was far from being a wilting flower and in fact thumbed her nose at the Parisian gentry and when the Nazis came ignored them as intruders. Chanel refused to conform to mundane entrapments of the establishment and would not even show up for a client's reservation, saying unabashedly, "A client seen is a client lost. Make yourself available and it will cost allure." Is that unique in the world of fashion? But Coco understood the esoteric nature of fashion and it wasn't about products but about the essence. To have an aura of mystique one must act special to be special. Early in life Coco admitted to having lost herself in the reverie of Colette's romance novels, becoming a likeness of a waif transformed into a fairy princess. Such fantasy-mentoring is the secret of the Jungian and Campbellian power.

Paradox pervaded Coco's adventurous life. She brazenly told *Vogue*, "I've been in business without being a businesswoman." This femme fatale was as sensuous as a female could be yet made her mark and fortune by adopting a masculine persona that was in total contrast to her femininity. This androgynous woman of the world was designing clothes for Parisian elegance yet adorned them with masculine lines and colors. Androgyny played an enormous role in her life and work and in many respects is what made her rich and famous. She had the temerity to show up at Ascot adorned in short hair and masculine attire or even pants in an era when self-respecting women were all frills and tradition. When the social set arrived in gowns and lace dresses she appeared in opposition. Poet Jean Cocteau called her a "pederast."

One of the real paradoxes of the Coco Chanel story is that she became what she hated. Coco detested needy men looking for a woman to pay their way. Yet she became one of those women who paid the tariff for dozens of male gigolos. Flaky males with a title and breeding were her Achilles heel. They offered her what this girl from the orphanage could never have and the well-read and well-bred were part of her life once she had made her House of Chanel of import in Paris. She funded the works of Igor Stravinsky including the *Rite of Spring* while sleeping with the gigolo. The ballet maestro Sergei Diaghilev and Grand Duke Dmitri were her boy toys long before women were into such dalliances. Mysticism dominated Coco's life and gave her the capacity to survive as an uneducated urchin in Parisian couture.

Mythical-Hero-Mentoring as Path to Power

Coco Chanel & Joseph Campbell were Poster People for Hero-Mentoring

Coco Chanel and Joseph Campbell personify the theory that mythical heroes can be the mentoring catalyst for achieving eminence. Both were far more surreal than real and it propelled them to the top. For them life was one big mystical feast that cast them as more ethereal than real. Coco became the queen of couture, Campbell the father of modern myth.

Coco used a fantasy mentality to go from a rural French orphanage to the celebrated salons of Paris. The trek was one of a peasant girl to a duchess with a move from the poorhouse to the penthouse. She jumped on that intrepid stallion named Possibility

and left that nag Tradition in the stable. Coco was dealt a very poor hand but played it with great panache. It left her with a heritage most would proclaim a royal flush.

After Coco had made it to the top Vogue *and the other chic magazines delved into her past but she refused to divulge the real her and insisted on remaining outside reality. She told the press that her early mentors were aunts when they were the nuns from the orphanage. The "aunts" taught her to read and to sew and the nuances of woman-kind. Then she escaped into the fantasy life of a girl just like her who had also made it to Gay Paree—Claudine, who was really the author Colette. Chanel loved to escape from harsh reality into the provocative romances fashioned by Colette. It didn't take long for Coco to become her fantasy, blazing a trail of entrepreneurial genius and leaving frustrated males in her wake. From street urchin to the palaces of power was her path due to an ability to disdain reality. Her dynasty was built as much by her mythical mentoring as from a frenetic work ethic.*

The urchin Coco transformed herself into a Horatio Alger heroine. The transforma-tion was not overnight and it wasn't easy as the snobbish Parisian aristocrats snubbed and demeaned her. She refused to be hurt and began turning the tables on her car-riage trade clientele. Long before it was justified or affordable Coco had a Rolls Royce with footman to travel the one block from her hotel residence to her office. Once she was an accepted part of the Parisian elite she was difficult to cope with. "The darling (rich bitch) has no shame. She is like a preying mantis" would be her description of the women who bought her wares.

That long climb to fame and fortune took its toll in the sense she never married or bore children, not unlike present-day Oprah. She was a charismatic damsel of couture that had made it to the pinnacle of Parisian culture, not an easy ascent and it didn't come without great pain. The trip would lead her to cynical sarcasm in the media with her proclaiming, "I'd rather be respected than respectable." With great insight into the wiles and wares of her clientele she told Vogue, *"A woman is always afraid of being blackmailed by her maid but has total confidence in her* venduese—*fashion consult-ant." Her way of saying she had evolved into the role of confidante.*

Joseph Campbell had a different calling and a far different cultural divide to cross but the essence of the crossing was not all that different. Campbell would study and study and become a renowned college professor at the prestigious Sarah Lawrence girls' col-lege. Despite adversaries he used teaching to pay the bills to support his worldwide research into myth. Campbell was accused by the establishment of getting lost in the reverie of hero-worship. But it never deterred him from seeking the truth of myth as an unconscious motivator of man. Campbell never knew Coco but her life validates his theories about leaving the real world to enter the far more satisfying one of fantasy and myth.

Campbell was one of the most erudite Americans ever. His words gave us all permission to retreat into our own inner being:

"Myths are life's potentialities, innately unconscious and powerful guides to the life of the spirit—our ticket to the spirit. Myths are metaphorical references of the will."

The Power of Myth *offered us permission to go outside reality to find solace. It was such permission that led George Lucas to ignore the sage advice of Hollywood moguls and create his all-time masterpiece* Star Wars. Lucas has admitted that the epic classic would never have been produced had it not been for his hero Joseph Campbell. *After* Star Wars *had become a hit Lucas told the media: "If it were not for Joseph Campbell I would still be writing* Star Wars. Hero *was enlightening to me. When Ben Kenobi says to Skywalker, `Turn off your computer, turn off your machine, get in touch with your feelings,' he was getting in touch with his inner being."*

Such permission from others is necessary to go beyond our self-imposed limits programmed by the establishment. Myths can prove magical in that they inspire from within and give permission to not listen to those who would prefer we remain in the flock. They can be the catalysts to self-actualizing and innovating. Hero-mentors show us the way. It is up to us to listen. Fantasy-mentoring is little else than elevating myth above rationality.

In a PBS special hosted by Bill Moyer Campbell waxed eloquent on his findings, saying, "I think of mythology as the homeland of the muses, the inspirers of art, the inspirers of poetry. To see life as a poem and yourself participating in a poem is what the myth does for you." He ended with:

"Each individual must find the myth that is fundamental to his internalized needs. Every society invents first magic and then religion and the myth becomes part of its religion."

▼

CHAPTER 2

THE EMINENT CHASE MYTHICAL MAVENS— NEVER MONEY

Obsession with the almighty buck only ensures you won't get much

Socrates said 2450 years ago, "I say that money does not bring virtue, but rather that from being virtuous one can attain money." (Plato's Apology)

"The drive to make money is inherently entropic. You have to decide if you want to make money or make sense since the two are mutually exclusive."
Buckminster Fuller, *Critical Path* (1981)

"I don't care so much about making my fortune, as I do for getting ahead of the other fellows. I care more about how to change the world."
Thomas Edison, Wizard of Menlo Park

Superstars and Supermen don't chase money. Money is the way score is kept in capitalism and that makes it a result of doing well, not a goal that should be pursued. Trying too hard to get money will prove counterproductive to getting it. What happens is you focus on the goal rather than the fundamentals that are critical to obtaining the goal. In both arenas the chase is far more titillating than the catch. Sounds weird but true! Focusing on the target leads to all kinds of bad decisions and self-serving moves. People become too enamored with goals and begin chasing instant gratification and the quick win. Really big wins take time and nurturing whether they are finding a soulmate or a successful profession. Those into quick hits and instant success are the ones always attributing super success to luck. The trek to fame and fortune is long and arduous—about twenty years in most cases. Get rich quick schemes are destined for failure so beware getting caught up in that trap.

The Wall Street mantra says, "Bulls make money, bears make money, but pigs never make money." That is not only profound but the truth. Psychologist Mihaly Csikszentmihalyi studied creativity relative to personality and concluded in *Creativity* (1996), "Money can't buy happiness, but happiness can buy money—sadness decreases prefrontal cortical activity, while happiness increases it." There are myriad studies that have shown that money does not buy happiness no matter how much you get. So stop focusing on something that cannot make you happy. That happens to be the process that can lead to money. Money buys freedom and independence and the right to live life on your terms. Those who have earned enough money to ignore convention are often the most content of all people. The sad commentary in most societies is that people hate their jobs precisely because they are working for the money.

In Zen Buddhism true wisdom comes from *emptying the mind*. The Samurai are taught that the true path to nirvana is more spiritual than physical or mental and that is true of money. In the West money is cherished as the panacea for happiness. It is not! Asians know this fundamental truth. The mantra of the Samurai warrior goes, "When you wield a sword and are conscious of wielding a sword your offense will be unstable." This sage advice is dedicated to the fact that we can't achieve until we stop trying to achieve. Cut off your head and your system will function quite well whether it is in romance, money, or sports. Why is the head the problem? Because your rational thoughts are laden with all kinds of programmed stuff, what ifs: "Will I get hurt?," "Can I recover if this doesn't work out?" Getting mired into what might be bad invariably leads to the bad. Until you stop thinking and go with the flow, as the Samurais were saying, you will be a pawn of your own fears. In all problems are the solutions.

The ignorant are never equipped with enough experience to solve difficult problems whether it is facing down a business adversary, hitting a tough tennis backhand, or playing a 4-no-trump hand in bridge. Anyone who allows fear to intercede in any venue is on the road to failure. Research has shown us that all the past experiences for positive solutions are stored in the unconscious, assuming one has sufficient experience in any give field. Just allow the unconscious to lead you—listen to your gut—and you will find you will prevail far better than listening to your conscious mind.

Those fearful fools who permit the mind to interfere with the process tend to lose due to their own anxiety. They become lost in their own negative imagery. Why? Fear becomes their enemy while they think it is their ally. Psychologists have labeled this *The Wallenda Factor* due to what happened to the great wonder of wire-walking Karl Wallenda. Karl was fearless and had walked the high wires without fear or safety nets for many years. As his fame spread so did his mental toughness. But it all ended one eerie day when he altered his mental state. That was the day his brilliant career ended along with his life. In 1978 Wallenda fell to his death. When interviewed his wife told the media, "This was the first day I ever remember him speaking of falling. Until now he never even considered it." She told the press that prior to that day he had focused on succeeding but never on *falling*. The moral is that success is based on *concentrating on positives—what works*—and never, ever, *negatives—what might not work*. We all know someone who was so petrified of failure that their life ended up being a horrid failure.

The Zone Is about the Metaphysical, Never the Physical

The irony of the futility of trying desperately to achieve ultimate success is not the drill. To achieve is to get into a state of what sports psychologists call "relaxed concentration." Focus on what it takes to achieve is good. Focusing on success is bad. Highly successful people are never goal-focused but opportunity-focused. They have practiced their professions enough to stop practicing when the gun sounds and just give free rein to the body, mind, and soul to do their thing. Entering that place described as the Zone by athletes, known to scientists as a state of flow, is about marrying the physical, mental, emotional,and spiritual into one synergistic state. In an interview by the *New York Times Magazine* the great soccer player Pele described such a state he would find himself in when at his peak performance, a place he said was a "near mystical state." When there Pele said it was a euphoric, mindless kind of place:

"It was a strange calm…it was a type of euphoria; I felt I could run all day without tiring, that I could dribble through any of their team or all of them, that I could almost pass through them physically. I felt I could not be hurt. It was a very strange feeling and one I had not felt before. Perhaps it was merely confidence, but I have felt confident many times without that strange feeling of invincibility."

Pele often said that while playing soccer he was not competing on the field but above the field of play. This is true of all successful people who are driven. Preeminent golfers never see water hazards or ravines. That doesn't say they are oblivious to them or arrogant but they are able to remove them as a deterrent. All world-class athletes are often found in a state when nothing goes wrong. They can't miss a shot no matter how difficult. This doesn't happen often but when it does even they are mesmerized by the moment. The one thing they all say is that it was a purely metaphysical state—that did not include the conscious mind or emotions.

Fear is not always the enemy. It can also be a motivating influence. It is only a detriment when it is permitted to interfere with successful execution. There are myriads of examples of highly successful people who were petrified of failure in whom that fear led to their overachieving. Ted Turner admitted to this, as has Michael Jordan. But when fear becomes the focal point of living the living becomes diseased by the fear. Those who play not to lose are life's losers. Those who play to win are the winners. If a person can limit their anxiety to doing well they will do better than normal. The irony of fear is that people are more paralyzed by the thought of personal humiliation than by the act itself. Combat soldiers have every nerve ending telling them to Run! But the fear of being labeled a coward causes them to stay and fight.

Innovative Entrepreneurs Never Chase Money

Those who chase dreams like intrepid warriors often end up with more money than they ever dreamed of having but ironically, never once concentrated on getting it. Henry Ford, Oprah Winfrey, and Bill Gates said they never made one decision based on the money. In 2003 Oprah became the first black billionaire and told Larry King, "I never did it for money. My television show was my calling in life."

When Michael Dell was in premed at the University of Texas his father was appalled when he dropped out to compete with the titans of the computer industry. The computer business had eaten the lunch of such titans as NCR, Control Data, and Xerox and though the life of a physician may not be quite as glamorous it was a sure way of living a prosperous and safe life. His dad wanted to know why he would throw away such a chance to become an entrepreneur. Why drop out of school in the freshman year to chase a dream? Michael never listened to the sage advice and by age thirty-two was a billionaire. It was a good thing this multibillionaire never listened to reason.

Money had always come in a distant second to dreams for Albert Einstein, who said, "Money is a jailer that enslaves you instead of a tool that empowers you." The power of solving life's mysteries was of far more import to young Einstein than making big bucks. Did he find much support for his ideas at first? Hardly! In fact no university would hire him and he was forced to write his famous papers on relativity while working for the Swiss Postal Service doing patent work. Before him the Renaissance visionary Leonardo had a similar position on money. He wrote in his notebooks, "He who possesses most is most afraid to lose." A profound insight that is still valid. This is why the Fortune 500 firms are the least likely to make a major breakthrough. They have so much they spend inordinate amounts of time and energy protecting what they have and will not bet the place on a new idea. That is why the three major networks—run by hired guns—were afraid to bet a nickel on a 24-hour news network. The young gun Ted Turner bet all he had on CNN. It is also why Apple produced the first programmable PC and not IBM. Why didn't Barnes & Noble start selling books online instead of Amazon? Same reason! It is why 18-year-olds are in foxholes. They do not yet have an asset base or family to put in jeopardy. What these wunderkinds did was work to be the very best they could be and the money came in bundles. In a study on the firms that remained viable over one whole century in America James Collins in *Built to Last* (1997) reported:

Contrary to business school doctrine we did not find maximizing shareholder wealth or profit maximization as the dominant driving force or primary objective through the history of most visionary companies.

These words are blasphemous in most traditional business schools, which continue to preach a mantra of profits or death. The paradox of such thinking is that the more profits a firm or individual accumulates the less they are willing to risk it, as Leonardo pointed out 500 years ago. Such behavior is seldom true of visionaries who continue to dance with the damsel risk who brought them to the profitability dance.

MBAs trained in the art of worshipping at the altar of earnings per share and quarterly profits often get lost in their own reverie. Why? They focus on the wrong things and get caught up in the instant gratification game of EPS and price-earnings ratios. Such behavior led to the demise of Arthur Anderson,

Enron, WorldCom, Tyco, Adelphia, and Marsh-McLennan. Booking pro-forma earnings as real and capitalizing expenses landed the principals in jail. When the bottom-line becomes the most important focus of management they are paving the way for disaster.

Henry Ford was the consummate example of a man with a long-term perspective that wins by a willingness to lose. Henry wanted to build a People's Car priced for the masses so his hourly workers could afford to own one. In 1914 he priced the Model T below cost to make it affordable by the masses. That led to a lawsuit by his CFO and shareholders who were in the game for money not long-term viability. When Ford priced the Model T at $340, or $60 below his manufacturing cost the Wall Street Journal and others said he had gone mad. Yeah! Mad like a fox. The fifth-grade dropout didn't know how to spell price elasticity but intuitively knew that with more volume his costs would drop precipitously. Economists now teach that for each doubling of steady-state volume costs drop by 30 percent. Within five years of Ford's unprecedented move for the right reasons he was building half the cars in the world and was a billionaire.

Big Winners Always Sacrifice a Safe Present for an Opportunistic Future

The brazen but brilliant Jeff Bezos offered validation to Ford's strategy when he told the media, "The landscape of people who do new things and expect them to be profitable quickly is littered with corpses." When starting Bezos knew that what makes you profitable in the early days is counterproductive to what is right for the long run. The firms with instant profitability tend to have done what is expedient to gain profitability and that is *not* taking losses to build market share, distribution channels, brand equity, and all the things that make a firm successful in the long term. Wall Street pundits demeaned him for all those early losses and especially when he said that Wall Street wanted him profitable so they could tout the stock and make money and were never interested in what was best for Amazon.com as a viable company. They almost threw up when they read his prospectus, which said, "We intend to lose a lot of money for a long time."

Bezos's logic proved best and by 2004 Amazon.com would become the largest online retailer in the world. Short-term mavens may do well in the short term but tend to self-destruct in the long. Their decisions are antithetic to building an infrastructure with staying power. Mass-market businesses economies of scale are critical to survival. Strategies that inhibit it are self-destructive. Jeff Bezos sacrificed early to have the ability to survive later. Wall Street hounded him to become profitable for five years until he posted his first profits in 2003. Bezos was savvy enough to see through their rhetoric. In those halcyon days Bezos was aware that his mortal enemy in the book business was Barnes & Noble and he didn't have anything close to their resources to compete without building a dominant online clientele.

Broadcast TV's wunderkind Norman Lear wrote, "Short-term thinking is the social disease of our time." SEC attorney Barry Barbash wrote about the cause of the Enron and Worldcom debacles in 2004 saying, "The obsession on Wall Street with short-term earnings targets gave executives an incentive to say and do whatever was necessary to meet quarterly expectations." One fallout of the Enron debacle led to a Duke University study that found that nefarious CFOs and CEOs were so short-term-focused that three-fourths of them admitted to sacrificing future potential to drive up present stock price:

"Seventy-eight percent of CFOs recently surveyed admitted they would sacrifice economic value to achieve smooth earnings. Financial engineering is not accounting."

Bucky Fuller was a man who personally suffered at the hands of self-serving business types whose god was money. This led him to write extensively of a fictional firm he named Obnoxico Inc.—more recently seen in the documentary film The Corporation. In this metaphoric firm executives were motivated by the almight buck and to hell with the environment and people. In his landmark work *Critical Path* Fuller wrote, "All money-making is undesirable. You have to decide whether you want to make money or make sense since the two are mutually exclusive." Many of Fuller's predictions came true with the debacles of Enron and Worldcom. Nefarious executives in these firms placed personal greed ahead of honesty, integrity, shareholders, and their employees. They booked phantom sales and capitalized expenses to push up the stock price. This Machiavellian need to win at all costs gives capitalism a bad name. Anyone who has ever spent a million dollars starting up a business knows that all that money should not be expensed against first-year earnings. Firms have start-up costs that need to be capitalized, but like all such things the nefarious short-term denizens use such concepts to look good quick. Such executives are not only kidding themselves but will be wearing orange jumpsuits to dinner. Executives with integrity never allow the numbers to get in the way of what is right.

In most cases hired hands are guiltier of such behavior than entrepreneurs who have their own money and reputation at risk. Henry Ford was more willing to suffer near-term losses than his hired CFO. This was also true in the case of Walt Disney, Sam Walton, Richard Branson, and Ted Turner. Entrepreneur types seem to be more willing to sacrifice the future for the present. Hired hands tend to be more self-serving and worship at the altar of the present in total disregard for the future. This creates an anomaly for new business ventures. Those who have their own money and future at stake tend to be far more inclined to opt for the long run than the hired hands. When raising venture capital it has been found that those who paint the rosiest picture are the ones funded. Those individuals with more moral trepidation tend to be more grounded but are not nearly as likely to get funded. The unscrupulous Bernie Ebbers was indicted for $4 billion in expense fraud. Tyco's Kozlowski was indicted over his wife's $2 million birthday toga party and for $2 billion in fraud. They were funded because they guarantee quick gains.

Pursue Your Bliss Not Bucks & Power Ensues

Personified by Bucky Fuller & Oprah Winfrey

No one was ever so infuriated with mercenary corporate types—those who place quick bucks over all else including integrity and personnel—than the father of the geodesic dome Buckminster Fuller. In his late twenties Bucky was fired for placing innovation above quick profits. He never got over the self-serving mentality of corporate boards and decided to leave this world. Bucky walked to Lake Michigan intent on ending his life, but sitting there and reviewing the facts led him to conclude that he wasn't wrong. The greed-mongers were! He decided to drop out and not speak to another human being for two years until he could clear his system of their diabolical influence.

A Renaissance Man emerged from that self-inflicted sensory deprivation during which he never even spoke to his wife but did talk in a one-way conversation with a newborn daughter. Fuller's interface with self-serving hypocrites led to him concocting a fictional firm he named Obnoxico operated by greedy executives with help from what he referred to as Legally-Pigally's. The recent scandals at Tyco, Enron, and Worldcom give validation to Fuller's words. "All money making is undesirable," screamed the visionary inventor, but few listened. He went on to write:

"The drive to make money is inherently entropic. You have to decide if you want to make money or make sense, since the two are mutually exclusive."

Even being granted a government patent was an ego-based quest that seldom paid off, according to a man who authored 25 books and held over 2000 patents. Fuller pontificated on the waste of patents saying:

"I do my best to discourage others from taking out patents which almost never pay off to the inventor. Most of my patents have come into public use long after my relevant patent rights have expired" (Fuller p. 149)

Have there been a few patent holders who have benefited? Of course! Patents are the consummate barrier to entry against competition for an invention. But the sad commentary is that the cost to defend a patent in the twenty-first century averages about $600,000 per battle. What young inventor can afford to go the mat with the large corporations with teams of lawyers to play that silly game? Not many! The huge financial success of Gatorade with its vast royalty stream and the pop-top can patent that earned Jay Morton $58 million were astounding successes. But in most cases patents do not pay off, especially for small firms without the time or money to spend in court. Even if the patent is airtight the big guys tell their engineers to design around the patent. If a start-up firm would spend their money on marketing and building a sales distribution network the money would be far better spent than to funding a patent that is virtually impossible to defend, especially against the big guys.

Oprah Winfrey spent her whole business career chasing dreams not money. The chase was not in vain as she became the first black billionaire in 2002 and has kept making a dent in the Horatio Alger myths with her incredible success story. Oprah has repeatedly told the media that money was never important and that she would be doing what she is doing regardless of the pay.

Oprah left Nashville to become a black news anchor in Baltimore. It was not her thing and after a few months she was fired for being ineffective. Like Walt Disney and Bucky Fuller before her the firing opened the doors to her ultimate fame and fortune. After suffering from an abusive relationship and a trip down drug lane, she became a co-talk show host in Baltimore to rave reviews. Success led to a job offer in Chicago to compete with the incomparable *Phil Donahue Show*. As they say, the rest is history. Within months she was beating Donahue in the all-important ratings game. With her contract due to be renegotiated she retained a lawyer. But when he began bargaining too hard she told him, "Look, I would do this for nothing, so don't jeopardize my job." The astounded attorney didn't understand but backed off and she still got paid real well for something she did far better than well.

Mythical Mantras of Fame & Fortune

**Bucky Fuller chose to make sense.
Oprah would have done it for nothing!**

Renaissance inventor Buckminster Fuller—father of the geodesic dome—and wunderkind talk show host Oprah Winfrey personify a mythical dance to fame and fortune. These two diverse personalities, one the quintessential introvert who went two years without uttering one word to anyone including his wife, the other the classic extrovert who has made a fortune by pontificating on TV, both went through an epiphany after being fired in their twenties and both attempted suicide. Both came back with a strong business ethic and integrity that had far more to do with execution than about making money. Each was hell-bent on chasing a philosophical dream with passion. These mythical marvels worked hard, listened well, permitted their minds to wander into ethereal zones where mere mortals seldom go, and that led them to unbelievable success. Never was this more apparent than in Fuller's inimitable words, "Innovation is the manifestation of the invisible." Oprah also has a philosophical sense of life and success often saying:

"My legacy is qualitative. I believe in my own possibilities and move with the flow. I take life's clues and let the universe handle the details"

These innovative doers pursued long-range heartfelt dreams rather than the instant gratification that is so key for much of the world. As a young man Fuller lost a young daughter to disease. Within a short time he was fired for being too innovative by self-serving short-term-thinking board members. Fuller then rebelled in a quintessential John Galt-like escape into a philosophical world of objectivism and creativity. For two years Bucky introspected and tried to come to terms with life's vagaries. That renegade escape into ethereal space was safe but offered him scientific sanctity. It took an experience of facing death in those icy waters of Lake Michigan to clarify his mind. Bucky was transformed into a Renaissance inventor.

What is strange is that Oprah went through a similar transformation after being fired from her news anchor job in Baltimore. Also staring at suicide over her failure, she was no longer petrified of the worst since she had already experienced the bottom. This made her trek to the top far less problematic. Each of these wunderkinds stopped listening to the world's users and came to grips with their inner power. Introspection can prove providential and is paramount to success when operating out on the edge of societal values.

The fantasy-hero behind Bucky's sense of self was the mythical hero of Sherwood Forest, Robin Hood. During his youth Fuller had become enamored of the heroic and humanitarian exploits of Robin Hood. The boy found Robin's penchant for stealing from the rich—the users in his mind—to give to the poor highly inspirational. Robin Hood became his mythical hero-mentor that would become a model for his own frenetic life lived in the fast lane of technology. In many ways Fuller patterned his own life after the likeness of his fantasy hero, as shown in his words written when he was sixty:

My most influential mythical hero was Robin Hood. Later I would take away Robin Hood's longbow, staff, and checkbook, and gave him only scientific textbooks, microscopes, calculating machines, transits, and industrialization's tooling. I made him substitute new inanimate forms for animate reforms (Critical Path p. 134).

For Fuller the ultimate sin was to give up your values and your soul for money. Fuller's life was spent developing and inventing and giving his ideas for the common good. As he aged, Arthur C. Clarke, the scientific fiction writer wrote, "Bucky is first engineering saint."

Oprah had a similar love affair with heroines out of books. At a Miami ABA book show in 1994 she told the audience, "I owe everything in my life to books. Books were my way to escape to another person's life." This mythical mentoring began for Oprah as a teenager. During her teens she spoke of hiding in a Milwaukee closet reading inspirational books by flashlight so as not to be laughed at by her half-sisters. At 19 she was hired as a part-time news anchor in Nashville, Tennessee. Oprah was petrified that first day. She didn't know how to act so she told herself to not be Oprah but be like her idol Barbara Walters. "Just act as Barbara would act," she told herself. She walked out that first night not as this terrified young black girl but as the world-renowned Barbara Walters. It worked! She had successfully removed herself from what was and became what might be.

CHAPTER 3

▼

HAPPINESS COMES FROM FOLLOWING YOUR BLISS

Happiness cannot be pursued; it ensues from chasing dreams

"Don't aim for success—the more you aim at it and make it a target, the more you're going to miss it. For success like happiness cannot be pursued; it must ensue as the unintended side-effect of one's personal dedication to a course greater than oneself."
In Search of Meaning (Victor Frankl 1959)

"Money can't buy happiness, but happiness can buy money—sadness decreases prefrontal cortical activity, while happiness increases it."
Mihaly Csikszentmihalyi

Superstars don't chase happiness any more than they chase money or romance. They chase dreams and happiness ensues as the by-product of a successful chase. Everyone remembers that day when everything they said was right on, everything they did was correct, and every tennis or golf ball they struck was divine. Oh! To return to that magical place that psychologists describe as a flow state and athletes call the Zone. That is happiness! Research shows that the key to that magical place lies deep within our psyche. That place is where the physical, emotional, mental, and spiritual are aligned in time and space. It is akin to the spatial term syzygy. For the uninitiated this is when celestial bodies align in space, such as occurs during a solar eclipse. In such alignments all things are perfect. For man the body, mind, heart, and soul congeal into a magical persona.

Remember those '70s lyrics *Don't Worry, Be Happy?* They implored us to stop playing the victim and adopt a positive veneer. Victims permit energy vampires to drain them and they often spread the negativity germs to others. Are you an agent of the positive or the negative? Victims always seem to have that dark cloud hovering over their heads and it impacts everything in their path. They see themselves as survivors since every event is a calamity. Winners have the reverse impact on others and always seem to have a smile and a positive attitude.

Studies have found that happiness and even strength result from an optimistic demeanor. Being positive increases positive energy flow and being negative decreases energy flow. Ever notice how the depressed sleep an inordinate amount of time compared to the normal population? That is due to the negative energy flowing through their systems. It turns out that health and happiness are actually a self-fulfilling prophecy that emanates from within. If you don't smile you can't be happy and if you don't frown you can't be anxious. Sounds weird but it is absolutely true.

Ever watch paraplegics with a perpetual smile on their face? They have all kinds of reasons to be miserable but they are happy. Such individuals have found solace in their wheelchair. Most people erroneously believe that to be happy one must be healthy and have big bucks, a beautiful mate, wonderful job, or other externalities. That is patently not true. Happiness is a function of pursuing some deep-seated passion as was the case for such visionaries as Mahatma Gandhi, Mother Teresa, and Dr. Seuss.

Pursue Your Bliss to Find Health & Happiness

How could Mother Teresa find happiness in the slums of Calcutta living like a pauper surrounded by death and suffering? Easy! She was chasing her dream of helping the severely disadvantaged. She was not chasing the dreams of her parents, teachers, or even the church. When one chases someone else's dreams they are setting themselves up for strife and anxiety. Pleasure or peace emanates from doing what we love not what someone else loves. Such was the path of Mahatma Gandhi. Despite living the life of a pauper he was perfectly content leading the cause for Indian independence. Peace and happiness come from dancing with dame passion that we have always found exciting.

One irony of the art of happiness is that we are never aware of being happy until long after we were. The state of happiness occurs when we are doing our thing without a care in the world. In retrospect we recognize that was the time of bliss. But most pour souls become hedonistic and attempt to speed up the state by resorting to stimulants like drugs, booze, or some external titillation. All they are doing is resorting to the agent of their demise. The paradox for such people is that by trying too hard they are ensuring they don't ever get what they truly want. You just can't be happy by trying to be happy, so stop trying. This is axiomatic personally and professionally. Trying to find love ensures you will not find it. Lust is often confused with love, as a quick fix for your needs. Trying to hit the perfect golf or tennis shot will leave you frustrated as well. Stop chasing the goal and just concentrate on the fundamentals that cause the goal to be met. Reflect on some past period of elation or happiness. Were you trying to be ecstatic? No chance! You were doing what you loved and it was working. Self-actualizing people are not trying to become self-actualized. They are lost in the reverie of their dreams, and that elevates them to such an ethereal state. Only on reflection does it hit you that past experience was more surreal than real.

The Hedonism Paradox was first discussed in literature by philosopher Henry Sidgwick. In his work *The Methods of Ethics* he characterized happiness as the goal but the result of something beyond the goal. During the passionate chase is when happiness occurs. Looking for the consummate titillation is what destroys most drug addicts. They are so enamored of instant gratification it ends up destroying both body and soul. During the vigil of living and surviving we seldom realize the journey is more important than the destination. This dichotomy was validated by Hermann Hesse in *Sidhartha*. The Buddha spent his life chasing goals to wake up at the end of life to find out that the journey was the essence not the goals. Studies have shown those who play the lottery and finally win are never happier. They have a larger home, bigger cars, and more good-time friends, but are no happier than when they were poor.

The art of happiness is about becoming lost in some quest like art, sports, or philosophic causes. It is about total abandonment of the *me* to the reverie of the *we*. It is often called the Life Force in the Western world. Psychologist Csikszentmihalyi called it being in the *flow*. Abraham Maslow called it *self-actualization*. The Chinese call it *chi*, Hawaiians *mana*, Indians *prana*. Athletes refer to being in *the Zone*. French intellectual Bergson spoke of such a place as *élan vital*. Freudian psychologist Wilhelm Reich wrote extensively on being elevated into an orgasmic zone of pure happiness due to Orgone Energy. All of these are about abandonment of the real and going into that surreal place where we are empowered. When we arrive we know it but are not sure why we leave or how to return. When normal we just want to find the secret genie with the magical key. The pathway to that elevated state of being could bring someone untold wealth. John Stuart Mill waxed profound on the subject when he wrote:

"Those only are happy who have minds fixed on some object other than their own happiness. Aiming thus at something else, they find happiness along the way. Ask yourself whether you are happy and you cease to be so."

As Mill told us, success and happiness can be deluding. When we think we know we actually don't. What makes us happy is often something that appears to be a problem, but when we solve great dilemmas we feel better about ourselves and happiness is possible. The struggle to find our bliss is often tedious and time-consuming. Once we achieve our goals they tend to be tougher to maintain. That is as true of contentment as it is of power. Once on top there is a universal tendency to stop doing what we were doing and to enjoy the fruits of our toil. We stop dancing with the damsels that got us there. We relax and lose focus. That makes us vulnerable no matter the discipline. In 1990 IBM was the king of the hill in the highly competitive computer world with record earnings. Two years later it lost more money than any U.S. firm in history and was teetering on the brink of extinction. Successful people and firms seldom if ever consider the downside and it makes them more vulnerable for it. Success is when we are the most vulnerable. Once you have conquered something is when the reflection must be most ardent.

The Paradox of Happiness for Those in the Fast Lane

Studies show that dopamine—the brain's reward accountant—rewards those willing to live on the precipice. What happens chemically is that the brain releases a dopamine cocktail making one happy far beyond what would occur if one were playing it safe. That is why people gamble. It is also the motivating force behind macho skiers jumping brazenly off cornices or skydivers pushing the limits. Dangerous new ventures drive the human animal to take risks that are viewed as unreasonable for the high-testosterone types and stupid by more grounded individuals. The irony of all this is that the pathway to happiness is about risking not about playing it safe. Paradoxically, the vast majority of people adamantly refuse to live life on the edge and look at those who do as a bit loony. Success is highly correlated to ambiguity.

Let's explore something simple like colors and their diverse nature. The word *blue* is paradoxical in that it has a plethora of meanings many of which are opposite. Blue can be used to describe birds, colors, or moods. Poets use the word to conjure up a feeling of sadness or depression. Composers and lyricists turn to it to connote a *blue mood* with a whole genre of music called the *blues*. Others with an upbeat bent have used blue to connote a positive state as Irving Berlin did in the classic *Blue Skies*. The color projects unconscious motivations that vary dramatically depending on the context of the individual experiencing it. Political wannabes no matter their agenda rarely dare show up in front of their constituency wearing anything but the traditional dark blue suit, white shirt, and red power tie. Why? Blue is the embodiment of strength and stability. The irony is that blue connotes either powerful, sad, pretty, happy, or passive depending on one's perspective.

Consider the paradox explored in depth by French philosopher Albert Camus. In his monumental existentialist work *The Myth of Sisyphus* he portrayed a lonely man endlessly pushing a rock up a hill only to have it roll back down. "Sisyphus is the happiest man alive," Camus would write, "because he doesn't know his dilemma." "Ignorance is bliss" was the moral of the French philosopher who saw nihilism running rampant in the twentieth century world in which he existed. This was understandable since Camus was given a death sentence in his teens when diagnosed with tuberculosis. There was no cure in that era and in a frenetic attempt to cram a lot of living into an abbreviated life he took out his frustrations in words. Many Camus fans such as Hollywood's crass Jack Nicholson lived on the precipice just as did Camus. Nicholson earned the nickname "alienated man" à la the Joker due to playing renegade protagonists in the movies. Nicholson truly identified with the message of a world out of touch and adopted Camus as his mythical hero. He would tell the *New York Times*, "The actor is Camus' ideal existential hero—the man who lives more lives is in a better position than the guy who lives just one." Nicholson referred to himself as Dr. Devil, an irreverent provocateur, and refused film roles that were not about eccentric intellectuals. Such self-insight led to more Academy Awards than any other actor in history.

To Be Happy Get Passionate

Historians and anthropologists have labeled people who were happy as hunters. Not just those who earn their living fishing or who work as African game hunters.

They were referring to those intrepid spirits who hunted for cures, artists looking to paint the great work of art, the writer hunting for the ideas for the great American novel, or the musician hunting for the perfect lyric for the tune. The search is about innovators looking for a new paradigm shift or entrepreneurs hunting for a new market opportunity. The reason these types are so happy is that they are deeply immersed in their work to the point it isn't work but a passion. In states of ecstasy there are no time clocks, time is irrelevant to the magic of the moment.

Do hunter types think of their career choice as work? Hardly! They have a passion for their jobs and it shows in their productivity, hours of toil, and most importantly in their personal lifestyle and longevity. Passionate people work feverishly and sometimes refuse to sleep in the standard sense of the word. Thomas Edison, Walt Disney, Dr. Seuss, and Bucky Fuller slept on their desks or took catnaps. If there was a problem on a Sunday night they were there. These types have more energy and more drive than the normal population and tend to live longer. Those two things appear to be in opposition but they are not, as those who have no reason to get up later in life one day will not. Those passionate about their professions like Bob Hope, Irving Berlin, Frank Lloyd Wright, or Mother Teresa tend to outlive their ascetic peers.

Another irony of work is that those who work for money alone are inclined to detest work even if it is their chosen profession. These people can't wait to retire. In contrast, the passionate worker never retires and seldom even considers it as a viable option. The positive energy that flows through their systems daily arms them for a long and productive life. Those who are dissatisfied and unhappy also have an energy flow but it is negative and often lethal. Passionate artisans like Picasso, Irving Berlin, Frank Lloyd Wright, and Coco Chanel not only worked until the day they died, they outlived the life expectancy in their era by a huge amount. And it had little to do with lifestyle; most of these individuals lived life in the fast lane with fast cars, women, and a diet that matched. All produced until the day they died, with Frank Lloyd Wright creating the Guggenheim Museum at age ninety and one-third of the output of his life after 80. That is precisely why he lived well into his nineties. The same scenario was true of Picasso and Irving Berlin, who were still conducting business deals well into their nineties.

Crises & Creativity = Happiness

The rain makes most people appreciate rainbows. Think about this concept. If you have ever had a near-death experience you appreciate sunsets far more than those who've never had to avoid a death-dance. Had Fred Smith of Federal Express fame not been born a cripple it is unlikely he would have been so successful in life. That is a pretty bold statement but the data from psychological studies offer much credence to what it is probably true. In a similar manner, had Coco Chanel not been an orphan it is unlikely she would have built an empire in couture. Lance Armstrong has told the media that he would never have won one Tour de France, let alone six, had he not been afflicted with cancer.

Taking this to a more philosophic and national arena, it is also true that if volcanoes had not violently erupted in the middle of the Pacific Ocean the glorious Hawaiian beaches would not exist. If hurricanes did not blow away pollution and tear down the weakened vegetation the world's beaches would not be nearly so golden. In similar ways tsunamis wash away that which was too weak to survive the waves and reclaim those shorelines for nature. Good often results from evil, a concept not often appreciated or recognized by most people. Even the ravishes of war have their upside as happened with the destruction of Japan and Germany during the Second World War. It forced them to rebuild and become the most dominant economic forces in the last half of the twentieth century.

Those not growing are dying. There is nothing static in the world. When young Walt Disney got fired and then had to file bankruptcy, it led to his move to California and the start of Disney Studios. The sad commentary of this precept is that when tragedy strikes many weak individuals crawl into a bottle or give up due to the calamity. Much evidence exists today to prove that breakdown does lead to breakthrough, but that is lost on the vast majority of the population. The textbook definition of innovation is *creative destruction*. In the profound words of psychologist Stephen Wolinsky, "Change is security. The idea of permanence is chaos."

Most people are unaware that fear is the enemy, not chaos or trauma. When shit happens, which it always does, those who permit it to destroy them are at fault. Many people get fired, but most like Bucky Fuller do not pull the panic button and self-destruct. Fear is the Achilles heel of all growth and change. An example is the fact that most people are more afraid of a shark bite than the flu. A close look at the statistical probability of dying from the flu compared to dying from a shark bite reveals that the former is highly likely and the latter is highly unlikely, even for those who spend hours in the ocean. People should be far more concerned about the flu but are not because it seems passive in comparison to the virulence of a shark. The reason is that we are wired for survival in the wilds. The image of sharks is stark and triggers those brain sensors. The more abstract concept of the flu does not initiate the same response as things with a lethal image like sharks. Scientists tell us that our brains are wired so that the amygdala portion, the emotional center, gets information before the prefrontal cortex (reasoning). This predisposes us to seek safety first by placating the emotions. The chance of dying by a shark attack is 1 in 281 million, or 2000 times less than the chance of dying from the flu. In this world, fear is the mortal enemy.

Happiness in a Frenetic Web World

In the prophetic words of Buckminster Fuller, "Truth is approximate. Truth is a tendency." Happiness is similar in that it is amorphous, a happening occurring as you chase opportunities that push your buttons. Contrary to popular opinion joy has little or nothing to do with succeeding. It has far more to do with the remorse of losing. Happiness ensues as the by-product of the pursuit of positive dreams—going within to find contentment. It allows us to be happy on our own as independent entities that are not dependent on others to feel good or safe. So many people cannot feel good alone but identify their own happiness by some external force or individual. Independence is golden when it comes to finding happiness. To deal with the trauma of someone dying or leaving you the only way to move forward is to find contentment within and after dealing with the grieving period chase some dream. In other words:

Until you give up what you have, you can't have what you don't—in relationships or in business; wipe out the past or you can't move on to a better future.

People often turn to alcohol to feel good despite the fact it is a depressant. Others overeat to sate inner inadequacies but that cure is far more deleterious than the short-term euphoria of food. We attend movies to feel good, but that escape is but a temporary respite from reality. Escapes are an attempt to not have to deal with the reality. Therefore they don't work. Alcoholics escape into a reverie that alters their consciousness in the short run but destroys their livers and brains in the long run. Writer Horace Walpole offered sage insight into self-delusions when he said, "Those who *think* see life as a comedy. Those who *feel* see it as a tragedy." He had intuitively sensed what psychologists now know: addictive behavior types tend to be emotionally weak. Feeling types tend to become addicted to drugs, alcohol, and obesity.

Eminent visionaries tend to be obsessive and excel because of a passion for their profession. They seldom are addicted to external crutches like booze or drugs because they are addicted to some dream. Pablo Picasso and Margaret Mead were obsessive visionaries with a passion for their work. They overachieved but were addicted to some dream that dominated every waking moment of their life. Gregory Bateson told the media that the reason his marriage to Margaret Mead couldn't work was her obsessive behavior and work ethic. Mead was candid, saying, "I can't stop pushing," and the marriage ended. Picasso had a volcanic lust for life and painting and told his third wife, "I sacrifice everything, including you, to my painting." Such people never have to have stimulants to turn them on and seldom use depressants to slow them down. There is no time in their life for whining or blaming others for their dilemmas. Fantasy opportunity is their drug of choice.

Our environment has a huge impact on our happiness. Hanging around whiners and losers can prove antithetic to joy. Energy vampires drain us. Life is way too short to hang around with losers. Validation comes from psychologist Mark Rosenzweig, a research scientist studying behavior at the University of California, who said, "Bright rats placed in impoverished environments lose their brightness and dull rats placed in enriched environments lose their dullness. Bright rats placed in enriched environments double their brightness edge over dull rats and vice versa."

The above is shown in the life and success of Isadora Duncan, the mother of modern dance. Duncan was an obsessive advocate of mind over matter. In her autobiography Isadora spoke of her years in San Francisco, where she was permitted freedom to roam and learn about life on the street. She repeatedly said it was the cause of her creativity. Isadora's mother permitted her to chase her own dreams no matter where they led. At age ten she opened her first dance studio and in her teens ran off to join the New York Theater and then off to the London Theater. In her autobiography Isadora wrote on her freedom:

"As a child I was never subjected to the continual don'ts. It is certainly to this
wild untrammeled life of my childhood that I owe the inspiration of the dance
I created, which was but an expression of freedom" (Isadora Duncan bio)

Positive Thinking & Fun on the Golf Course

Golf is a strange game with an appeal that belies the difficulty and frustration that playing the game elicits. Just wander around any course and you will witness wild eruptions of positive emotions when a birdie drops into the cup and of total frustration when the ball finds the water hazard. The game conjures up the comedy and tragedies of the theater or what I like to call the Greek pleasure-pain principle. Without the joy of a great shot the pain could not be tolerated. The pleasure of a birdie is offset by the pain of a triple bogie. A similar analogy exists in the game of war and peace. Peace is hard to imagine in the midst of the killing during wartime and killing is soon forgotten after years of tranquil living. Good health is also seldom appreciated until we don't have it or become deathly ill.

For millions on the golf links the pain seems to far exceed the pleasure. Golf is very expensive, not only the equipment, but also the cost of joining a club or just playing eighteen holes. Today the cost is in the hundreds of dollars for one round, forgetting the cost of the clubs. In addition the average player loses another $20 per round in balls plus the cost of carts, tips, and bets. The game was designed to frustrate players with deep bunkers, water hazards, and rough. Only the most dedicated fanatics master the increasingly difficult courses with millions of dedicated advocates playing for years without ever breaking 100. But they return for the chance to redeem themselves. In the inimitable words of the chairman of Callaway Golf:

"Nearly three million of the 26 million adult golfers in the U.S. quit each
year (National Golf Foundation). It is so difficult that about two-thirds of
those who try the game quit because they don't think they will ever be able to
play the game respectably."

Energy & Happiness—A Zero-Sum Game

Passionate people look for reasons not to remain in bed longer than necessary for the body to recoup its energy. Depressed individuals look for reasons not to get out of bed as the thought of coping is too much for them. One is titillated by life and its possibilities. The other is paralyzed by life's challenges. This is why energized types are dynamic doers and depressed types are lethargic whiners.

A person has only so much energy. It is either positive or negative. Every moment spent on negative stuff weakens and drains us of our vitality. Every moment spent on positives is energizing. This zero-sum game demands that one spend time accentuating the positive and eliminating the negative, to mimic the old song lyrics. Because every moment spent on negatives removes a moment of positive.

Energy is about brain waves—the ability to balance the emotions of optimism and pessimism. In the inimitable words of psychiatrist John Diamond in *Life Energy* (1990), "Optimizing potential is about balancing the cerebral hemispheres—eliminating the negative and promoting the positive." In other words, being what we are and what we aren't can help make us be more than we could otherwise be. Sounds trite, but it's true! Opposites can make us whole. Extroverts can find their balance by taking a book to the beach alone and not speaking to anyone for an afternoon. If you are competitive to a fault tell yourself it is okay to lose for a change. If you are compulsive about making sure every "t" is crossed and "i" is dotted relax and permit yourself to allow incompleteness in your life.

Permission to be different is about removing fear of failure from everyday living. Happiness is about the absence of fear and the removal of negative energy. When we are in a state of consternation we are not able to be happy no matter what positive things take place. Fear is also laying in wait for those in control of their destiny—those called Internal Locus of Control types. For them fear or even adversity is merely a catalyst for a greater opportunity. Internal Types take charge of their destiny. They feel they are in control of what happens. Research shows they rebound better from adversity than *External* types and are not debilitated when a boss or authority figures says no. They just don't listen and do it there way. When you are in control you can't be out of control. Happiness comes from not permitting negativity to live in you, which is the dilemma faced by External Locus of Control types.

Adopting a mantra of positivity is critical to a joyful life. This isn't some recent insight. Twenty-five hundred years ago the Greeks visited the Oracle at Delphi and were told *Know Thyself.* The message was aimed at them looking within for the secrets to their success. Most people don't. It is easier to cast blame elsewhere, to blame their parents or boss or fate than to admit their own errors. The eminent are more inclined to look at life's negatives and learn from them. Here are a few principles that may help in self-programming.

Negate the Negative via the Positive

- Never hang with losers—tell 'em you've used up your quota of negativity this week

- Never allow others to manage your destiny—when in charge take charge

- Never chase money—like happiness it is a byproduct of living optimistically

- Never take the easy road—there are no wins at the end

- Never let 'em see you sweat—it empowers adversaries

- Never drink decaf—you need to be a bit manic to catch the brass ring

- Never opt for safe havens—if too easy there are no big wins

- Never equivocate—chase dreams with singular passion

- Never choose instant gratification—it's fools gold like fast-food

- Never quit until you are spent—and you'll never lose although you may run out of time

Get Happy by Being Proactive, Not Reactive

Maria Montessori & Theodor (Dr. Seuss) Geisel Paved the Way

Happiness for both Maria Montessori and Dr. Seuss came in their frenetic search for freeing the child within. Both spent a lifetime trying to eliminate age-old educational stereotypes. Montessori made her mark by educating children who were considered not educatable. Dr. Seuss was more concerned about making reading an art and fun instead of a dreaded undertaking. Both would cast an enormous spell over education and epistemology. Both challenged educational convention and left their imprint on millions of children. Both violated tradition and the establishment in espousing their ideas. Reading Dr. Seuss is a trip into the wonderful world of the surreal that appeals to the imagination of the child. Being educated in a Montessori school frees children to explore and find their own niche by having the right to find their own mysteries to solve. They are not tethered to a chair or told what to learn but learn at their own rate.

The Prophet of Pedagogy (Montessori) and the adored destroyer of Dick & Jane readers (Theodor Geisel) were dedicated to their work to the exclusion of all else. Dr. Seuss and Montessori refused to be distracted or even to pay attention to conventional wisdom. It was this approach that permitted them to alter paradigms. Their daring took time but it paid big dividends. Both detested the dinosaurs who attempted to destroy their ideas. Were they happy? Hardly! Both paid dearly for daring to be different but in reflection both happily pursued their work until well into their eighties. Dr. Seuss's long-suffering wife Helen told the media, "He's unhappy while he's working on a book but even less happy when he isn't." Dr. Seuss often escaped the vagaries of working all-night vigils on a new book by painting all night. When asked why he painted he retorted, "I paint as a psychosis deterrent—to keep from going batty." But one of the great tributes came from the top dog at Random House, Bennett Cerf, who told the press, "Of all our writers Ted alone is a genius." Those were pretty powerful words for a publishing house with the likes of Eugene O'Neill, William Faulkner, John O'Hara, Ayn Rand, and James Michener.

The sad life story of Montessori is that she was a woman without a country. Her progressive ideas and books were at odds with the Fascism of mid-century Europe where Mussolini and Hitler disdained all forms of freedom, let alone that of a child. The Messiah of Education ran from Fascism and took up residence first in Spain then in England, Denmark, and India. This didn't impede her preaching on the need for allowing children freedom to grow and learn. Maria wrote, "Education is social engineering," and went on to say, "Children work, not out of fear of punishment, or out of anticipation of rewards, but for the sheer pleasure of the activity." Dictatorships in the classroom or in politics were antithetical to the Montessori Method. In her system the child was permitted to learn without coercion or restraint.

Montessori was the first female physician in Italy. But she paid a horrid price for her audacity to choose a career in a male-dominated world. Maria was not permitted to work in a hospital for fear she would have to treat a man in turn-of-the-century Italy. Consequently, the maven maverick was given idiot children to nurture to keep her out of the way. The power brokers underestimated Montessori, who took those children that were called idiots and fed by throwing food into their rooms, and had them reading and writing at normal rates within the year. She achieved this miraculous achievement by doing little else than changing their environment and motivating them to grow.

In a similar departure from the established ways Ted Geisel dropped out of art school within hours after being told to draw within the lines. This man-child adamantly refused to grow up and it is what made him so innovative in writing books for young children. He was on their level, with a great understanding of how they chose to interface with the world. It was Geisel's immaturity that made him such a genius in the world of letters for children. Remaining a child—he asked for a Lionel train set for his sixtieth birthday—kept him in tune with children. In his memoirs he wrote, "When I dropped out of Oxford I decided to be a child. My books do not insult the intelligence of children because I'm on their level." The childish imagination made him rich and famous and the destroyer of the Dick & Jane books.

Mystical Majesty of Maria Montessori & Dr. Seuss

Happiness lies in the mind of the beholder. Chase fantasies and dreams and one can not only be happy but will never work since work is your passion. What makes such people whole is what makes them happy. Dr. Seuss and Maria Montessori epitomize individuals with the temerity to chase their passions no matter if it is politically correct. Their refusal to abide by convention is what made them special and contributed to their altering the paradigms of the educational process.

The eccentric Geisel was always considered odd. The Dartmouth school paper labeled him the school's "Least Likely to Succeed." Ironically, he far surpassed any of those who wrote those antiprophetic words. Shows what the establishment knows about the creative process. Graduating with a passion for drawing, he promptly enrolled in an art school, like Walt Disney had some years earlier, and like the father of Mickey Mouse lasted a very short time. The teacher told Geisel, "There are rules that every artist must abide by and you will never be successful if you break them." Thinking about that rejection for drawing outside the lines he promptly packed his things and walked out and said, "I was free forever from art-by-the-rule books."

In a similar way Maria Montessori was rebuffed for daring to think outside the lines in Victorian Italy. It would appear her life was miserable but for her it was a constant adventure. Attending engineering school as the only woman she decided to attend the Rome Medical School and when turned down by the dean for being female she appealed to the Pope and gained entry.

*After graduating and working as a medical doctor in Rome Maria found herself preg-
nant by a young physician. His family refused to accept Maria, forcing her to bear the
child out of wedlock, a real no-no in that era in Italy, and to raise the child as a
nephew in faraway Florence. Maria had been rejected by her old-fashioned father for
wanting to be a medical doctor. Then she was ridiculed by the male physicians at the
University of Rome. And once again she was rejected when told she could not practice
medicine like other physicians. For most people it would have been too much when she
was rejected by her lover's family. And then the political party headed by Mussolini
found her belief in the freedom of the child to be inconsistent with their political
dogma and she was forced to leave Italy to practice her profession across Europe and
Asia.*

*Many lesser individuals would have dropped out or crawled into a bottle but the
highly mystical Montessori never capitulated. She wrote unceasingly of her passion on
childhood education until in her eighties. This only child who early on decided to pursue life with gusto was used to rejection. She had been groomed by a strong mother to
be self-sufficient. That led her to enroll in an all-boys science academy, to the chagrin
of the officials and her father. Later she enrolled in engineering school in college,
which infuriated her father and other paternalists in Rome. When she opted for a
career in medicine it was the last straw and her father did not speak to her for years.
At the University of Rome's Medical School she was told to become a teacher like other
girls. She refused to listen and that is what made her great.*

*The voracious reader was a devotee of Positivism philosophy. When forced to resign
her position at the University of Rome due to pregnancy she became lost in the works
of French writers Rousseau and Frederick Froebel. The famous Froebel blocks became
tools in her educational work and later in the Montessori Schools. Maria spent time in
France studying early childhood education under French psychologists Itard and
Seguin. After much study she became a philosopher of education in her own right with
insights such as, "No one can be free unless he is independent."*

*The pedagogue of education questioned everything and later wrote of her success say-
ing, "I could have done anything." Her life and work have a strong Nietzschean and
Promethean quality. This can be seen by her strong words like, "Moral education
demands a Superman. More important than a method is a master." This offers insight
into Maria's dedication to experiential and pragmatic educational approaches—what
works is good. Permitting students to be free to pursue their own ideas and desires
proved to be a revolutionary concept at the time. The archaic programmed education
in more traditional venues was adversarial; they couldn't comprehend allowing chil-*

dren to learn on their own. At the Casa da Bambini in Rome, Montessori's original test group for the Montessori Method, the children were in power and permitted the "mental freedom to take what they needed." Maria proved that freedom is power and it must be pursued at all cost to find truth.

Geisel was as deviant as Montessori in his approach to writing books for children. It permitted him to become famous under the pseudonym Dr. Seuss, to offer validation and a certain mystique to his work. He was a big kid who never grew up. While on vacation the good Doctor would romp in the pool like a ten-year-old even while functioning as the CEO of Beginner Books. In his position he could not refrain from zany antics like telling his staff, "Adults are obsolete children."

In a complete defiance of office decorum Dr. Seuss would create signs for the office doors of his staff like some madcap seven-year-old. The creative signs offered insight into the management: "Dr. Violet Valerie Vowel—Divisional Director of Consonants." Dr. Seuss reported to Phyllis Cerf, the wife of CEO Bennett Cerf. Phyllis referred to him as "a happy genius." But when she tried to control his maniacal words and pictures with a more constrained rhetoric the two came to an impasse and rather than lose his famed writer Cerf terminated his wife.

For Dr. Seuss nothing was off-limits. The perpetual kid escaped into an inner reverie that made him as happy as when he was twelve at the zoo in Springfield, Massachusetts. Once during a media interview he mentioned that work was killing him and making him unhappy since he was unable to sleep. The reporter asked why a man of his wealth didn't just stop working so hard. Dr. Seuss responded, "I would be more miserable if I were not doing this."

▼

CHAPTER 4

WONDER WOMEN IGNORE CONVENTIONAL WISDOM

Experts have such a personal investment in what *is*, they can't see what *might be*!

"He who doesn't know, knows. He who thinks he knows, doesn't know!"
Joseph Campbell

"Only by stepping outside logic can one make the leap to enlightenment"
Douglas Hofstadter

"Your thoughts have the power to alter the physiological response of your muscles"
John Diamond, Behavior Kinesiology

The eminent are nonconformist supermen who chase dreams rather the dogma of others. The reason is they intuitively understand that experts have such a psychological investment in what is traditional they have little or no understanding of what might be possible. Thomas Kuhn spoke of such behavior in his landmark work *The Structure of Scientific Revolutions*, in which he coined the term *paradigm shift*. Kuhn wrote, "All new paradigm shifts were resisted by experts for approximately thirty years—a whole generation." The experts can self-destruct over their own arrogant need to be right and defend their area of expertise to avoid suffering personal inadequacy. Thomas Edison was a brilliant inventor who transformed the world with his light bulb and work on direct current devices, but he went to his grave defending direct current over Tesla's alternating current for distribution of electrical energy. Einstein was guilty of the same myopia in his position on quantum theory. The intuitive child-man was convinced we become too enamored with knowledge to know how to innovate, saying:

"The gift of fantasy has meant more to me than any talent for absorbing positive knowledge. Once you grow up you know too much, far too much. I think physicists are the Peter Pans of the human race. They never grow up and keep their curiosity."

As Einstein said, we are often so smart we are stupid. Why? We know too much for our own good and it causes us to lose our childish curiosity. Until Roger Bannister broke the elusive four-minute mile no runner set it as a possible goal. The barrier was so ingrained in the thinking of track and field athletes no one ever considered trying it, but when it was broken high school runners all over the world began breaking it. Studies have shown that the salesperson who doesn't know where not to go often emerges with the big deals. Breaking traditional dogmas is what creativity is all about. The Pike Syndrome demonstrates why this is true. When northern pike are separated from the minnows located just beyond the glass barrier they become conditioned not to go there. That is what happens to humans due to early conditioning. The pike will actually die after the glass is removed rather than swim to their food. Like the pike people often are found self-destructing from within due to spurious past beliefs.

Self-serving attitudes or too much negative conditioning is the death knell for innovation. In such things the mind is the traffic cop hindering progress. It tries to protect us from adversaries but in the process obstructs creativity. It does so even when we don't want to be protected. The secret is to know when to listen to that cognitive input and when to ignore it. Families and loved ones can also limit us by their interest in our safety. In an attempt to keep us out of harm's way they will offer advice that is not only bad but can prove tragic. When Walt Disney showed his brother Roy his idea for the first animated cartoon film, *Snow White*, Roy responded, "You're trying to ruin us." Later when he brought in the plans for an amusement park—Disneyland—his brother threatened to have him committed.

Hollywood demeaned Walt's idea of a full-length animated film, *Snow White and the Seven Dwarves*, calling it Disney's Folly—not unlike Seward's Folly. Banks backed off and the firm almost went bankrupt. One of the legends of Tinseltown, Louis B. Mayer of MGM, told the media "Who'd pay to see a fairy princess when they can see Joan Crawford's boobs for the same price at the box office" (Landrum 1996 p. 343). Walt had a nervous collapse but prevailed and on its release that folly of a film earned $8 million in the first 18 months at a time when tickets sold for 25 cents at the box office. *Time* called it "a masterpiece" and *Variety* said it was the "all-time box office champ." By 1990 the classic had earned over $100 million and when it was reintroduced in 1994 it became the all-time best-selling video. What if Walt had listened to the experts?

In 1977 when I showed my mother the prototype of Chuck E. Cheese she turned to me and said, "Honey! When are you going to get a real job?" Such well-meaning comments are born of ignorance and fear of the new and innovative. Only one to three percent of the population buys into new ideas with the rest dismissing them as the work of an eccentric. An example of this precept was when the prestigious *Washington Post* (Burns 1980) wrote scathing editorials on the stupidity of Ted Turner's 24-hour news idea called CNN. The journal said, "Industry doubts that Ted Turner knows his ass from a hole in the ground. CNN just can't be done." Turner didn't listen. In fact, the renegade bet every bit of his $100 million net worth on his brainchild. His temerity paid off. He is now a billionaire, and both his name and that of his news network are famous. What if he had listened to the networks and the *Wall Street Journal* who called him crazy?

New Age writer Anton Wilson offered insight into the paradox of experts not being in tune with reality when he wrote in *Prometheus Rising* (1997):

Participants in a large organization must be very, very careful that they are in accord with the reality-tunnel of those above them. In such authoritarian situations it is important to see what the top dogs see; it is inconvenient, and possibly dangerous, to see what is objectively happening.

Shamans Keep Dancing with the Gorilla They Created

Once Shamans bet all on an idea they must continue to dance with the gorilla they created or chance being destroyed by it. That merely perpetuates idiotic ideas such as school testing after the school year has been completed to justify promotions to the next grade or graduation. The truth is that the teachers have that responsibility, based on what has occurred in the classroom, not some bureaucrat playing CYA games. Give the authority to the principals to decide who is retained or passed. If they can't, or won't, do it, then relieve them of the responsibility. Educators are now sanctifying tests as the paragon of outcome assessment to justify their teaching methodology and programs. That is ludicrous.

The purpose of education is to teach kids to grow, to learn to think on their feet, and to learn new concepts that can be used on the streets of life. The purpose is not to pass tests for accountability for retention or promotion. Year-end testing is self-serving for the educational hierarchy who don't know how to deal with incompetent teachers. Students have already been tested during the school year so adding further tests to see if they qualify to pass is not only redundant but counter to the educational process. What if a student does exceptionally well during the school year and flunks the final test due to some other variable? What if they can't make it to that test? The time used for such tests takes away from the time that could be used to prepare the student for life after school. The problem is that educational officials won't defy the system for fear of being destroyed by that gorilla they have created so they may keep playing the game. Those at the top don't see the truth. Most often they are too ignorant to get it or far too self-serving to deal with it.

A Blind Man Often Sees beyond Those with Sight

Studies indicate that the majority of our actions emanate from the unconscious, not the conscious. In other words, our behavior, wants and desires, and even passions emanate from within. Our consciousness only shows us what is blatantly obvious. Even our eyes can deceive us, as is shown below in the necker cube experiment. Visionaries and savants seem to have a sixth sense. Those who have lost a limb know this as they still have feeling where nothing exists. We record images in our minds and those images remain the same over time despite changes that have occurred. Attending a high school reunion after many years brings this to the fore; we still have stored the picture of the person from that long-ago visage. The new image now updates our memory bank. *We are blind to the fact we are blind.* Slow people are just not aware of their lethargy, dumb people do not relate to their ineptitude unless forced to solve some intellectual problem, and even obese people don't see themselves as they really are.

Think about your drive to work today. Do you remember it? Probably not! In particular you are oblivious of environmental details along the route. The reason is that our brains go on remote control to keep us from overdosing on data and sensory inputs since there are just too many for us due to latent inhibition. *Necker cubes* are an example of this reality paradox. They are proof of the optical illusion or the way the eyes are out of synch with our brains. Ogle them and they flip-flop as you concentrate. Your right-brain will perceive the forward protrusion to be to the lower left while your left-brain sees the forward protrusion to the upper right. If you continue to concentrate your perception begins to play games with you. The images switch back and forth in a bizarre but surreal sensory phantasmagoria. What is taking place is what psychologists describe as a whole-brain state or cerebral balancing.

On close examination the middle and right cubes take on an illusory image. The lines that delineate the forward protrusion—to the left or the right—becomes altered and configured in a way that would be impossible for a real cube to exist. This paradoxical vision is real as drawn even if implausible to the human eye. Remember these cubes the next time you are confronted with an enigmatic puzzle.

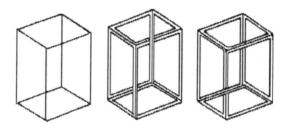

Such images are often beyond man's logical sense or visual perception. The mystery is sensory and is why we were so moved by the magical movements of Disney's characters Dopey, Grumpy, Doc, Sneezy, Bashful, Happy, and Sleepy singing "Heigh ho, heigh ho, it's off to work we go." Walt saw the vision but it was lost on those Hollywood know-it-all's like Harry Cohn, Jack Warner, and Louis B. Mayer. They knew too much and were lost in their own reality tunnel. Innovation is more likely to lie well outside what is perceptually obvious, but most experts are too immersed in what is to see what might be.

Arrogance—The Panacea of Ignorance

In the insightful words of Georgiei Gurdjieff, "If you want to lose your faith, make friends with a priest." The moral of his words were that it is easy to become lost in priestly dogma to the point of losing contact with objective reality. Watch those steeped in number-crunching to the point they often become lost in their own analysis-paralysis. Everything is evaluated quantitatively by such people, to the detriment of the qualitative. When we become too good at anything we can get lost in our own myopia. The absolute in any venue is a dangerous mind field. When the medical world bled patients in the nineteenth century they thought they were on the right path to a cure but were way off course due to their lack of vision.

When in power, people tend to become self-deluded, often believing in their own omnipotence. They start believing they were predestined for their position as in the case of Napoleon, Hitler, and Stalin—all arrogant power brokers who felt they were messianic. Napoleon became so enamored with his power that he proclaimed, "Nothing that happened to me that I did not foresee. I can divine everything in the future" (Hershman & Lieb p. 148). Wow! Hitler's megalomania went so far as to say, "Extraordinary geniuses permit of no consideration for ordinary mankind. I never make a mistake" (H&L p. 78). In his *Short Biography* Stalin claimed, "A genius cannot help but be right. Everyone can err but Stalin never errs."

Top dogs often conjure up rules and regulations to keep the flock in line. Those rules become sacrosanct for their followers. They frighten their flock with hell and then promise them salvation if they will just give them power. The same is found in large corporations where budgets are used to ensure that no one violates the dictates from the top. Are budgets good tools? Sure! But when used to control and eliminate originality they become the enemy of growth. Telling employees they can't because it's not in the budget is akin to marching backward into the dark ages of merchandising. What if violating the budget doubles sales or triples profits? That is lost on those wanting to maintain control no matter the cost.

Expertise can program us to remain in the status quo or pay the price of personal loss in the eyes of our associates. Academics are often guilty of becoming lost in their own dogma. This was true when the prestigious *Scientific American* wrote an editorial decrying the Wright Brothers' flight as a hoax. Arrogant omniscience led Mother Church to imprison Galileo for daring to say the Earth was not the center of the galaxy. As ludicrous as it may sound the Sorbonne in Paris called Diderot's encyclopedia a heresy.

Engineering experts called Edison a dangerous wannabe inventor for trying to develop the light bulb. Professor Silvanus P. Thompson said, "Edison's bulb idea is doomed to failure and shows the most airy ignorance for the fundamental principles of electricity and dynamics." Dr. Henry Morton of Stevens Institute told the press, "The Edison incandescent bulb is an absurd claim attributed by sheer ignorance and charlatan." But the most arcane of such arrogant claims was when a young Philo Farnsworth visited Motorola in Chicago with what he described as a talking radio. Executives refused to talk to the kook and sent a secretary to the lobby to dispatch the crazy kid and warned her to beware of weapons and knives. Farnsworth's television invention was just too far outside the mainstream for experts to believe possible.

Intuitive Insight Is Often like Magic

Radical rationality has been proven to be contra to innovation. To become innovative one must rely on the gut. Jonas Salk liked to say, "It is always with excitement that I wake up in the morning wondering what my intuition will toss up to me, like gifts from the sea. I work with it and rely on it. It's my partner." Einstein spoke often about his intuitive powers that he considered far more valuable than his mind. Mozart told of his gut leading to far more compositions than logic saying:

> *"When I am traveling in a carriage, or walking after a good meal, or during the night when I cannot sleep, it is on such occasions that ideas flow best and most abundantly"*

Valerie Hunt, an internationally recognized human energy guru, in her work *Infinite Mind* (1996) said, "Any sufficiently advanced technology is indistinguishable from magic. Ultimate reality is contacted, not through the physical sense of the material world, but through deep intuition." Philosopher and mathematician Bertrand Russell had the most profound insight into the magic of creativity saying, "The sense of certainty and revelation comes before any definite belief." Great artists often have a special predilection for starting at the end not the beginning. They begin their innovative search with answers and then proceed to solutions during the journey. Leonardo wrote in his notebooks, "First start with the end." Michelangelo spoke of staring at a block of marble and seeing David in the rock. The finished work was only a matter of removing the unnecessary parts that kept David from being revealed.

Rejection Inspires Innovators

George Bernard Shaw was considered the greatest playwright since Shakespeare. It was no accident that his first six novels were rejected outright. Half a century later H. L. Mencken spoke of Shaw's early work as his greatest contributions to the world of letters. No less than 27 different publishers rejected Dr. Seuss's first children's book, *And to Think That I Saw It on Mulberry Street.* No fewer than nine myopic publishers told J. K Rowling that *Harry Potter and the Philosopher's Stone* was not marketable as a children's book and had "no commercial value." Within ten years the Potter books had unprecedented appeal, with sales of half a billion, and Rowling was worth more than the Queen of England. What if she had scrapped her book due to the experts' opinions?

This implausibility of expert opinion in literature appears to have peaked in 1997 when a New Zealand study on bad writing found that the worst writers were actually those who taught the subject—prestigious academics. In one sense that finding is surprising, but in another it is not at all. Professors become so grounded in what is important to APA style that they groom students to pay more attention to structure than content. For them words are sacrosanct despite the fact that humans are known to think in images not in words. Yet every college professor grades down if the student dares show a graphic image to enhance their point. Syntax and grammar become godly with effective communications lost in their personal arrogance. The New Zealand contest on bad writing ironically concluded that those who wrote what was bad were the very ones who taught what was good. The worst writer of all was a professor of comparative literature at Duke University named Frederic Jameson.

Innovators Prefer Form over Function—Opposite Experts

Experts have a long history of falling in love with what you know.
There's an adage in the physical sciences: "If a great researcher in a field, near the end of a long and successful career, says something is possible, he is almost

always right. If a great researcher in a field, near the end of a long and success-ful career, says something is impossible, he is almost always wrong." The death knell for innovation is becoming so smart you know what can't work. Experts are the ones who poisoned Socrates for teaching the youth of Athens to "know thyself." They were also the academic know-it-alls who denied Stephen Spiel-berg entrance into USC's prestigious film school, not once but twice, because of his C average in high school. This was despite his having won the Arizona State Film Festival Award at age seventeen for *Escape to Nowhere*. Spielberg was evaluated on his high school merits without consideration for his potential of artistry in a world of artistry. Dumb! Similar logic would cause the majority of American institutions of higher learning to reject Bill Gates as a professor in their CIT programs. Why? He doesn't have the required 18 hours of graduate credits.

The struggling writer James Michener wrote of his adventures in the Pacific theater toward the end of World War II and titled his manuscript *South Pacific*. An agent was aghast and told the schoolteacher, wannabe writer, "You have no future as a writer." Ironically, within a week *South Pacific* won the Pulitzer Prize for Literature. In one short week Michener went from remorse to ecstasy. An even more dramatic example of expert myopia comes from the world of music. The most prolific songwriter in American history, a Russian Jew, could not read or write music. Irving Berlin wrote the most endearing American classics—*Alexander's Ragtime Band, There's No Business like Show Business, White Christmas, God Bless America,* and *Easter Parade*. *God Bless America* has often been considered as the song to replace the national anthem since it is considered more patriotic and more in tune with the American spirit. It is not surprising then to find that Frank Sinatra, Judy Garland, and Elvis Presley were incapable of reading music.

Paradoxical Power

The more we *are* something the less we have *to be* that something and con-versely the *less* you are the more you have to act like you *are*. Such logic had President John F. Kennedy picking up dates in his Plymouth with no money in his pocket. Those mired in the projects conversely show up in their mort-gaged Cadillac. Wannabes need symbols of acceptance while those with the pedigrees can forgo the vestiges of affluence. Those requiring validation of being smart join MENSA and more often than not the rooms are filled with those without gainful employment. Ever look closely at the resume of a recent high school grad? It is two or three pages describing their experience in the band, clubs, and inconsequential part-time jobs. A resume of Bill Gates will suffice with a one-liner: "I know a lot about operating software." The more we know about any subject the more succinct we can be in describing that knowledge. The less knowledge we possess the more we tend to pontificate. C. Northcott Parkinson in his classic cynicism on experts wrote in Parkinson's Laws on the inverse relationship between the complexity of something and its acceptance by so-called experts. He spoke of a nuclear reactor receiving board approval in 90 seconds while a bicycle rack took three hours since everyone knew a lot about bicycles and virtually nothing about a nuclear reactor.

Diversity Is Paradoxical

There is an irony in the life of the diverse. The *haves* want what the *don't haves* have and the *have nots* want what the *haves* have. What? A British study in 2005 found that women with an IQ sixteen points higher than the norm had a 40 percent less chance of marrying while a man with such credentials had a 35 percent greater chance of marrying. Young girls fantasize about marrying a man whom she can change while men fantasize about marrying a woman who never changes from that girlish nature. Ironically, guys seldom change and women always do.

Whites tend to dress down to appear cool while blacks dress up to look cool. Whites go to beauty salons to have their hair curled while blacks go to salons to have their hair straightened. Blacks desire thin lips while whites have plastic surgery to get a full-lip look. Whites are at the beach trying to be darker while those who are dark are looking for ways to look lighter. In Asia affluence for women is a full figure while in America it is in vogue for them to be model-slim. For centuries men have placed attractive women on pedestals when an average woman with brains, talent, and integrity would be far better suited for the role. Conversely, a woman opts for the guy with big bucks despite his shortcomings as a father or husband.

A Cultural Anomaly: Wanting What You Don't Have

- Bright women have a lower chance of marrying while bright men have a greater chance

- Women chase men with big bucks even if they are the worst possible mate or father

- Men chase women with great looks even if they are not nice

- Whites go to tanning salons to get dark; blacks prefer being lighter—Michael Jackson and Oprah prayed to be white when young and Jackson spent megabucks trying to make it happen

- Whites go to beauty salons to get curly hair; blacks have salons to make their hair straight

- Being model-thin in the U.S. is a sign of affluence; being plump in Asia is a sign of affluence

- Whites have plastic surgery to get a full-lip look; blacks have lip reductions

- The most common surgery is to round the eyes

- Asians and Whites see small families as a sign of prestige and go ballistic if their daughters come home pregnant without being married; Hispanics see large families as a sign of prestige and find pride if a daughter comes home pregnant

- Whites dress down to look cool; blacks dress up to look cool (black males have historically led in setting fashion)

The Path to Power Comes from Listening to Your Internal Genie

Albert Einstein & Golda Meir

World-renowned physicist Albert Einstein was about as analytically oriented as a person can be. But despite his expertise with numbers he bowed deeply to his intuitive side that led him to say, "Intuition is the gift of the gods, logic is its faithful servant." He would write that, "Imagination is more important than knowledge. Anything that is truly great is created in the mind of one individual laboring in freedom."

A poignant example of Einstein's faith in the intuitive process was his use of aphorisms at Princeton. Each day he implored physics doctoral students to stop idolizing numbers and listen to the gut insights that unfold daily. He admonished them to stop worshipping at the altar of the quantitative with these prophetic words written on the blackboard: "Not everything that counts can be counted, and not everything that can be counted, counts." Einstein married time, energy, and space and led physics to stop marching to the concrete sequential, saying, "A theory can be proven by experiment, but no path leads from experiment to a theory."

Einstein was considered a marginal student at best. A German headmaster told his father that he would not amount to much. The teacher didn't get the student since his curiosity refused to allow him to adapt or spend time on useless conformity. Like most gifted children Einstein was more interested in looking for what might be than what had been. Unfortunately, most schools groom children to adapt and study the past rather than chase the future. Mediocrity results from an educational process that is politically correct for the norm rather than the gifted. Teachers who can use the textbook theories to demonstrate what it means on the street of hard knocks are far more in tune with imaginative children.

Due to Einstein's defiant nature, when he earned his doctorate he was not considered special and was unable to find a teaching position at any of the Swiss or German universities. In fact he was so marginal in the eyes of academics he was forced to work in the Swiss Post Office working on patents. It is in this unlikely environment that Einstein wrote his landmark thesis on the Theory of Relativity, the famous $E = MC^2$. Scientists of that era were not impressed. He had not proven his theory in the laboratory; thus they said it was the work of an eccentric wannabe. Academics panned the Theory of Relativity for over a decade until it was finally validated in 1919. That is when Einstein was awarded the Nobel Prize in Physics for the photoelectric effect. A similar refutation was found in the work and life of Nobel-winning mathematician John Nash, who was a student of Einstein's.

Golda Meir, the first female Prime Minister of Israel, went through a similar fight for freedom when her father told her to marry and bear children instead of trying to chase mystical dreams. Golda didn't listen and left home as a teenager to live with an older sister. When her dreams came to fruition and Golda found herself as the head of the Israeli state, she like Einstein gave free rein to her intuitive powers and it helped save the young nation. To the chagrin of her male cabinet members she let her female intuition serve her. In March of 1973 Golda was reading reports about Russians suddenly leaving Arab territories. This triggered a sense of foreboding just before the Yom Kippur holiday in October, and she called a cabinet meeting. The males were not thrilled and told her to stop being a woman. Golda gushed, "Look, I have a terrible feeling that this has all happened before. It reminds me of 1967. I think it means something." The all-male cabinet scoffed at her feminine intuition saying, "Don't worry. There won't be a war." Golda was right and there was a war, one that came close to destroying the nation. Golda would write, "I should have listened to my heart and ordered a call-up" (Landrum 1994 p. 290). When the media asked how 350,000 Jews defeated 4 million Arabs, Golda responded, "We had a secret weapon, No alternative!"

Mythical mentoring was a key element in the success of Golda. The Golden Girl was born in Russia and came to America at five and was reared in Milwaukee. Ever since her early years of hearing the taunts of "death to the Christ killers" in Kiev she was infatuated with Zionism, living for the day she could be part of the reincarnation of an Israeli State in Palestine. Schoolfriends in Milwaukee gave her the nickname Zionut due to her impassioned speeches at fund-raising events. Golda adopted a motto of, "If you will it, it is no fairy tale." The young firebrand earned the epithet Golden Girl for her passion and sensuality. That seems a strange epithet when seeing her later in life but as a young woman Golda was a femme fatale. During her heyday she raised millions to arm her new nation. A political adversary, David Ben Gurion, heard her speak and gushed, "I trembled at her daring words."

The 1972 Olympic massacre of Israeli athletes took place during Golda's regime as Prime Minister. True to her competitive spirit this matronly lady put together a counterterrorist group called The Unit. Their mantra was *Wrath of God*, aimed at avenging the senseless killings by the PLO of innocent athletes. Eleven athletes perished senselessly but within a few years each of those responsible was hunted down and killed without remorse. The young girl from Milwaukee was an advocate of the biblical chant, "An eye for an eye," and sent a lasting message to her enemies that if you kill, expect to be killed.

Mythical Magic of Cognitive Motivation

Albert Einstein & Golda Meir Were the Embodiment of Mythical Magic

Both Einstein and Golda Meir were advocates of listening to their gut. These two paid close attention to the essence of the situation rather than just looking at the hard facts. This is somewhat interesting in that Einstein was trained in the science of physics and Golda was reared in a paternalistic home environment where woman were revered but not heard. But Einstein had always disdained his cherished numbers for the mysteries of life. Curiosity and childish imaginative ideas were the fuel to his success. He even named his boat Intuition. *When asked about his ability to intuit solutions he said:*

"The really valuable thing is intuition."

The German-born physicist was derided for his eccentricities by the media and scientists but he saw the essence without ever getting lost in the stuff. When he landed in America escaping the Nazi onslaught in Europe a reporter asked him how far it was to the moon. Einstein said, "I have no idea." The smart-ass reporter retorted, "But Mr. Einstein, you are lauded as the world's most brilliant mind." The ever-loquacious Einstein looked at the pundit and said, "I know where to find such petty facts if I need them but don't care to litter my mind with such trivia."

After Einstein had submitted his ground-breaking thesis on relativity to the Switzerland Polytechnique he was refused a position in their school as a wayward intellectual. Most scientists were incapable of understanding his brilliant thesis on time, space, and energy. Many laughed at his complex theory that had been concocted by envisioning himself riding on a rocket through space. Later he would write, "I used childlike questions, and then proceeded to answer them. The most beautiful thing we can experience is the mysterious."

Rejection like Einstein endured most of his life was also founding the life and work of Golda Meir. During the 1973 Yom Kippur War Israel was threatened with annihilation by four million Arabs who had but one goal—to remove the Jewish religious zealots from Palestine. The years of struggle the Golden Girl had already endured had groomed her for dealing with the threat like only someone can who has stared at their mortality from childhood. As the first Israeli Prime Minister Golda appeared to be vulnerable but persevered via controlled aggression. Those haunting pogroms of a Russian childhood had armed her for the titanic Holy War with the Arabs.

"I can honestly say," wrote Golda in her memoir, "that I was never deflected from doing something because I thought I might fail." When King Abdullah of Jordan agreed to meet with a top Israeli parliament member none of the males volunteered. Crossing the Sinai desert was a suicidal mission for a Jew, and doing it dressed as a Muslim wife as she did was just as risky, as her Jewish comrades would have slit her throat. The intrepid Golda crawled across the dreaded sea of sand when in mid-life to meet with King Abdullah. She saw it as a chance to solidify their nation and her life was a small sacrifice. Close friends warned her that the chances of survival were minimal. She responded, "I would walk to hell if there was a chance to save one Jewish soldier's life" (Landrum 1994 p. 287). She went and the rest is history.

CHAPTER 5

▼

TITANS ARE PASSIONATE
TO A FAULT—GET
EXCITED OR CHANGE

Pass the Tumescence Test of Creativity or Pay a Price

"Unsatisfied libido is responsible for producing all art and literature."
Sigmund Freud

"Most virtue is a demand for greater seduction."
Natalie Barney

"Falling in love is a matter, not of magic, but of psychology. Once you understand your target's psychology you are better able to cast a magical spell. The seducer sees love not as sacred, but as warfare, where all is fair."
Robert Greene, *The Art of Seduction*

Superstars are often passionate mystics. Their passion is often paradoxical in that they are motivated by some inner fantasy or dream that elevates them above the pack. Success is the by-product of a passion for something not among the obvious needs of ordinary men. The key to all success is to listen to what your heart says and go there without thinking. Getting excited is the seed of all eminence. If you can't get excited about your job go find another. If your life isn't titillating alter it immediately. If you don't have a seductive nature about each day then you are not chasing the right dreams or anything worth chasing. If you are not willing to bet it all for some dream the dream isn't worth spending your valuable energy on.

Can you pass the tumescence test for life? If you don't get excited about your job, mate, or life you are not playing in the right ballpark. Mania for a mission is the catalyst for all progress. Those who get too excited can self-destruct by their zeal. Excess is empowering and destructive. The eminent live life right on the precipice but have the ability not to fall into the oblivion below. Most people are unwilling or unable to go to the edge, but not so for the superstars. The energy is either upbeat or downbeat. One makes us, the other breaks us.

Passion is what differentiates the also-rans from the winners. Passionate people are proactive and make things happen. The docile watch what is happening and wonder what happened. Even when things don't go well and you blow it you will be heard above the surrounding din. Everyone communicates quite well when impassioned. If you go too far the passion becomes self-destructive. At the zoo the frenetic monkey cage draws far bigger crowds than the passive alligators. The reason is that energy attracts and lethargy detracts. This is axiomatic for both humans and animals.

Evangelists offer us an example of what it means to have a powerful force within to pursue. They are often negative but we can learn from their passions. Evangelistic mavens succeed by promising everlasting peace and tranquility if you give your body, soul, and money to them to use as needed. Millions of people in all cultures have bought into such pitches with the most arcane those of twentieth century gurus Jim Jones of The People's Temple, David Koresh of The Branch Davidians, and Marshall Applewhite of Heaven's Gate infamy. The source of this charismatic appeal and power is finding the weak and disenfranchised. Then, frighten them with hell and promise them salvation, and studies indicate that they will follow you virtually anywhere. Here are some of the ploys.

Correlation between Libidinal Energy & Creativity

"Innovative people are sensuous." These were the profound words from social psychologist Frederick Herzberg. They describe what took place in the minds and hearts of the world's great innovators like Catherine the Great, Napoleon, Dostoevsky, Bertrand Russell, Balzac, Isadora Duncan, and Howard Hughes. Balzac wrote, "My orgies take the form of books," what Henri Bergson had spoken of as the *élan vital*. Isadora Duncan said, "I fell in love with males at eleven and I have never ceased to be madly in love." Even Golda Meir was not removed from this as her nickname in Tel Aviv was "Meir the Mattress" due to her nonstop liaisons with world leaders. Nikola Tesla, arguably the world's most brilliant engineer, never married or even slept with a woman but said in his memoirs, "I work in a frenetic passion. I knew I would perish if I failed." Other giants who remained single but sublimated their passions into their work were Leonardo da Vinci, Michelangelo, Sir Isaac Newton, Francis Bacon, and Nietzsche. Tesla felt marriage would drain him of vital energy writing, "I do not think you can name many great inventions that have been made by married men."

Charisma & Passion—Gurus Show Us the Way

Psychiatrist Anthony Storr wrote extensively on the motivations of gurus in *Saints, Sinners & Madmen* (1996). Storr found, "Gurus claim to have been granted a special, spiritual insight, which transformed his life." Most of them offer safety and hospice for the disenfranchised if they will just succumb to the guru's will. But in all such submissions there is a price to pay. There are no free lunches and when you become a disciple you often must sacrifice your sense of self or even more. The guru promises salvation and it is a haughty prize and is why trains to *Traditionville* are empty but those on the way to *Shangri La* are full. Robert Green in *The Art of Seduction* (2001) offered insight into the guru's message when he said, "Your words must lift people into the clouds where it is easy for them to lose their way."

Charismatic Power & the Seductive Process

- HAVE PURPOSE: Grab hold of a mystical vision that appeals to followers

- BE MYSTERIOUS: Enchantment comes from the unknown

- BE UNINHIBITED: Never compromise; go where mere mortals fear; take the journey with unbridled sexual possibilities

- BE ELOQUENT: Use powerful words and concepts to impart your emotional message like Napoleon, Carl Jung, and Hitler

- USE THEATRICS:

  To communicate with disciples don sartorial robes in order to appear larger-than-life with a saintly persona

- EGOISTIC FERVOR:

  Believe and people will follow to any Promised Land

- BE REAL & OPEN:

  Vulnerable people attract legions to their side

- BE ADVENTUROUS:

  Unconventionality is exciting and thrilling for those wallowing in mediocrity; brazen courage is magical

- USE MAGNETISM:

  Look into the eyes of the magic man to find power

All product or romantic sales pitches must be encapsulated in a passionate rhetoric that knows no bounds. The vagaries of reality cannot be confused with the goal. The reason is that all queries must have their emotional needs satisfied verbally and physically and the most successful ones offer a mythical escape from the present to a Utopian future. Seductions that are too obvious come to a poor end and will fall on deaf ears. When a man with a raging libido attempts to seduce a lovely lady it must be done with panache and style. Just like trying to hit a home run in baseball or a hole-in-one in golf, trying too hard ends in frustration. Home runs, like seductions, most often happen when you are not trying to hit them but when you are in a relaxed state of consummate focus and concentration. Stop trying and you will succeed more than you ever dreamed. A perfectly satisfied person cannot be seduced.

Seductive Semantics for Serious Sybarites

Be *avant-garde* and you'll be desirable. Be *brazenly cocky* and you will be pursued. Be *entertaining* and you'll be loved. Be *charismatic* and you'll be followed. Be *unavailable* and you'll be chased. Be *mysterious* and you'll be cherished. Be *energetic* and you'll have disciples. Be *passionate* and you'll be prized. Be *attentive* and you'll be prolific. The will wanes in the face of outlandish expectations, so *back off* dude. Remember that fantasy is far more appealing than reality. Romantic liaisons, no matter how brazen, are always preferable to safe seductions.

Metaphorical duplicity underlies all seductions whether on the field of play or when trying to play the field. Seductive or poetic communiqués have a better chance of hitting their mark than direct innuendos. Speak to the subject's inner needs and imagery, such things like emotional calamities are far more grabbing than non-emotional diatribes on what's good for you to eat. Speak to milady about how she makes you feel and she will help gain an identity with you and start feeling you as somebody. Emotional dialogue leads to sympathetic seductions. Coming on like a needy macho man is counterproductive to any liaison. Desperate men become desperate loners. Only when you don't need do you become needed.

Business Sales Seductions

New product launches go through a seductive dance just like romantic liaisons. Asking for seed monies seldom results in getting seed money since it is born of need. Until a potential investor becomes emotionally involved in the product or business he will not become a player or an investor. It is a game of greed versus fear and the greed had better be ten times greater than the fear.

If a prospective investor believes you need the money the chance of getting money becomes virtually nil. It's all about jumping on a moving winner with little downside and if that is not true or believed no one gets on the train. Until the chasm between the fear of losing and the elation of great wealth is bridged the entrepreneur goes wanting. No one invests because of a business plan with huge future gains. But no one will invest without one either. The numbers are but a justification to do what someone has already emotionally bought into and are there to validate their buy-in. Passionate rhetoric from a winner with potential is critical to victory. In the words of Robert Green in *The Art of Seduction* (2001):

> ***Lift people's thoughts into the clouds and they will relax, their defenses will come down, and it will be that much easier to maneuver and lead them astray. Your words become a kind of elevating drug.***

Seductions that are too obvious fail. Those who win are the ones with a devil-may-care attitude. Winners act like it's boarding time, off to another exotic adventure, pontificating, "Get on the train or it's leaving to some adventure without you as a participant." This is not gender specific. But women seem to be far more prone to buy into an adventurous tryst than men due to their more romantic mentality. Such convoluted logic is perplexing to traditional types who take words and actions quite literally.

Passionate Duplicity Trumps Candid Integrity

Many studies have shown that successful business types are less than candid in their pitches. During the time I was developing a business plan to fund the expansion of the Chuck E. Cheese concept of family entertainment the chairman, Nolan Bushnell, told me to stop being so honest with the projections. He said, "Gene, stop allowing the truth to interfere with what is needed to raise $30 million. Just put in the plan that we will surpass Pizza Hut in three years." I responded, "But Nolan they have spent a couple decades building 8000 stores. We have seven." With a twinkle of insight he responded, "People discount the numbers anyway. So let's give them numbers that justify their need for greed." In retrospect, candor would have proven unsuccessful.

Though not in tune with ethical standards in business or close to being politically correct, too much integrity is not correlated with raising big bucks for new risky business ventures. That is why middle Machiavellian types on tests have always made the best leaders. Great leaders must have enough integrity so they are not always using guile and deception to hurt others, but not enough of it to dissuade them from going down that pothole-ridden road. You can't have someone in front that you can't trust but you must have someone who can bamboozle a little bit to get the pack off dead center.

Zany wunderkinds like Thomas Edison, Henry Ford, and Walt Disney were deceptive enough to get financial backing for their projects. So were Coco Chanel and Martha Stewart. Why? They never permitted the number-crunchers to interfere with their cause. It takes a certain amount of bravado to hit the lotto of life and such individuals have it. The Don Juans are prevaricators of dreams, snake-oil salesman with a penchant for passion. Just look at the history of such gurus. Adolph Hitler, Jim Jones, and David Koresh were deluded. They used charisma to open doors and to mesmerize. Fantasy escape was their appeal and even though they were deluded we can learn from their approach.

Catherine the Great, Napoleon, and Hitler took over nations of which they were not even citizens due to charismatic and flamboyant power. They spoke of castles in the sky that appealed to the multitudes that put them in office. Nationalism and power for the masses were their platform and it sold well. Once granted power they often didn't bother to respect the platform but that is the ploy of Machiavellian types. Hitler's political sales pitch was simple: "Elect me and I will destroy the evil Red Menace from the East, end inflation, give you jobs, and protect you from the evil Jewish money mongers." The German people bought his words and gave him power. And later they paid the price of their naiveté although the military buildup did end inflation and they did have jobs.

The Paradox of Passion—Provocative to the Point of Perversity

Isadora Duncan became the anointed Mother of Modern Dance. The diva on a devilish mission wrote of her inner passions that erupted on stage and cast an aura of provocative daring. She wrote in her memoir, "Most virtue is a demand for greater seduction." Isadora spent most of her provocative life in Paris where the body is a temple more than a vessel. The horrid truth is that nations without all the puritanical laws and harangues America has have far fewer rapes and molestations. Paris permits nudity, as does much of Europe and especially Scandinavia, yet they do not have the same degree of sexual problems as the more puritanical America. During the era when Isadora preferred to dance with flowing lace exposing much of her body she was disdained in her home country but found solace in Europe.

The freedom of the dance that Isadora personified was her path to the top and ultimately led to her demise. This wild child loved with abandon and became a victim of her freedom-loving nature. Isadora died as she lived when a free-flowing scarf became entangled in the axle of a sports car in southern France and snapped her lovely neck. Isadora Duncan was an iconoclast who dared what most feared and her passion defined her dance and her memory. The dance diva wrote, "The seduction of Nietzsche's philosophy ravished my being."

The paradox of passion that was Isadora is pervasive in the media. They spin what sells. Which Martha Stewart did you believe in her defense of lying to the SEC? The one who said she was just trying to protect herself or the one who said her handbag was not a haute couture $6000 bag but the only one she owned? What? That is tantamount to saying she was also wearing her only pair of shoes to court. Don't think so, coach. Both men and women are guilty of such illusory images but the most egregious seem to be those naive females who hang huge

Christian crosses between their exposed breasts. Classically, the larger the cross the larger the cleavage due to breast implants. What a dichotomy! And it isn't just women who do this. Look at those rock stars on the make seducing groupies with crosses around their necks or in diamond-studded earrings.

Crosses adorning cleavage for seduction is a dichotomy lost on this writer. What motivates people to use such perverse duplicity? Crosses are sacred icons and certainly incite some emotional response. They conjure up positive imagery and when used as a weapon to seduce seem a bit out of synch with the belief in a greater power that would obviously see through that kind of subterfuge. Disarming a victim with words and symbols is understandable although questionable ethics, but the use of religion for seduction is somewhat insidious. The message is, "Look dude, I'm a God-fearing lady thus safe to sleep with." The whole game appears beyond the pale of a truly rational being.

The irony of seduction often belies logic. Women fear men who would use them and then leave them. Men are turned off by mercenary women looking for a meal ticket. Thus a game of guess my goals ensues. Machismo seldom admits they dislike aggressive women but they do. Women cower from males on the make but it is what they want and why they spend much of their life trying to look appealing. Women love needy men but they are the most needy with security rampant in their plans for a mate. Diabolical males often take advantage of this feminine weakness. Research shows this to be the case for men who find themselves in pinstripes. The girl next door can be found writing them love letters and offering solace and love to rapists and killers. This was the case for America's most notorious serial killer Ted Bundy. A woman named Carol Blue contacted him in a Florida prison, married him, and had his child. Both Menendez brothers were married in prison despite the fact they admitted killing both parents in cold blood. Women have written about the sexy eyes and demeanor of Osama Bin Laden and speak of fantasizing over him as a lover. Nurturing females are enamored of saving such monsters, a state lost on most men. A *San Francisco Chronicle* article appeared on January 6, 2002, titled *The Mysogynist's Mystique* by Shobhaa De:

"Sadly, for me I've always found misogynists sexy—you think they can be undone by your interest, that you will be the exception. The more evil and corrupt the greater the esteem for the woman"

Want Real Romance? Remove the Head!

Observant singles have long since found that the essence of romance is in the chase not in the catch. The chase involves dining and dancing, conversing on titillating subjects, petting and kissing. For the goal-oriented male this is part of what is necessary to achieve the goal. It is very costly and time-consuming but important and in retrospect is what romance is really about. For most women such ritual is the goal, not the bedroom scene that is the goal of the male. The dichotomy of thinking here is that men go for the score while women go for the romantic chase. When young this chase for the female involves catching a mate with potential for marriage and fatherhood. For the young male this chase is oriented around a woman who can play housewife and mother. The majority of males don't want to hear about romantic journeys but successful destinations. For the female the whole trip is about the journey. The women tend to be more right in this arena as journeys are far more titillating than endings. This dichotomy is the genesis of most marital problems. Robert Greene in *The Art of Seduction* (2001) wrote of this:

> **"Falling in love is a matter, not of magic, but of psychology. Once you understand your target's psychology you are better able to cast a magical spell. The seducer sees love not as sacred, but as warfare, where all is fair."**

Males and females, à la *Desperate Housewives*, play games with radically different values. A woman will stop playing any game that may destroy a valued relationship. What do the males do? To hell with the relationship! Win the game no matter the casualties. This is true in games of tennis, bridge, or life. Ever witness a game of mixed doubles in tennis? Men argue vehemently over a call while the women say forget it and let's just have fun. Goals are good to have—male seduction or female rings—but once formulated should be suspended during the seductive dance for romance. Focusing on the journey is far more rewarding than getting lost in the goal. Women tend to get this far better than men.

In gamesmanship *what ifs* cause distress and inevitably lead to stress. *What ifs* are born in the head and cause a person to become tentative, press, or become anxious. In such situations remove the questioning head and all cognitive thinking and just keep on dancing with dame success that brought you to the dance. *What ifs* interfere with the body's natural ability to function effectively. They are akin to well-meaning parents telling you to take the safe path. Both interfere with normal homeostatic functioning. Listen to the gut when you don't absolutely know the correct path. Don't worry, just do. Want to take off for Tahiti for your fortieth birthday bash? Dreaming won't make it happen. The way to get there is to work hard, save money, and then buy the ticket. Talking about it just won't get the job done.

Fear of Failure Is in the Head

Athletes know the importance of execution and fundamentals. If you don't execute well all the talent in the world is worthless. At crunch time athletes who worry lose. Those who execute effectively win. An example is hitting a long drive in golf. Once the body is trained to do the task engaging the head only disrupts the muscle memory that knows instinctually what to do. Cognitive meddling messes up the process. I was once skiing with an advanced skier who came to the top of a steep incline, stopped, and looked down and froze. She had negotiated this slope many times without a problem or trauma, but this time she permitted her head to interfere. Once she looked down and kept looking down all the unconscious fears took over and she sat down and began to cry. Once that happens the ability for the body to function normally has been lost and failure becomes a self-fulfilling prophecy.

Thinking is the fuel of failure. It is counterintuitive but it is true. Thinking about failing distorts reality. And then the dominant neurological process is fear of failing. People who try not to fail are the ones who fail. Those who only look for reasons to succeed are far more inclined to win. Most people are oblivious of this fundamental premise, even those experienced football coaches who start using "prevent defenses" in lieu of doing what got them the lead in the first place.

Men often fear rejection by beautiful women. That is precisely why most will ask a less attractive one to dance instead of the *femme fatale*. Most women are unaware of the morbid fear men have of crossing a dance floor to ask a woman to dance. If rejected that walk back is forever. Males are rational and do not think a woman would be there if she didn't want to dance, but they get lost in rationality, since she is there to pursue possible relationships, not to dance. In his mind if he isn't attempting a seduction why the rejection? Most women would be shocked how devastating it is when they say no to a male. This is key to why brilliant attractive heterosexual men like Nietzsche and Tesla disdained the mating game.

Trauma can be a catalyst. When actress Sharon Stone turned 45, old for a femme fatale actress, she also went through a horrid divorce, was told her father had inoperable cancer, was diagnosed with a life-threatening brain aneurysm, and it all led to an epiphany. Those people without a positive sense of self would self-destruct and crawl into a bottle. Sharon used the crises to transform herself. In a 2004 interview she appeared before the media as a giggling woman-child and told them, "I'm in Happy Land. Life is too short for anything. I'm now in my girly state and enjoying it immensely."

Fear is debilitating because it brings about exactly what you don't want. The reason is the unconscious has been imprinted with the negative, permitting no positive. That makes fear the problem, not the problem at hand. As the bumper stickers say *Shit Happens!* And that is a universal truth. Problems are not the enemy but fear itself, as FDR said so eloquently during the height of the Great Depression. The victims who worry about everything are their own worst enemy. They keep getting what they worry about getting because it permeates their system. Sound paradoxical? It is! Only a person can stare down fear as if it were not there will prevail. Those who permit fear to dominate their lives are crippled by it. After her flirtation with death Sharon Stone told the media that she had reemerged as a "vagina with an attitude." She told one talk show host that the good-old-boys in Hollywood now treat her differently. Before, she said, she had been treated as a brainless beauty but once she changed they changed. Once they discovered that she was unwilling to be used she stopped being used. Stop whimpering and be heard and it may just happen should be the mantra of choice for women on the move.

Once a person is willing to walk away from fear or a relationship neither holds any power. To maintain a relationship it is imperative to give freedom to the other party. When one party has too much need the other begins to feel the pressure and the relationship begins to unravel. Males showing up in a singles bar with a raging libido are waving a red flag at their quarry and are destined for rejection. The frenetic male asking every woman in the joint to dance is so obvious he is immediately labeled loser by the women no matter his true status. That self-confident dude at the bar chatting with friends comes across as desirable due to a devil-may-care persona. He is nonthreatening and often becomes the prey. What a contrast between the two. The minute a female asks Mr. Nonchalant to dance the battle of seduction is over. In this psychological mating game he who speaks first loses.

The High Heat Paradox in the Game of Sex

In the game of sex success begets success. In the struggle for dominance and power those who succeed in seductions have increased sexual energy and become more and more of what they are—dominant Alpha Males from a behavioral perspective. The converse is also true. Decreased sexual energy accompanies defeat. When a male walrus is beaten by the dominant male they become impotent. Some males in the animal kingdom lose the color that attracts the opposite sex once beaten. Women seem to be the variable in this game of power. Whether they are consciously aware of it they use sexual attraction to gain power.

In high heat women can make men look like wimps. They do what men merely talk about. In the locker room men brag about their ability to perform while swinging precariously from a chandelier. Women will actually do it when sufficiently aroused. Men swagger and talk about doing it in front of a battalion but when push comes to shove the women will actually do it while the guy wilts. When sufficiently aroused a woman is the wild uninhibited beast with a jungle sense of adventure and the macho male is a bewildered milquetoast trying to understand what happened. Men go rational while women go emotional in high heat. Men caught with their proverbial pants down are suddenly discharged. Women, however, are different. In high heat females are fully capable of sating their passion while the world watches.

British psychiatrist Anthony Storr offered insight into this when he said, "Love is a totally irrational experience, a kind of madness, the normal prototype of the psychosis." Are lovers often "moonstruck" to the point of acting irrationally? Absolutely! Despite a puritanical upbringing, Bertrand Russell wrote extensively on the irony of sexual behavior and the prudish policies that are hypocritical at best. Ranting on the subject of free love and religious dogmatism led to him lose a lucrative Oxford teaching position and be banned from New York City. The philosopher of logic wrote, "Where sex is repressed only work remains, and a gospel of work for work's sake, never produced any work worth doing" (*Marriage & Morals* 1987). Another philosophic insight went, "The degree of one's emotion varies inversely with one's knowledge of the facts—the less you know the hotter you get."

Repressed Psychological Urges of Creative Geniuses

One biographer wrote extensively on Walt Disney's repressed sexuality. He spoke of Mickey Mouse and Donald Duck as Walt's alter egos. These opposite tendencies were in synch with Walt's wild mood swings that were due to his obsessive-compulsive nature and his bipolar personality. When Walt was up he was way up. When he was down he was incapacitated. Bipolar personalities are more provocative than the norm although in Walt passion was sublimated into his animated characters. Uncle Walt's numerous emotional collapses and suicidal behavior spawned his creativity. It appears his superego, to use a Freudian term, was imbued in Mickey—*chaste, humble, cerebral, asexual, in control,* and *adored by all.* In contrast Donald Duck was created later and embodies Walt's more devious nature or what Freud would have labeled Walt's id. Donald Duck had a more Machiavellian nature and was *dark, volatile, emotional, sexual, out of control,* and *angry.*

Like Disney, Leonardo da Vinci also sublimated his inner passions into his work. Volumes have been written about the androgyny of *Mona Lisa.* Her famous smile was a true anomaly—the masculine and the feminine interconnecting in one enigmatic facial expression. One side of the Mona Lisa's face is smiling. The other is austere. The work of art is a dichotomy of gender, passion, and androgyny portraying good and evil, compassion and cruelty, seduction and innocence, the fleeting and the eternal, the yin and the yang. And it is all about Leonardo the ambidextrous macho man and tender *artiste.*

Leonardo lived a life of ambiguity in opposition to authority with an adamant refusal to conform to anything or anyone, even the Pope. Leonardo exuded both the masculine and the feminine. He was a perfectionist but also a flake. He was happy and sad, mysterious but obvious, rational while being dysfunctional, and able to paint equally well with either hand. Freud analyzed Leonardo and made the point that he remained a child his whole life yet was a man's man with arms of steel. Leonardo painted the *Last Supper* left-handed but on tiring would then paint right-handed. As with most geniuses he always started with the end not at the beginning. The frustrated Pope Leo complained, "Alas! This man begins by thinking of the end of the work before the beginning."

British Prime Minister Winston Churchill, hardly a sex symbol, said it best, "Before you can inspire with emotion, you must be swamped with it yourself."

The table below offers some insight into this as well as some paradoxes on passion and sexual proclivity. Some of these are validated by Freud who wrote of sex as the basis of all behavior yet after age forty never had sex with his wife. Another paradox is that Carl Jung, a man whose father was an Anglican Bishop, preached polygamy and free love and had the gall to move his mistress into his home to live with his wife and children. This paradox has been quite apparent in the life and work of Madonna, who has been sacrilegious in her use of icons in her rock videos and desecrated all things in her *Sex Book* and *Truth & Dare* movie. Bestiality, S&M, homosexuality and *ménage a trois* have been fair game for her yet she now writes children's books.

Paradox of Passion & Sex

- Attempts to appear sexy produces the opposite effect—look at those 50-somethings sans bra or the older guys at the beach adorned in speedos

- The best chance of getting a date is not looking for one

- Any woman who insists she is a lady probably isn't

- Chasing kills men faster than scoring—why married men live longer

- Until you are willing to walk away from a deal or relationship you will never make the best deal

- Androgyny is key to power—the most successful females have a masculine nature and the most effective males are sensitively feminine

- In the struggle for dominance sexual energy is enhanced; those beaten have lower sexual energy

- What is most prohibited by the Church is typically what is most desired in the bedroom

- Impotence is an absolute function of trying too hard (not punny)

- Males talk a big game about sexual potency but women in high heat make them look like wimps

- Males are more voyeuristic; women more prone to exhibitionism

Energy & the Mating Game

Psychiatrists studying behavioral kinesiology have found that negative energy undermines the ability to be effective. John Diamond said it best when he wrote "If our Life Energy is high, others will benefit from close contact with us; if it is low our relationships with others become part of the problem." Victims often conjure up all kinds of spurious reasons not to risk getting hurt or rejected by the opposite sex. In high school Hitler became totally taken by a girl who he assumed—due to eye contact—was his true love. The pathologically shy Hitler never said one word to the girl but began fantasizing about her and conjured up all kinds of liaisons in his mind that were but imaginative trysts. When she became engaged to another boy he was devastated and felt jilted despite not having spoken to her. His energized passion was internalized but never externalized. According to psychiatrist John Diamond, "All illness starts as a problem on the energy level. About 95% of the population tests low on Life Energy." This will be dealt with at length in a later chapter. Our mythical passions can make us and break us as can be seen in the lives and loves of Carl Jung and Madonna.

Passion Is the Consummate Path to Power

Validated by no less than Carl Jung and Madonna

As bizarre as it may sound the renowned psychotherapist Carl Jung and the Bimbo of Babylon Madonna were quite similar, especially in their romantic liaisons. Both were blessed or afflicted with insatiable libidinal energy that would dominate their lives and loves. This comes as a profound shock to most people. Their mythical sense bordered on the arcane. Jung flirted with mysticism. Madonna was enamored of the ancient Judaic Kabala. Both were spiritual mystics that never turned down any opportunity to sate their passions. And both used fantasy as the fuel to success in their given disciplines. Jung rose to become the expert of modern personality and a charismatic psychotherapist. The Material Girl Madonna Ciccone lived out her *Electra* image as a wannabe male with aggressive masculine-like seductions permeating her life. Her manager told reporters, "She seduces men like men seduce women."

Jung and Madonna were the products of two divergent cultures. Jung was highly educated in medicine and psychology. In contrast Madonna had little formal education but was a voracious reader and fan of mythical lore. Both were

Promethean types—intuitive-thinkers as Jungian personality types. These types tend to be curious and love new knowledge. Prometheans look deep within to find the meaning of things and what makes them tick. Such people spend an inordinate amount of time and energy pursuing new opportunities. Jung was the son of an Anglican Bishop but would become a mesmerizing guru with disciples from all over the world doting on his every word. Jung's early interest in his inner behaviors led to his Personality Types. In his work *Psychology & Alchemy* he wrote, "Everything can be explained from one idea—the personality—and all my work has been related to this one theme." From childhood Jung was driven to find what it was in his personality that made him different. He spent his life searching for the answer and said, "A creative person has little power over his own life. He is not free. He is captive and drawn by his daimon."

Jung's daimon originated within a raging curiosity. Those unconscious drives and needs worried him and led to him focusing his research on what caused them. I have described them as *success imprints* and *failure imprints* from past experiences. Jung worked closely with Sigmund Freud and became the first President of the International Psychiatric Institute. A raging libidinal drive was sated but he had to justify it by pushing the emotional and psychological benefits of polygamy and free love, writing, "Free love will save the world." Many of Jung's hypotheses were based on a Collective Unconscious that drives us and the inner needs postulated by an Archetypal personality of maleness and femaleness. It was deep within that area he called the syzygy that these drives were manifested. Psychological healing was part of being able to allow free rein to our mystical heritage, leading him to say, "Fantasies can unite the conscious and unconscious."

Myth and alchemy dominated Jung's life. "The more myth we are capable of making conscious," he would preach, "the more life we integrate." In 1913 he saw himself becoming the likeness of a Mithraic lion-headed god. This was in December 1913 when the Mithraic mysteries—an ancient form of Aryan spirituality—were in vogue. Out of this mysticism grew his theories of *synchronicities*—there are no accidents and other principles like *Active Imagination—See it to be it!* and *Individuation—visionary insights leading to epiphanies.* Irreverence for convention spawned his need to research personality. "Neurosis is essentially an escape from a challenging life event," Jung wrote. An example is his anthem, "Sexuality is the *sine qua non* of spirituality—one only exists through the other."

For Jung, sating the passions was key to living a life of optimal health. But moving his patient, lover, and assistant Toni Wolff into his home with his wife and kids was beyond the pale even for the most liberal practitioners. Freud was appalled. But the mesmerizing spell Jung cast over his long-suffering wife and disciples was immense. The daughter of John D. Rockefeller, Edith Rockefeller McCormick, left her husband and children to visit Jung in Switzerland and didn't return for ten years. Edith donated $2 million to further Jung's work. Other stories of Jung's soirees were beyond the pale of research and progress. Biographer Richard Noll (1997 p. 98) spoke of fantasy dominating Jung's life and work, saying, "Jung became the charismatic leader of his own mystery cult. Sexual energy surged through him with a power that frightened him."

Madonna was unaware of Jungian psychology but like him she was also steeped in mysticism. The Material Girl lived life on the edge, telling one magazine, "Free love will save the world." Not as psychologically savvy as Jung but still way beyond the norm Madonna pushed the limits when she published her *Sex Book* in 1992. The *Like a Virgin* gal was equally as daring as Jung but not nearly so scholarly. In her intrepid trek to conquer the world of entertainment she shocked and titillated without remorse. This quintessential love child struggled to survive during those early days in Manhattan. This vegetarian was a health faddist who often ate out of garbage cans to survive. When in high heat it would be sated by either gender as the situation demanded.

Madonna self-produced, directed, and starred in a XXX movie, *Truth & Dare*—a blatant documentary of on-the-edge sensual entertainment. The Bimbo of Babylon admitted to the world in an MTV interview on October 21, 1992, her true philosophical reasoning:

"I would like to offset the sexual mores of society. My behavior, videos, book **(Sex)**, *are all aimed at changing those behaviors. Our society is beset by an evangelic scrutiny of what's right and wrong. I am determined to change it if I can."*

In one interview she justified her eccentric behavior saying, "How could I have turned out any different with the name Madonna." Often names can influence behavior. In her case the name Madonna became her rallying call to live life above mere mortals. A name like Madonna carries with it many mythical connotations for a woman. They permeate the soul as well as the need to be special. In one early MTV interview (1992) she admitted, "My mother is like a fantasy to me. She is the perfect picture of a human being, like Jesus Christ."

The Material Girl reengineered herself so many times it became a media fixation. The mother of reinvention knew that entertainment is faddish. Without change you become stale. Success in that fickle world is about what have you done lately. Her talent was always marginal at best so she had to be special or chance being gone. This woman named after the consummate mom refused to allow offspring to impede her trek to the top with numerous abortions in her twenties. When nearing forty she decided to opt for motherhood and bore two lovely children, one out of wedlock with a boy-toy trainer, and the second with a ten-year-younger British husband, Guy Ritchie. Then the transformed former sex kitten began authoring children's books to the amazement of the media.

A mythical persona always pervaded Madonna's perverse actions but in her forties she went to Israel to study the derivation of the occult spirituality of the Kabala. In her 1998 album *Ray of Light* she offered lyrics and philosophy from her newfound spirituality and began sporting the Red String to show her allegiance to the spiritual world of the ancient past. This mystical Hebrew dogma permeated her life and actions and she became the guru for other Hollywood wannabes Demi Moore and Britney Spears.

Mythical Mentoring—The Catalyst for Passion

Carl Jung & Madonna—Poster Children of Passion

The compelling persona of Carl Jung led to a long list of female disciples who found the Swiss psychotherapist mesmerizing. Such charismatic power can attract a wide following and cast fear into the establishment, who won't understand. Jung attracted legions of disciples. Many left their homes and husbands to be near their guru. Edith Rockefeller, married to tycoon Harold McCormick of International Harvester fame, went to Zurich in 1913 and didn't return home until 1921. In a similar flight from conformity Madonna quit college at 19 and left for the Manhattan Mecca of entertainment and also never again returned except for a visit.

The Archetype was Jung's name for what lies within that drives us to depart from consensus. The psychotherapist would have said that Madonna's archetype was Promethean with a driving force from deep within that needed to titillate at all costs. He would have implored her to chase her vision and not listen to dissenting advice.

In 1913 Jung admitted to having experienced an epiphany while in a state of emotional turmoil. This trauma took place right after he had broken with his mentor Freud. He called it a "visionary ecstasy" and would write of it as a "psychotic experience" that led to an epiphany. This scientist became convinced that he was the product of an Aryan mystery cult known as the Mithraic Mysteries. In 1997 biographer Richard Noll said.

"Jung became the charismatic leader of his own mystery cult having transformed himself into the lion headed god Aion."

Not coincidentally it was during his period of collapse that Jung developed virtually all of his breakthrough concepts: Personality Types, Syzygy, Archetypes, Synchronicities, Individuation, and Active Imagination. In his memoirs Jung wrote of having "intense visionary experiences" (Landrum 2001 p. 147). During his breakdown he rationalized his constant affairs with patients and disciples saying, "The prerequisite of a good marriage is the license to be unfaithful." It was during this period that he moved his mistress Toni Wolff into his home.

In a similar way Madonna's life has been a trip down mystical lane. She always was beset with an ethereal nature and looking for empowerment. That would not come until her forties when the Roman Catholic girl who wanted to be a nun became enchanted with the ancient Judaic spirituality called Kabala. Hollywood pals can now be seen adorning themselves with Red Strings to protect them from "the evil eye" and living by the Kabala tenets:

☼ *Take responsibility for your actions*
☼ *Life is about spiritual transformation from a reactive to proactive being*
☼ *Fill the world of darkness with light—positive energy*
☼ *Never lay blame on other people—it is yours so deal with it [Internal Locus of Control]*
The negative traits found in others are merely your own reflections of your negative traits—fix yourself before attempting to fix others

The anomaly of this vixen with a Christian name is her quest for spirituality. Like Jung she has justified many questionable sexual soirees as a means of spiritual cleansing. They left a trail of lovers in their wake. Freud accused his one-time disciple of being an "Aryan Christ" with a "colossal narcissistic and god complex." Both Madonna and Jung had Machiavellian natures and used devoted disciples to sate their passions and achieve their goals.

Jung and Madonna defied convention despite puritanical upbringings. Jung was reared in the household of an Anglican Bishop but became a mystical Buddhist type. The Catholic Madonna has become a spiritual Jew. During her early years she denigrated religious dogma in sacrilegious rock videos defiling crosses and sacred icons of the church. It is evident that she has been trying to find the truth of a higher being and has pushed the windows of convention in that quest. Madonna told Vanity Fair, *"I have not resolved my Electra Complex. The end of 'Oh Father' video where I'm dancing on my mother's grave, is an attempt to embrace and accept my mother's death."*

CHAPTER 6

▼

SUPERMEN ARE WEAK ENOUGH TO BE STRONG

Everyone's Greatest Strength Is Their Greatest Weakness

"Exertion makes weak people strong, sloth makes strong people weak."
Socrates

"Creative people seem to harbor opposite tendencies. They are more likely to have not only the strengths of their own gender but those of the other."
Mihaly Csikszentmihalyi, *Creativity* (1996)

"Men prefer acting powerfully, women traditionally show more interest in being strong."
David McClelland, *The Achieving Society* (1961)

A parable in Corinthians 12:10 admonishes, "When I am weak, then I am strong." This is but further validation that when on bottom we are more motivated to move upward. Conversely, when on top we are the most vulnerable. Servant leadership falls into this arena. Insecurity is motivational, as is adversity. The fear of failure drives individuals much more than some positive reward. They will not necessarily push the limits to be #1 but sure will not to end up last. People who know they are good in a given arena don't necessarily try as hard as those who know they are weak and attempt to not be embarrassed.

The paradox of strength is that we become complacent or actually get lost in our own reverie. Those who are capable of talking their way through any closed door often don't know when to stop talking once in and are often guilty of talking their way right back out. In business the number-crunching freaks that use numbers to justify all things good and bad tend to self-destruct by their analysis-paralysis that drives everyone crazy. IBM's great strength was engineering and manufacturing but in the personal computer business it almost did them in. They refused to go offshore like upstart Dell Computers and others and started believing their strength would protect them. Well it almost destroyed them.

Weakness can often be strength since we try harder on those things we know we can't do. When we fail a test we seldom forget it but always forget those that we aced. When we fall off that bike we learn more from that experience than when we don't fall. Trauma has a way of awakening our inner spirit to fight harder. Studies have shown that breakdown does lead to breakthrough and if we have been to the bottom the trek to the top becomes far easier. Fear of failing is not the issue. It is more about the fear of loss of image or not measuring up that drives us to try to avoid failure. This is the paradox of being strong as there is always someone stronger and we often become content when things are too easy.

Vulnerability of Super Success

Those at the very top in any discipline are by far the most vulnerable. Why? They have made it and can now relax and enjoy the spoils of victory. Wrong! They are now the targets for the world's wannabes. Why is Oprah constantly on top in the talk show ratings? Because, as she has so eloquently put it, "I always act as if I'm #10 because the minute I act like #1 I'm at risk of becoming #10." Winning in sports or in the world of business has a similar predilection. The guard comes down as soon as you become the CEO or President. Audacity begins to permeate the mental and the emotional and vulnerability is now setting in. The irony of this is that it is not because they have done anything wrong but they stop feeling they have to do as many things right. Such people self-destruct from a reduced craving for the gold ring. They stop dancing with dame desire that brought them to their present state of excellence.

Complacency must constantly be attacked so as not to lose focus on life's objectives. When smugness is attacked it is no longer a weakness. The vast majority avoid weaknesses and go with the proven methods. Just watch those weekend warriors on the tennis court running around their backhand to hit a forehand. What happens? Their forehands get better and better while their backhands get worse and worse. The fear of taking a chance gets in the way of improvement in all disciplines.

Expectancy theory studies show that when we expect more of others or even ourselves it becomes a self-fulfilling prophecy. Studies show that athletes training with another athlete achieve more than if they trained alone due to the unspoken motivation. Intrinsic inspiration is at work without us even knowing it is. This is similar to Expectancy Theory, which has shown that coaches with higher expectations receive higher performance from their players. University of California psychologist Robert Rosenthal says, "Expectations become a self-fulfilling prophecy." The study shows that teachers who expect more get more and even scientists expecting rats to run a maze faster find them running faster. A 2003 study resulted in the following results, some of which are truly amazing:

"Teachers who expect better intellectual performance from their students get it. When coaches expect better athletic performance from their athletes they tend to get it. When behavior researchers are led to expect a certain response from their research subjects they tend to get it." (**Wall Street Journal** *Nov. 7, 2003 Sharon Begley p. B1*)

This data is pretty amazing but nothing compared to the finding that a human-rat motivation without extrinsic rewards works as well. Researchers discovered that rats were highly influenced by the expectations of the scientists. In other words, the attitude of the research scientist was the only variable in success. They found that "Behavioral researchers expecting a certain response tend to get it." The researchers selected two groups of similar scientists and gave one group exceptional rats that could run faster after generations of breeding. They gave the second group inferior rats who were dullards in running the maze and asked the two to run repeated tests to see how they fared. As expected the superior rats performed 65 percent better. But the scientists had been duped. All the rats were exactly the same. The only variable was the expectations of the scientists conducting the research. The mental attitude and positive energy flow of those in charge had influenced the rats' performance. Wow!

The Anomaly of Power vs. Force—Strength & Weakness

Remember that no matter how strong or powerful you become there is always someone out there who is stronger. No matter how many rockets or nuclear weapons one nation has some other nation can out-arm them given enough time and money. Those who permit themselves to get into a one-dimensional race for power are destined to die by their delusion. Conversely, becoming content is also not good. Those who become complacent are doomed, as are those too enamored with their own potency. Those who are too satisfied are waning since in a dynamic world one is always moving up or moving down. It is a constant battle of power versus force but research has shown that power is all about empowerment.

Success is a function of synthesizing the mind, heart, body, and spirit to do your very best. When you are multi-dimensional adversaries begin wondering where to attack. The well-rounded individual can hit forehands and backhands, see the qualitative as well as the quantitative in a system, deal with the local and the global. Few individuals ever achieve such cerebral centering or optimization of their emotional and physical. Carl Jung wrote of this extensively, admonishing his macho disciples to tap into their feminine side and his female disciples to tap into their masculine side. This takes you into a higher state of consciousness that psychiatrist David Hawkins found to be the road to enlightenment.

In the inimitable words of Hawkins in *Power & Force* (2002), "Power makes you strong. Force makes you weak." For empowerment is all about giving up fear, anger, and guilt and pursuing the higher qualities of love, reason, and peace. He admonished us to "transcend limitations and dethrone the mind from its tyranny as a sole arbiter of reality." This is about eliminating the negative and accentuating the positive, as the lyrics once told us. When the will is in control the body follows faithfully. That is the true path to power for anyone in any profession. Hawkins offered us profound wisdom:

"Universal energy knows more than it knows it knows. Positive and negative muscle responses occur within the body independent of a subject's opinion."
(Hawkins p. 30)

Hawkins encouraged athletes to beware of relying on just the body to win a contest. In *Power vs. Force* he wrote, "It isn't one's environment, but one's attitude that determines whether one will be defeated or be victorious." Hawkins was speaking to the ability of man to rise above the ordinary, that mediocre place where he says 85 percent of the world is stuck. It's where fear, greed, pride, anger, and guilt dominate all behavior. When energized we are empowered to rise above such a negative life. Omnipotence is possible when we find peace within. To get there it is necessary to start thinking differently and to stop allowing fear and greed to dominate one's life. "The competitor motivated by pride or greed," he says, "will go weak at the moment of the starting gate." In his system one must rise into a higher state of energy and human consciousness to grab the gold no matter the contest:

> *"High states of consciousness are frequently experienced by athletes—sublime states of peace and joy. Transcendence from mediocrity to eminence often occurs at a point just beyond the apparent limit of an athlete's ability."*
> *(Hawkins p. 172)*

Paradox of Personality—Beware What Makes You Special

The sordid truth is that we all live and die by our own personality quirks. We often think we are unique but everyone is different albeit in various ways. They are driven by varying forces within—95 percent of all thinking is an unconscious act due to some early imprint. I have found from years of interacting with creative visionaries and those who ridicule them that there are three major categories of people: Proactive types, Reactive types, and Inactive types. Proactives make things happen, Reactives watch them happen and Inactives just wonder what happened. There is no right or wrong, just different. But you don't want a Proactive changing a proven production process just as you don't want Inactive types heading up R & D. One thing is for certain: life is too short to drink cheap wine or to depend on losers for your livelihood.

Personality can be our savior or our nemesis. Those incapable of tolerating risk never take enough chances to become a real success. They spend too much time and energy avoiding failure to ever succeed. Those afraid of adversity avoid confrontations and it destroys any ability to move forward. Politicians often attempt to cast fear into their constituency to win votes. They constantly pontificate on the problems of unemployment, exchange rates, shipping jobs offshore, and stock market shifts. This is mental masturbation since capitalism has always been a wave-like series of ups and downs that are as predictable as morning following night. Those who can't stand setbacks should not be in business.

The MBA personality types at WorldCom and Enron used their number-crunching savvy to manipulate numbers and capitalize expenses to make profits look better so more people wanted to buy the stock. The bottom line in all things is that most people do what benefits them no matter what they say or what spin they put on it. In a study at Duke University 78 percent of the CFOs studied admitted to sacrificing the future—"economic value" in their words—in order to look good. Chairman Ken Lay of Enron said he didn't know what was happening in the multi-billon dollar scam of stockholders. Since when has ignorance become a viable defense, especially in the world of business?

Those debacles at Enron, Tyco and World.com that are now in the courts were predestined due to the worship of numbers and instant gratification at the expense of ethics and a long-term perspective. The top guns were obsessed with constantly raising stock price and it distorted their objectivity. Instead of making sure their firms were growing by ensuring sound revenues and cost management, they got lost in the reverie of their self-serving wins. Booking pro-forma numbers as sales resulted and it came back to haunt them. They never seem to have heard of the old maxim that there are no free lunches. Their duplicity worked for a while since they were smart enough to engage an auditing firm that was also earning hundreds of millions for looking the other way. They managed the numbers until the numbers managed them. The fact of life is that in capitalism earnings don't always go up. Trying to make them do so is pathological and becomes a self-destructive ploy.

Indicted Enron Chairman Ken Lay has played the ignorance card as a defense in his trial for duping stockholders out of billions. That may have been partially true since the top dog is always delegating such authority. But the bottom line is that no one can delegate responsibility. Eminent leaders know that they are ultimately responsible for their personnel and that is part of the job description. A leader can't have power and not have it. Martha Stewart made it to the top via a controlling nature that would in the end do her in. She was obsessed with controlling every nuance of her company Omnimedia Inc., and that led her to try and control her foible of stock ownership in ImClone. Such control led to perfectionism in her magazines and chocolate soufflés. But that perfectionist nature would not allow her to admit she goofed and lied to the authorities. The control-freak once admitted she could never become a patient of a psychiatrist since she could out-wit them. That power is what made her a billionaire, but it was also what led to her imprisonment. The cost? Her freedom, TV shows, CEO position for Omni-media, and $500 million in stock value.

"The very mania that gave Napoleon such advantages in battle," wrote one biog-rapher, "doomed him to waste the victories and destroy his empire." In a similar way overprotective parents tend to destroy their children's chances of growing up independent. By sheltering them they destroy their chance to learn how to solve problems. *The overprotective parent is the bane of creativity.* They try so hard to make their kid safe they destroy their ability to cope in a competitive world. Per-mit personnel and children to err and they learn to survive on the street. That is the nature of growing and learning.

Nietzsche spoke eloquently of a superman within man that could take him to the top. This message was lost on many who got caught up in his other words that they didn't truly understand like his "God is dead" thesis. What the great philos-opher was saying is that we all have been put here and are now alone and had bet-ter become the master of our destiny or pay a high price for waiting for a savior to bail us out. His words were a metaphorical message for man to become self-actu-alized since god is not standing in the wings to save you. His message was about man's inner power. This spiritual son of a minister wrote:

"Faith is always coveted most and needed most urgently where will is lacking; for will is the decisive sign of sovereignty and strength. The less one knows how to command, the more urgently one covets someone who commands, who commands severely—a god, prince, class, physician, father confessor, dogma or party consciences."

Our Greatest Strength Can Be Our Biggest Weakness

Maya Angelou & Jack Nicholson are Poster Children for Axiom

Two uniquely different personas rose to the top via a highly mythical sense of their destiny. The irony is that both are intellectual but without much formal education. Both were bright and introspective in their dealings and could not suf-fer fools gently. *Roots* Emmy winner Maya Angelou and renegade movie icon

Jack Nicholson danced to the tunes they heard from within. Neither was easily duped except for kindred spirits whose strength was also about a higher meaning in life.

These iconoclasts ventured into diverse roles with a mystical sense of their fate. Maya became a world-renowned poet and Bill Clinton's inaugural poet laureate in 1990 with the poem "On the Pulse of the Morning." This was after she had become a self-made best-selling author. Few people realize she got her start on the stage at a very young age, not unlike Jack Nicholson, who worked as an MGM mail boy at age eighteen. Neither attended one class in college yet both were bright enough to have gone through grad school. Maya actually became a tenured professor at Wake Forest University. Jack has been the recipient of a number of honorary doctorates for his huge contribution to the arts. The rebel thespian has also been nominated for more Oscars than any other actor in history.

Marguerite Angelo took the name Maya when her brother Bailey told everyone "she's mya-sister." Her love for him led to her adopting the name rather than some more formal soubriquet. Maya was essentially abandoned by both mother and father and reared by a paternal grandmother in Arkansas. But the intrepid Maya rose above those humble beginnings to become an award-winning entertainer, poet, and author. At seven she moved to St. Louis to live with her mother and her mother's boyfriend. The boyfriend raped her and when she was called on to testify in court went mute when he was killed by relatives. Maya blamed herself for the death of her molester. If not for the presence of a wonderful teacher in Arkansas she may have been scared for life. Bertha Flowers brought her out of her self-inflicted silence through books and poems. At eleven Flowers enticed Maya to recite passages from the Bible and then transformed her forever by getting her to memorize the flowing sounds from Edgar Allan Poe, William Shakespeare, and Charles Dickens. Once this extrovert began to talk she was never again silent. Winning the Horatio Alger Award in 1992—the consummate symbol of rags to riches—is testimony to her tenacity.

In her twenties Maya became a singer and dancer and toured Europe with a *Porgy & Bess* stage production. By that time language and words were very important to Maya. The uneducated girl from the Deep South taught herself to perform in seven different languages. It is hard to comprehend how she became fluent in French, Italian, Spanish, German, Arabic, and Fanti. That epiphany at twelve would become her pathway to the top. "Words mean more than what is set down on paper," she would write. "It takes a human voice to infuse them with shades of deeper meaning." The mystical land of letters became her solace. "When I read Shakespeare and heard that music," she remembered, "I couldn't believe it, that a white man could write so musically." She would write, "My mind resounded with the words and my blood raced to its rhythms."

Having visited the bottom more than once left its mark, leading her to write, "All my work, my life, is about survival. You may encounter many defeats, but you must not be defeated." Those inspiring words are behind her cathartic self-expression. The optimist with a pessimistic past would write, "The word *can't* didn't exist for me." Once the power of books infiltrated her she became lost in them. Later in life she offered tribute to books as her savior, writing, "*Crime and Punishment* changed my life." In her acclaimed first book, *I Know Why the Caged Bird Sings* (1970), she tells the emotional story of being raised in racist Arkansas where death permeated most of her daily life.

Maya Angelou and Jack Nicholson were both voracious readers who adored intellectual works by Camus, Dostoevsky, Kipling, and Wilhelm Reich. During Nicholson's days as a struggling B-film actor he became a fan of the existentialism of Albert Camus. Jack Nicholson was an anomaly to family, fiends, lovers, and outsiders. Those who knew him in those early days describe him as a quiet intellectual who dared be different. It is interesting that the parts he played were like him. During the down times Jack lost himself in Camus's nihilism. The bizarre twists of *The Myth of Sisyphus* enchanted him. The cynical philosophy of Camus is not that different from Jack the Devil. Trying to make sense of life and love on Sunset Strip is weird. Mythical escapes can offer solace as they did for Jack during twelve years as a struggling wannabe. He had repeatedly pushed uphill with rejection after rejection until he finally landed that role in *Easy Rider*. The counter-culture nature of Camus was deeply imprinted in Nickolson's dropout attorney character George Hansen. Pushing those insidious rocks up the movie hills kept Jack from self-destructing.

After Jack made it big in Hollywood he had to try to maintain a sense of normality and has always kept a silver tray at his entrance hall with torn $100 bills to let him know it is all fleeting. Playing the role of The Joker in *Batman* earned him more money for the time spent of any actor in Hollywood's illustrious history. But critics say he was deserving of every cent of that $60 million. Jack happens to be better at his craft than most yet he is an anomaly to ex-wives and directors.

This down-home guy maintains a low-key persona despite a life as an obsessive lothario. He is extremely well-read but detests intellectualizing. The unshaven guy on the sidelines at Lakers games is a true lover of sport and life. Those roles as the manic-depressive renegade are not just some fluke. He works diligently to pull them off.

In a moment of self-deprecation Nicholson told the media, "I'm a guy who's at odds with the establishment but whom they'd love to have to dinner." Dr. Devil is his self-image from the movie caricature of Lucifer as Daryl Van Horne in the film *The Witches of Eastwick* (1987). Few actors could have pulled off such a role with such conviction; his stellar performance was due to his "spiritual dimension," according to director George Miller. To prepare himself for the sexual comedy he read Dante's *Inferno* and a plethora of witchcraft materials to make audiences believe that he was "the devil."

Nicholson is also an ardent fan of Wilhelm Reich if for no other reason than rationalization for his rampant womanizing. Reich believed that *orgone (orgasmic) energy* had to be released. Jack has spent lots of money and energy making sure his is released. His *Playboy* interviews offered him a platform to justify his philandering, which he sees as the path to health and happiness. In a 1972 interview he said:

"If you're not releasing your sexual energy you are in trouble. It's not that sex is the primary element of the universe, but when it's unfulfilled it will affect you."

Such motivation led him to take weird trips in life and film roles. An example of his obsessive behavior occurred when he was signed to play a nude scene. That led the wild one to spend one whole month without clothes. No matter who showed up at his home Jack opened the door and greeted them stark naked. "I decided I would get over being self-conscious about nudity, so I lived in my house as a nudist. Once I decide to do something I don't do it partially, so I was nude no matter who came by" (*Playboy* Jan. 2004 p. 79). That even included a meeting with his daughter.

The misogynic Nicholson was thirty-four when a *Time* writer called to inform him that his mother was his grandmother and his real mom was his sister. It was revealed that his real dad was still living but that was as disquieting to him as his sister-mom and grandmother were. Jack refused to see his dad because he didn't want to destroy a family life in which he was the golden boy. He had been reared in a household full of women who molded him into a strong-willed womanizer. The same thing was found in the childhoods of Picasso, Howard Hughes, and Bill Clinton. Director George Miller of *Witches of Eastwick* (1987) spoke of Jack having strong female qualities saying, "He goes with the flow which I find very female. You can't be a great actor unless you've got that great flow and nurturing. I think that's why females are attracted to him." This quality is what Carl Jung described as syzygy—tapping into your female side.

Jack told *Playboy*, "My films are all autobiographical." This was never more true than in his role as Melvin Udall in *As Good As It Gets* (1997), an obsessive-compulsive with an antisocial but acerbic wit that broke up the audience. The break that truly made Jack Nicholson came in 1969 when he was in his early thirties and about to stop acting. His role as the cool disenchanted lawyer on a Harley in *Easy Rider* stole the show. The term *Easy Rider* is a euphemism for a whore's old man who has the easy ride. As Jonathan in *Carnal Knowledge* Jack played a mindless malcontent on a sexual mission to sate his needs no matter the cost to the women. If that doesn't depict the Nicholson personality nothing does. Michael Douglas, who cast him in *Cuckoo's Nest* said, "I've never been more impressed with any actor in my life." When Jack says, "The next woman who takes me on is gonna light up like a pinball machine and pay off in silver dollars," it gave testament to a sex-crazed antisocial. When asked to portray a sociopath in *Cuckoo's Nest* the perfectionist flew to Portland, Oregon, and started hanging out in a mental institution with cold-blooded killers on death row. The move was to ensure that he knew exactly what sociopaths were like and how they thought and acted. After many weeks of this moribund life his girlfriend at the time Angelica Huston became alarmed at his change. She told him he was becoming as bizarre as those with whom he was associating. After a few more days she packed up and left, telling him, "You're acting crazy" (Thompson 1997 p. 139). It worked. He earned his first Academy Award. And of course the man who could handle the truth was terrific as Colonel Jessup in Aaron Sorkin's *A Few Good Men*.

Mythical Meaning of Strength—The Will to Win

Maya Angelou & Jack Nicholson Tapped Weaknesses to Get to the Top

The powerful personas of Maya Angelou and Jack Nicholson offer insight into that long tedious trek to the top. Both have an eerie mythical sense of life and used it to

make it. Maya is an indomitable spirit that could not be denied in her intrepid jour-
ney out of the Arkansas hills to become the guru of Oprah Winfrey. Jack Nicholson
attacked his demons on his trip to the top.

These two wunderkinds validate the fact that money, breeding, and formal education,
although a nice way to start out, are unnecessary credentials for becoming rich and
famous. They demonstrate better than most that the heart and the head are all that is
needed. Maya and Jack played the cards they were dealt and played them with
panache. Both had the presence to play the cards in their hand and not try to be some-
thing they were not. Jack seemed to know intuitively that he had to play himself no
matter the money or the appeal of the role. The zany antisocial has made such parts
his personal typecasting.

Maya Angelou's life and work were even more steeped in mythical lore than Jack's.
The *New York Times Book Review called her writing a "genius of serial autobiog-*
raphy." That genius was born and bred in the mystical mentoring of a mind that
refused to bow to what others thought. She told the media, "There is a world of differ-
ence between truth and facts. Facts can obscure the truth. You can tell so many facts
that you fill the stage but haven't got one iota of truth." After her inaugural poem she
told reporters:

"A hero/shero encourages people to see the good inside themselves and
expand it. Frederick Douglas and Eleanor Roosevelt confronted societies
that did not believe in their ideas. I try to act as I would want my hero/shero
to act" (Landrum, 1997)

Mysticism pervaded Maya's trek through life. Only a passionate woman with gusto
has the moxie to make it in both entertaining and writing. Testimony to her tenacity
was a memorable moment when she was still struggling in New York City with a
young son. When a Harlem gang leader put a contract out on her teenage son this
iron-willed mother became concerned. Only a woman with inner power would track
down a fearless gang leader who killed for kicks. She brazenly walked into his tene-
ment, busted through the door of his room where he was with his girlfriend, pulled a
revolver from her purse and pointing it at his head told him, "If one blade of my son's
hair is touched I will blow your brains out, then your girlfriends, then your family
and every fucking roach in this place." She turned and walked out and that was the
end of that problem.

Jack Nicholson had a long lurid love affair with philosophers and the supernatural psychotherapist Wilhelm Reich. The radical Reich promoted a concept called Orgone Energy that he felt was central to living a healthy life both physically and emotionally. Reich's theory that the optimum life is one lived via Orgasmic Energy turned Jack on.

In 1975 Jack told the New York Times, *"The actor is Camus' ideal existential hero—the man who lives more lives is in a better position than the guy who lives just one." For Jack, Camus was an anti-hero like him. In speaking of his role as The Joker he said, "Batman is Nietzsche for kids." Such a surrealistic comic-book style permitted him to portray iconoclasts as real. A mystic-like persona earned him accolades from the Hollywood elite with actors like Eddie Murphy saying, "He was brilliant. Nobody can mess with that guy."*

Nicholson brought a new era to Hollywood but it took a long time for him to find himself. Traditionalists saw him as a bright space cadet. But Jack would bring a Chaplinesque comedy to the movies, a mix of passion and pathos that makes life more real. Taking chaos and making it palatable and funny proved titillating for movie fans. The madcap is actually very smart—scoring in the top 2 percent as a high school senior in a national college entrance exam for chemical engineering. For him Hollywood was a testing lab for his philosophic bent. He finally decided to quit making movies when by accident he struck a chord by making money with Easy Rider. His form of pathos was more mythical than real and could no more be separated from him than his thinning hair. It is what has made him and his work special.

When Jack was struggling to rise out of the B movie matrix in his early thirties he wrote screen plays and thought that would be his final place in Hollywood. The roles dominated by sex, drugs, and rock 'n' roll culture were potions for his psyche. During this era he wrote a screenplay touting drugs as the panacea for escaping the rigors of life in the slow lane. He titled it The Trip *(1976) and it touted the whole seventies theme of tuning in, turning on (with grass and LSD), and dropping out. When he showed the screenplay to his future costar in* Easy Rider *Peter Fonda the actor was floored and gushed, "That is the greatest script I have ever read. I think Fellini wrote it." During their filming of* Easy Rider *he told* Playboy *(1972) they smoked 105 joints of Mexican grass to show they were really out of the mainstream.*

As with most creative types Nicholson lived life right on the edge. An avid sportsman, Jack owns a place in Aspen where he skis with his lady friends. One of his pals says, "Jack skis like a kamikaze, a total wild man on the mountain." This is the same guy who refuses makeup, a total anomaly for someone earning millions in show business where greasepaint is not only a ritual but a necessity. The reason he says is to not distort the real Jack, who should be seen with all the flaws.

―――――――――― ▼ ――――――――――

CHAPTER 7

SUPERSTARS ARE SO DUMB
THEY ARE SMART

If you don't know you can, you can't; if you don't know you can't, you can!

"Naiveté is the most important attribute of genius."
Goethe

"If our civilization fails it will be due to stupidity rather than evil."
Carl Jung, psychotherapist

"The whole problem with the world is that fools and fanatics are so certain of themselves; wise people are so full of doubts."
Bertrand Russell

Wonder Women are often too stupid to know they can't climb high precipices and that is precisely why they can. In the inimitable words of Joseph Campbell *"He who doesn't know,* knows. *He who thinks he knows,* doesn't know." The sad commentary on this is that the world's dumb-dumbs are prone to pontificate on what is right and wrong and thus are guilty of believing their own BS. And those with great insight often remain silent. Bertrand Russell said it well, "Fools and fanatics are so certain while wise people are so full of doubts." Russell was speaking about his own life, in which he spent so much time battling with self-serving bureaucrats. After much soul-searching he became fed up enough to become politically incorrect (though always logically exacting). For Russell people were far more paradoxical than his famous paradox on analytical philosophy.

Russell was perplexed by having his most passionate drives stymied by religious fanatics and evangelistic dialogue. Like most young men reared in the Victorian era he had been told that if he touched himself he would go blind. On top of the Adam and Eve myth he was appalled of such ignorance by so-called learned individuals. Puritanical pandering during his early years led to his rebellion. Pendulums always swing farther to one side due to having been too far on the other. Had the brilliant Russell not been told stupid dogmas it is unlikely he would have been so mutinous once he found out he had been lied to by those he respected. As a young man with a raging libido he was told to pray when he was excited and that would suffice to stifle those horrid urges. That led to his insurgent adulthood where he spent much of his time fighting the ludicrous dogmas of Christianity. This logician was far ahead of his time and saw through the spurious attempts to keep him in line. It led to his unashamed arguments for free love, polygamy, working women, marital freedom, and the freedom of all consenting adults to pursue life's pleasures. "Men are born ignorant, not stupid," he loved to say but "they are made stupid by education."

Very smart people are destined to pay a price for thinking outside the box. The establishment will find you blasphemous or threatening. Average people don't like intellectual arguments that they don't get. Conversely, smart people can sometimes lose it when forced to conform to senseless conformity. Russell personified this frustration with logical nonsense.

Education Is about Thinking—Not Conforming

One irony of formal education for the masses is that it is designed for being average and leads inevitably to mediocrity. Children are taught what they can do and what they can't do and that infuriates the gifted like Walt Disney and Frank Lloyd Wright, who never made it through high school. One editorial spoke to this in *USA Today* (Dec. 16, 2004):

"Children are being taught that there is only one right answer, a track sure to breed conformity rather than ingenuity. Mounds of evidence suggest that children learn through active play."

The self-proclaimed Queen of Education Lou Ann Johnson wrote of the problem in 2004 saying, "Public schools are badly broken and we must stop preparing at-risk children for standardized tests and just teach—stop spending money on tests and spend it on improving the classroom environment." Touché! Maria

Montessori was an exponent of this approach to early learning when she wrote, "The free horse runs swifter than the one motivated by the whip or the carrot."

Freedom is what true learning is all about. Kids and adults alike will study vociferously in arenas of high interest and will ignore boring regurgitation of information for the sake of information or passing some kind of test to justify the educational institution giving it. In other words a non-evaluative atmosphere is key to learning, not the right-answer syndrome so prevalent in today's educational systems. Studies at UCLA and the University of Georgia have found that children lose half of their creative potential between the ages of five and seven and 99 percent of it by age forty. Why? They have been told No! and Don't! so often they give up the ghost of What if? Teachers are partially at fault as they have been trained to maintain order, to teach to the norm, to make kids conform to societal rules. Whose rules? The rules of the bureaucrats in charge! The truth of the creative and innovative process is about drawing outside the lines, questioning old ideas, not accepting conventional dogmas. Do you think Socrates, Leonardo, and Montessori were conformists? Or Einstein? Or even Uncle Walt Disney? Hardly!

Innovative types thoroughly understand that they are not in the business of doing it like Brand X or they will have their head handed to them. To be good in any new venture one must be ten times better and that demands being significantly different. It is critical to begin training students to learn to think and what the textbook theories mean on the street. What can I do with this information to change and grow? Educational psychologist Paul Torrance spent much of his life studying childhood psychology and found:

"IQ tests do not measure creativity. By depending on them we miss 70% of creativity. Most children start life with a valuable creative spark; most have it knocked out of them by the time they reach the 4th grade." (**Science Digest**)

What Torrance has preached is precisely why the United States scored 24th out of 29 nations in applying math skills to real-world problems according to a 2004 study by the Organization for Economic Cooperation & Development (NDN Dec. 8, 2004 p. 10A). The *Wall Street Journal* wrote an editorial on this and quoted Singapore educators since they repeatedly led the world in scoring on math skills. "Kids in Singapore learn to use visual tools to understand abstract concepts—to draw bars and other diagrams to visualize problems—a technique called bar-modeling." That is the way to become #1.

Another Smart Paradox is those legions of salespeople who know too much about the situation or client to walk in a given door. That stupid dude who walks in a door he should not often walks out with a huge sale. Bertrand Russell saw this paradox in educational delivery, but when he spoke of it he was fired from Cambridge. Russell was way ahead of his time. Conformity is safer but not in tune with a dynamic world where all information doubles every three years. Instead of trying to change Cambridge, Russell went out and opened his own nontraditional school to practice what he was preaching.

Russell recognized that students were being taught what was right and what was wrong to the detriment of their learning to cope in life. Isaac Asimov wrote an essay about this, "The Relativity of Wrong." Russell understood the world is not white or black but grey. Today imprinted ideologies are still rampant as can be seen by life in the Middle East. In Muslim nations those in charge decide—male power brokers—decide which individuals can go to school and women are not among them. Women are also not permitted to drive or show their faces in public. They are groomed to serve men, not because that is right or wrong, but because it is how they are postured in the hierarchy of a patriarchal society. In China students are not permitted to question a teacher even if they don't understand material. The end result is that students learn what they can achieve and what they can't due to the doctrine of the system. Russell founded the Beacon Hill School where "free thinking" and innovation were fundamental to learning.

Russell wrote an adversarial work titled *Why I Am Not a Christian* (1927) to show that those in charge were using self-serving dogma to keep their flock in line. Such hypocrisy incensed this curmudgeon. It wasn't so much that he was against people having their own belief systems as he was appalled at the way the clergy misled their members. The Beacon Hill School used progressive educational programs where logic and the meaning of words were of paramount importance to learning to think independently. Russell was dedicated to stopping the sages on educational stages who were only there for the purpose of furthering their own beliefs. He saw the children as the unwitting victims of such a system. Goethe said, "Naiveté is the most important attribute of genius" and his pupil Russell attempted to impart the importance of questioning.

Virtually all teachers have never spent time on the street to learn their craft and consequently are ill-prepared to align the meaning of theory to the practical. Professors locked into the safety of the classroom have a penchant for pontificating on do's and don'ts that have little relevance on the street. Pedagogical ignorance is 20–20 but not necessarily instructive. Such pedagogy is tantamount to marching backward in history. Few stories tell this better than that dastardly C from a Yale professor on a paper on overnight package delivery by Federal Express founder Fred Smith. As a junior Smith wrote his paper for an economics professor who told him it was well written but made no economic sense. What if Smith had listened to this horrid advice from an unknowing professor? FedEx would never have been born.

The Overprotective Parent Is the Bane of Innovation

Most parents want to do best by their children but are inclined to give them poor advice in the interest of protecting them from harm. They don't allow them to draw outside the lines or try anything new, and consequently the children never learn to deal with life's vagaries, which are mostly outside the lines. These well-meaning parents don't realize they are programming their children for mediocrity.

Such people are prone to preach what is good, what is safe, and what is dangerous. How do they know? They don't, but believe they do. Besides, what is safe is seldom what is best in any venue and at any age. Most great people became great by living on the precipice in all they did. Do you think it was safe for Oprah to quit college to take a job in the television business? Was it safe for Michael Dell to drop out of pre-med school to launch a computer business? Was it safe for Liz Claiborne to bet her life's savings at age forty-eight on a new clothing line? What if Walt Disney had listened to his brother who told him Disneyland was a stupid idea? And what is safe is usually not worth the time or energy to pursue. The reason is that risk and reward are inversely related. The more risk the greater the potential. The less risk the fewer rewards. When we reach age eighty the only things we regret are those risks we didn't have the guts to take.

It is not an accident that the world's billionaire computer gurus—Gates, Ellison, Jobs, and Dell—don't have a college education between them. That doesn't mean they don't know much about the business. They know far more than most MBAs. But they were too impatient to put up with the trivial nonsense of the formal education process. "Adapt or die" is the unstated message in most schools, but gifted minds like Albert Einstein and James Michener were unceremoniously thrown out of school. When billionaire Richard Branson quit high school in his junior year the headmaster told him, "Congratulations Branson. I predict you will go to prison or become a millionaire." He did both but it would be billions not millions.

Following the pack is safe but is not in the lexicon of the special or innovative. Old-time educators prefer to stifle creativity than risk disrupting influences in the classroom. That drives the gifted nuts. When forced to conform they drop out or find an environment more suited to their bent for curiosity. Socrates was poisoned for daring to teach the children of Athens to "Know thyself!" The model for contemporary schools is unfortunately not dramatically different than a nineteenth century factory with rows of students asked to sit in order and perform dutiful tasks without error. Over 100 years ago Maria Montessori saw this and created a school where the child had the freedom to explore and learn. Bertrand Russell saw it and created a nontraditional school. Both were castigated as renegades. But they didn't listen and Montessori actually refused to hire any teacher trained in the art because they knew way too much.

Defy Tradition to Find Utopia

Those too stupid to bow to conventional wisdom tend to hit life's lotteries. They have a tendency to take those mysterious roads and find pots of gold those not so daring miss. They are not so governed by tradition and consequently end up with untraditional wins—some good, some not so good. Walt Disney was so inclined as he refused to hire anyone with an art degree since he was unkindly asked to leave art school when young. In a similar disdain for formally trained engineers Soichiro Honda refused to hire anyone with an engineering degree at Honda Motors. Both were eminently successful, especially with nontraditional innovations that traditionalists disdained. Frank Lloyd Wright described this approach to the creative process when he told reporters, "I don't build a house without destroying the existing social order." Consider the below ironies of innovation due to lack of formal training:

Galileo was trained in medicine—not astronomy as was Luigi Galvani the inventor of the storage battery. Gregor Mendel and Charles Darwin were men of the cloth who altered the whole system of heredity and evolution. Balzac was trained as a lawyer but became the father of the modern novel. Trained as a philosopher, Karl Marx used his insight into the nature of man, to write the Communist Manifesto. Fyodor Dostoevsky was a military engineer but wrote the world's greatest psychological novel—Crime & Punish-

ment. *Montessori became the high priestess of pedagogy after training as a medical doctor. Michael Dell was in pre-med when he decided that he could beat powerhouse IBM at their own game so he dropped out and did it.*

Traditionalists know so much about how to be safe they know nothing about how to be truly successful. Why? They are so enamored of the status quo they can't break out of that mediocre mesa and visit those unknown vistas where eminence is waiting. Politicians fall into this category. They can be found pontificating in 2005 about the danger of exporting jobs, which is tantamount to marching backward in economic history. The world is growing smaller and trying to build a wall around America to gain votes is both inane and self-serving. Unfortunately, many of their constituents aren't savvy enough to see through their ignorance of a global economy.

No matter our expertise we can become irrelevant or obsolete or price ourselves out of the mainstream. That is the commentary on growth and change. If India is better suited to develop software so be it. Let them do that so we can do what is most economically feasible here. Americans have a history of innovative competence so we should innovate not do the mundane tasks that can be done cheaper elsewhere. Never do what you are not good at. Only do things at which you excel and life will be good. This may not be nice in the short run but is the economic reality in the long run. When candle makers are no longer in demand they better learn to develop light bulbs. If Wal-Mart can sell candy cheaper then the local candy store then that candy retailer had better find a niche in which they make a difference like low-carb candy.

It is axiomatic that the more we learn the more we know we don't know. That is the province of the well-read and is lost on the un-read. The learned psychiatrist David Hawkins said, "There's nothing the mind believes that isn't erroneous at a higher level of awareness" (Hawkins *Power vs. Force* p. 247). Mathematician philosopher Bertrand Russell saw the same inconsistency when he read *Gulliver's Travels* and said of the epiphany, "The account of the Yahoos had a profound effect upon me and I began to see humans in that light." As I like to say, *It is okay to not know and to not know it. It is not okay to not know and not admit it. And god forbid if you don't know, don't know it, and don't care.*

Box of Mediocrity Is Safe & Destined for Sameness

Those unwilling or psychologically incapable of functioning outside convention are destined to live and die by their lack of temerity. To be innovative it is imperative to take risks and live life close to the precipice. Mediocrity reigns supreme wherever it is sure and safe. Walt Disney and Dr. Seuss always drew outside the lines and it was their catalyst to fame and fortune. Did they pay a price for thumbing their nose at traditionalists? Sure! But it was worth the gamble as they lived life on their terms not on those of the narrow-minded who would have them conforming to mediocrity. Most people are unwilling to face such rejections. But not the superstars! They live by the eloquent words of George Bernard Shaw, who said, "The reasonable man adapts to the world; the unreasonable one persists in trying to adapt the world to himself. Therefore, all progress depends on the unreasonable man."

Until a person knows something real well they are not inclined to challenge the traditional ways in that discipline. They bow to what has worked in past. That makes knowledge of supreme importance to innovative solutions. This is precisely why virtually all change comes from the fringe. It is why Frank Lloyd Wright, Walt Disney, and Dr. Seuss were considered eccentrics by peers and even family. The following chart offers some insight into the slight differences between knowledge and Ignorance. It shows how each are in similar places but just deal with their plight differently.

All types are needed in any society. But if you prefer to be special you must function where special people function and that is not in that surety box of conformity. It is akin to being proactive versus inactive or having drive to be unique or the need to be the same. Neither is right or wrong, just different. It often boils down to a battle between innovation and xenophobia. What is risky versus what is sure. There is a need in all societies for people who will function blindly on cue and will not change the system. Banks have a need for tellers who always ask the appropriate questions. These are good citizens but are not the ones needed to deal with change.

Matrix of Knowledge & Ignorance

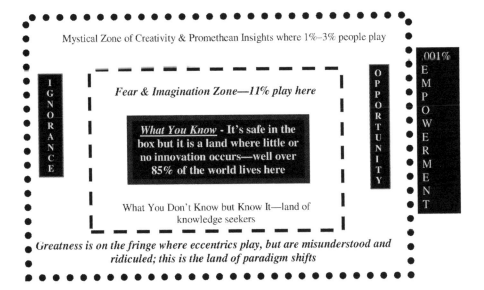

Changemasters are life's movers and shakers like Leonardo de Vinci, Frank Lloyd Wright, Isadora Duncan, Mahatma Gandhi, and Mother Theresa. The world's followers are in the vast majority, representing about 97% to 99% of the population. These are stable citizens needed to maintain order. They worship at the altar of surety and maintain stability. Those who lead change, however, are those zany wunderkinds who disdain budgets or conventional structures. Being in the Empowerment zone is why Mahatma Gandhi and Mother Teresa changed the world. They represent only 1% to 3% of the general population.

As shown in the graphic illustration above *the more we know about any discipline the more we are incapable of altering that discipline.* Why? Because we have such a psychological investment in what is it becomes mores difficult to see what might be. In business school we are taught if things are not meeting budget to cut back. Ironically, that is the worst possible strategy. When in trouble you have to spend more money promoting your wares, not less. The eminent don't cut back when things are tough they tend to expand. Ted Turner and Rupert Murdoch became media barons and billionaires using this strategy, as did Richard Branson of Virgin Atlantic. Branson told the press, "The only way to cope with a cash crisis is not to contract but to expand." When he couldn't pay the bills at Virgin Records he bought a chain of nightclubs, to the chagrin of his key executives. But his strategy led to a billion-dollar empire. Most people don't have that kind of temerity.

Early Adopters vs. Laggards—Opportunity vs. Xenophobia

Opinion leaders are always out in front of the pack. They pursue change rather than avoiding it. That is why they are often labeled *Innovators* and *Early Adopters* by psychologists. Their counterparts are *Laggards* who resist change with a passion. Risk-taking innovators make things happen while the risk-averse laggards watch things happen. Research studies show that *Laggards* take about ten times longer to buy into any new concept than *Early Adopters*. Change is debilitating for these types; they would rather do without than risk taking a chance on the new.

Innovators and *Early Adopters* are those adventuresome types who go for the gold even before they know exactly where to find it. They are less dogmatic than *Late Adopters* or *Laggards* who wait years for things to be proven prior to jumping into the fray. Virtually all professions fall into this personality distribution. If you are selling to dentists remember it is always the Early Adopters who buy first and the Laggards who will never buy until everyone else has. Each type follows predictable buying patterns. Ever wonder who hangs out in Sharper Image stores? Yea! It is the Innovator and Early Adopter types who tend to be better educated, younger, worldlier, and more socially active than Laggards.

Guidelines for the adoption process can be seen in the below chart. About 15 percent of the population in any discipline tends to fall into the Innovator and Early Adopter categories. That says that 85 percent are going to slam the door in your face. The irony is that Late Adopters and Laggards don't see themselves as behind the times. They think they are prudent since that is the safe path. But ignorance is bliss. Such people cherish the status quo and seldom get traffic tickets. They are not in a hurry and would not take chances to win the war of life. Innovators and Early Adopters are willing to lose in order to win and tend to have a higher incidence of traffic tickets as they are in a hurry to find their niche. Late Adopters and Laggards work in bureaucracies, live life in the slow lane, and follow policies even if they are stupid. They don't adapt well to change.

Diffusion & Adoption of New Ideas and Concepts

- Early Adopters have more formal education than later adopters

- They also have a higher socioeconomic backgrounds and have more interpersonal relations

- These types are far better read with more exposure to the mass media

- Early Adopters tend to be highly cosmopolitan and well traveled

- These types have more professional change agent contacts within their social environs

- More social participation in the community is always a clear factor

- Innovators have a very high comfort with ambiguity

- Such people have a much higher Internal Locus of Control (control of your destiny)

- Self-efficacy (confidence) is far higher for Innovators and Changemasters

Freedom to Be Different Drives Innovation

Freedom to explore, learn, and grow was the forte of spurned American engineer Edward Demming. When American industrialists refused to listen to him, Demming went to Japan and is credited with unleashing that Japanese juggernaut that landed in American living rooms beginning in 1960. This quality guru was a free thinker at odds with those Late Adopter types running American factories who disdained his ideas on quality control. While America wallowed in a love affair with doing it by the numbers Demming showed the Japanese the art of quality. It worked so well that America began to lose industry after industry to the Japanese, beginning with the radio industry and then spreading to the whole consumer electronics industry. Within two decades America went from producing over 90 percent of the world's consumer electronics to 10 percent. The very products America had invented—stereos, TV's, VCR's, calculators—became the backbone of the Japanese industrial empire. While America was landing on the moon Japan was landing in American living rooms. Just prior to his passing in the early nineties Demming documented the philosophy that had transformed a small sleeping nation:

"The source of innovation is freedom. You cannot plan to make a discovery. Discoveries and new knowledge come from freedom. When someone is responsible only to himself, he has only himself to satisfy, then you'll have invention, new thought, new product, new design, new ideas." (*Industry Week* Jan. 17, 1994 p. 24)

Paradoxically Money Is Not the Catalyst for Growth

When a firm spends more money on their R & D the expectation is to get more products to the market. Wrong! They get fewer to the market based on one research study that was made famous by Peter Senge's *The Fifth Discipline*. Is that bizarre or what? The reason for this is that increased budgets and spending increases the number of people and the conflagration in the middle impedes the process. New researchers and scientists create empires and make the organization less efficient than when it was smaller. Author Richard Daft said, "As R & D budgets increase product development decreases."

This anomaly is also true for investments. Long-term investments are always better than trading according to longitudinal research studies. Optimum investing should focus on industry fundamentals not on the near-term profits. Focusing on the short-term vagaries like interest rates, ROI, and P/E ratios is futile if the industry is under siege by new innovative products. But the surety-driven investors tend to take the safer path leaving the riskier one to the gut-feeling innovator types. Common stocks of start-ups over one 73-year study showed they were by far the most lucrative investment in contrast to the stocks of larger firms, government bonds, Treasury Bills, or long-term corporate bonds.

The Myth of Expertise as Path to Power

Bertrand Russell & Margaret Mead Show Us the Way!

Bertrand Russell and Margaret Mead were wunderkinds with a mythical sense of life and achievement. Neither permitted existing dogmas to interfere with their trek to the top. Both were academics, renegades, and were considered eccentric by the establishment. They spent much of their professional lives violating traditional ways and consequently were seen as weird by the establishment. And both were blasted for shocking romantic liaisons.

Russell was a dichotomy. This renowned professor at Cambridge repeatedly fell in love with women who were married to other professors or worked for him. The most notorious of his love interests was the wife of his celebrated collaborator on *Principia Mathematica* Lord Alfred North Whitehead. While a full professor at Cambridge Russell began touting the merits of free love, polygamy, and extramarital affairs plus the stupidity of war. During the heyday of Victorianism and British Imperialism this was heresy and cost him his job. Margaret Mead had a similar predilection. The first female Ph.D. in Anthropology engaged in blatant affairs with both men and women with whom she worked. Her most infamous liaison was with her mentor and teacher Ruth Benedict. Margaret was an indomitable spirit who always marched to the tune of her own rhythms despite traditional dogmas. It made her great and made her an enigma.

The parents of Margaret Mead were both Ph.D.'s. Despite their formal education backgrounds they home-schooled Margaret until high school. She learned the rudiments of writing, sewing, poetry, literature, and to play musical instruments from her grandmother. Keeping a journal forced her to look within what was transpiring around her and to document the nuances of life. She competed in sports and became an independent thinking woman long before that was in vogue. Reared in an agnostic household she rebelled and became an Episcopalian at age nine. Then to show her independence Margaret married an ordained minister. But the indomitable spirit embarked on blatant affairs prior to running off to Indonesia to do her doctoral work that was published as *Coming of Age in Samoa* (1928). This was a petite young woman who unashamedly traveled to the South Pacific to live and work in the jungle when most young women didn't even dare fly on a plane. Margaret is a poster child for exploration to build confidence and coping skills. It was imprinted during her youth when the family lived in sixty homes prior to her starting school. The haughty self-sufficiency of her adulthood can be traced back to those early years.

Mead was spiritual but passionate. When it came to romance no religious dogma was sufficient to interfere with her liaisons. She participated in numerous affairs while off on research assignments in the Far East. This is more interesting since she spent her life researching the behavior of young women and wrote her most redeeming works on the sexual behavior of remote cultures. Her ability to live outside the bounds of convention came from her belief that she was special. An example is the time she arrived at an airport without a ticket and finding no seats on the plane told the attendant, "But I'm Margaret Mead," fully expecting the airline attendant to find her a seat.

Russell earned a reputation as the philandering philosopher in his native London. Russell left the world a huge legacy of literary and philosophic works. Bright men like Russell and John Nash, memorialized in the book *A Beautiful Mind* and fictionalized in the movie of the same name, were philosophic mathematicians. When enamored of a young woman they didn't bother with a long courting period but very rationally spoke of their physical desires. They rationalized romance in order to find it. That is lost on the average female. The brighter ones often bought in for both Russell and Nash but it appears the appeal was more to the grey matter than the physical. Russell wrote extensively on his beliefs, blatantly saying, "I cannot know a woman until I sleep with her." But it turned out once he knew her he wanted to know others and this led to four marriages, the last at age eighty. His third was to a teacher at his nontraditional school many years his junior who bore him a child at age sixty-six.

The Russell Paradox was Russell's treatise on analytical philosophy. The brilliant iconoclast concocted an ethical system in tune with what he felt important for living a healthy and happy life. In 1945 at age seventy-three he was awarded the Nobel Prize in Literature for the world-acclaimed *The History of Philosophy*. His *Logical Paradox* was included in his magnum opus *Principia Mathematica,* developed with Alfred North Whitehead between 1910 and 1913. It was during this long and grueling effort that he fell madly in love with Whitehead's wife Evelyn. It mystified this renegade that he would not be permitted to pursue his passion despite her marriage. Logic was master for Russell. And he used it often to rationalize his own provocative nature. Russell's frustration of not being able to sleep with the woman he loved ended in a treatise titled *Ethics, Sex & Marriage*. In this he wrote on a subject out of synch with Victorian England:

> **"If marriage and paternity are to survive as social institutions some compromise is necessary between promiscuity and lifelong monogamy."**

Russell's radical invective on Victorian family life and war—he was a vocal pacifist—led to his firing from Cambridge and imprisonment in 1918. His timing was bad since England was at war with Germany. Fortunately, Russell was financially independent, having inherited enough money to live and love comfortably the rest of his life. The money gave him the freedom to speak his mind on many issues that irked those in power. And it led to many enemies and imprisonment during his long and embittered life. The establishment saw him as a threat. The liberals saw him as a refreshing intellectual.

During Russell's time in prison for pacifism during World War I Russell wrote two books, *Analysis of Mind* and *Introduction to Mathematical Philosophy*. And at age sixty-eight he was still the passionate pacifist pontificating against World War II. His campaign against traditional marriage led to his ban from New York City led by Bishop Manning's crusade against the blasphemer. Just how dangerous was this aging Brit in America? But the establishment tends to fear anything that goes against their dogmatic beliefs. Evangelists feared his scholarly intellect and ostracized him for much of his life. His passport was confiscated in New York City. Such mindless moves led to more scathing words on religious zealots.

Bright women were attracted to Russell and younger men to Mead. One of Russell's former married mistresses sent him flowers on his ninety-seventh birthday, to his eternal delight. Mead's second husband Reo Fortune, an Australian, told the media, "She is life force incarnate." After attending one of her lectures when she was a matronly monarch a young male in the audience gushed, "The sex appeal of her mind absolutely captivated me. If she pointed to me and said, You! You are the one. I would have gone with her anywhere."

Margaret Mead had a similar propensity as Russell. Both could piss off the Pope by their words. In Mead's case it was the doubters from traditional anthropology that were upset. Margaret was never diverted by adversarial theories. *Newsweek* was enamored of Mead's indomitable persona and wrote, "It never occurred to her that she wasn't destined to become the world's greatest female anthropologist." In her forties Mead split from Gregory Bateson, one of the world's most acclaimed anthropologists. On being queried in London on the reason for the breakup he said, "She was like a tugboat. She could sit down and write 3000 words by 11 o'clock in the morning and spend the rest of the day working at the museum. I couldn't keep up and she couldn't stop."

Mythical Magic on Being Smart by Being Stupid

Bertrand Russell & Margaret Mead—Mind over Matter

Bertrand Russell never conformed to any principle during his long life. This curmudgeon could not be bought or broken by societal mores. This made him unique and the

*darling of the media due to his insightful candor that was never constrained by politi-
cal correctness. The loquacious one could always be counted on to defy the correctness
of anything from war to virginity. His contribution to the world of letters was* The
Russell Paradox *in which he said, "The sense of certainty and revelation comes before
any definite belief."*

*The analytical philosopher correctly saw that, "Fear is at the bottom of all that is bad
in the world" due to the weak capitulating to those in power. He detested that such
people would sacrifice individual rights to the establishment. In one diatribe he said,
"Emotion varies inversely with one's knowledge—the less you know the hotter you
get."*

*Books were important for Russell as they were for Mead and inspired his trek to the
world of letters. "At age eleven, I began Euclid," he wrote, "This was one of the great
events of my life, as dazzling as first love. From that moment until I was thirty-eight
mathematics was my chief interest and my chief source of happiness." It led to a life of
philosophy exploration.*

*In a similar trek through intellectual insight and myth Margaret Mead became great
because she saw herself as great. Like Montessori she had a unique philosophy on formal education, admonishing educators that, "Children must be taught how to think,
not what to think." In her doctoral work that was published as the first of nine books,*
Coming of Age in Samoa *(1928), she earned worldwide acclaim as the first female
Ph.D. in Anthropology. In her books* Growing up in New Guinea *(1930) and* Sex
& Temperament *(1935) she spoke to the nature of behavior relative to nurture
rather than nature.*

*Rather than just concentrating on anthropology Mead became a student of behavior
with personality and nurturing key to much of her more noteworthy work. Mead was
a prolific writer who published 139 articles and 10 documentary films and received
40 awards and 28 honorary degrees.*

*This indomitable personality was a petite tigress who wore down macho males and
delighted living life on the edge both personally and professionally. Like Russell she
had a strong comfort with ambiguity and a strong sense of her destiny. It permitted her
to overcome many obstacles. The indomitable one adamantly refused to bear children
during her early child-bearing years and then decided to have a child at age 39.
Within a short time she placed her daughter stepparents as playing mother was interfering with her role as a world-famous anthropologist. An example of this strong sense*

of self was her refusal to take the name of any one of her four husbands, the last of which was the world-renowned Gregory Bateson. Psychologist Jean Houston tested Mead later in life and was amazed at the tie between her left and right hemispheres and wrote, "She could move in and out of her unconscious with ease." Her most noted talent was charisma as shown by her appeal to all types and nationalities.

CHAPTER 8

▼

ICONOCLASTS ARE
MANIACS ON A MISSION
TO THE IMPOSSIBLE

Great Intensity & Hyper-Activity Energizes
Superstars

"To measure up to all that is demanded of him, a man must overestimate his capacities." Goethe

"The man who consumes without producing is a parasite."
Ayn Rand, *We the Living*

"One characteristic of genius is the capacity for great intensity. To remain in power high energy is key."
Psychiatrist David Hawkins (2002 p. 107)

Peak performers in the twenty-first century will be quick or dead. They don't use snooze buttons. Energy is the variable that makes them special. In a world that is in double time one must be quick or pay the price of mediocrity. Bucky Fuller labeled the secret of functioning *ephemeralization*—getting more and more done in less and less time. George Gilder said something similar in his book on the history of the Internet in *Telecosm* (2000), "In a world of material abundance the only inexorable scarcity is time." Testimony to what is now happening is that the speed of travel increased 1000 times during the twentieth century. Communications increased 10 million times. Today's Web-world is about tempo. And that tempo had better be intense and positive. The message in such a world is, "get on the Web wave or find yourself wiped out in its wake." In other words, work as if you were double parked on the highway of life and you will make it. Those not so inclined will not be altering any paradigms or even reaching the pinnacle of success. Get excited or become mired in the wasteland of mediocrity.

Renaissance inventor Bucky Fuller lived life as if his next most precious project may not get finished so he feared going to bed for fear it would not get done. Bucky was so wired that he considered all things wrapped around speed—getting more and more done in less and less time. He labeled his system *ephemeralization,* striving to achieve more and more with less and less. The incredible overachiever was energy incarnate. His classic work *Critical Path* (1981) documented most of his brilliant ideas.

Rushing sickness is not a polite way to say it but it is the fuel to the top. Bucky Fuller's *dymaxion sleep* personifies such passion. This Type A+ workaholic trained himself to work for six hours, nap for thirty minutes, then work another six hours followed by another power nap and so on for months. This maniac could outwork and outthink men decades his junior. For men like Fuller time is a precious resource not to be squandered. Time for him was far more important than money. Although Fuller's lack of sleep didn't appear to impact his health or output, as he lived to be a vibrant eighty-eight.

The world is moving at warp speed. Every three years the totality of information in the world doubles and each day there are about 250 megabytes of new information for every human being on the planet. In such a world you either become part of the process or find yourself losing out to those with more energy and drive. Human potential guru David Hawkins said, "One characteristic of genius is the capacity for great intensity. To remain in power high energy is key."

Such feverish behavior never comes without some cost. Walt Disney paid dearly for his feverish activity, as did his friend and contemporary Howard Hughes. Both would drive themselves to the point of breakdown and then have to take a rest cure or face serious emotional trauma. Both worked around the clock many nights to complete some new project. Such men are willing to live with the downside of their frenetic behavior for the upside benefits. Most people are not so inclined. Leonardo da Vinci had a similar predilection, as did Thomas Edison and Balzac. Leonardo wrote in his notebooks, "Inactivity saps the rigors of the mind." Napoleon was less polite when he wrote, "I will lose a man but never a minute."

Visionaries Are Driven People

Prudent individuals set moderate goals. Visionaries set radical unrealistic goals. Once the prudent man meets his goals he is satisfied! Visionaries are never satisfied even when they can build that castle in the sky. They then go look for Utopia. Did Helena Rubinstein stop going to the office every day after becoming the richest woman in America? No! Did Picasso or Mother Teresa ever retire? No! Will Donald Trump ever stop betting it all for the next skyscraper? No chance! The moral of this is that overachieving zealots must have new mountains to climb or get lost in mediocrity or crawl into a bottle. New opportunities fuel their passions. Those who stop dreaming are on the way to dying. Cite the example of the Great A&P Tea Company. In 1960 they were the largest retailer in the world. Caught up in their own success they decided to protect their assets instead of using them to grow. They not only didn't prosper they fell off the radar screen within a decade. In a growth environment you grow or you die. They died.

Individuals who get turned on by life's possibilities must continue to risk for life to be palatable. Basking in success like A&P leads to atrophy. The less driven are content to stop risking and not grow but they pay the price, even if they are not aware of it. They become couch potatoes or waste their talents on inane wanderlust. People grow or deteriorate since there is no such thing as staying the same. Psychologists have found that muscles shrivel up without use and that the brain does the same. The emotional system lives by the same laws. When Thomas Edison had made his fortune he could have retired to his Ft. Myers estate and enjoyed the fruits of his past labors. But Edison was a driven man and kept up a feverish pace until the day he died. And that is precisely why he lived a long and productive life.

Success is tied inextricably to ardor. Zealots get more done and that is why they tend to alter the world. The less passionate are less likely to get ulcers or worse but their life is far less interesting. What they perceive as prudent becomes their downfall. Passion led Plato to open The Academy in Athens at age forty when the life expectancy was thirty-six. He operated it while training such stalwarts as Aristotle until he was eighty. Such passion for life and career are the fuel that permits long life. Hyper-actives live much longer than the average as they always have a reason to get up and get after it every day. We live in the Internet Age, a world of e-mail not snail-mail where cyberspeak is pervasive. Those who don't get on the e-wave are destined to be wiped out in its wake. The overachieving zealot Frederick Nietzsche said it eloquently, "The sedentary life is the very sin against the Holy Spirit."

Ayn Rand pushed the limits in the world of letters. Passion was her fuel to the top. Rand was dedicated to destroying Communism, that despicable system that had destroyed her family when she was a young girl in St. Petersburg, Russia. After defecting to America her whole life was based on destroying any system that robbed man of his right to succeed and fail. Her passionate philosophic diatribes never waned for forty years. They were couched in metaphors about railroads and buildings that tore at the soul of socialism. Howard Roark and John Galt had more to do with tearing that Berlin Wall down than all of the guns and political rhetoric in the free world. *The Fountainhead* was modeled after the rebellious architect Frank Lloyd Wright who she adored for his refusal to conform to traditional forces. But protagonist architect Howard Roark blew up his own innovative building rather than see it bastardized by a self-serving establishment. Those who would despoil and denigrate were "users" in the Rand lexicon. In the impassioned dialogue of Roark being prosecuted for a crime against nature Rand had him scream:

"The world is perishing from an orgy of self-sacrifice. The creator originates. The parasite borrows and mutilates. It is a world in which I cannot live."

Rand spent her life writing on the positive effects of permitting man to be free. In the classic *Atlas Shrugged* (1957) protagonist John Galt pontificates at length on the high price paid by mankind when self-serving bureaucrats are permitted to rule for the masses. Rands's quintessential self-actualized man Galt screams to the world in his famous radios speech:

"The man who accepts the role of a sacrificial animal, will not achieve the self-confidence necessary to uphold the validity of his mind—and the man who doubts the validity of his mind, will not achieve the self-esteem necessary to uphold the value of his person." (Sciabarra 305)

Freedom for man to win and lose, bet and fail, and not to be merely a pawn of a central government was Rand's philosophy of capitalism labeled Objectivism. Every word was aimed at showing the nihilistic nature of collectivism with rational human beings paying the price. On her passing in 1983 her casket was adorned with a ten-foot-high wreath of roses in the form of a dollar sign as the consummate capitalist.

Excess Can Be the Panacea of Productivity

People with too much time on their hands get in trouble whether they are eight or eighty. Obsessive people seldom get in the same trouble unless it is in getting traffic tickets or pushing the limits of some new endeavor. Excess is their secret to success and it leaves little time to indulge in booze, drugs, or crime. Those obsessing over breaking 100 on the golf course or improving their tennis serve are not often found closing the local taverns. Those preoccupied with a new product idea or business start-up don't need drugs for titillation. The eighteen-year-old dedicated to making the football or baseball team is not out stealing hubcaps or joining some gang. In contrast those who are retired with nothing to occupy their time often find themselves escaping into booze or food. The mother of modern dance, Isadora Duncan, was an obsessive woman. She wrote in her memoir, "I was so interested in my work I got into a state of static ecstasy." Such passion leaves little time for other things and the fatigue of excelling ensures those who do fall asleep immediately on hitting the bed.

Excess can be good or bad but when chasing a dream it is the fuel that makes it come true. Passionate people just get more done. When Mother Teresa was told she couldn't start a Society for the Poor in Calcutta she quit the Catholic order. When the power elite saw the young nun would not be dissuaded they capitulated. Had she been less driven she would have just been one more casualty of traditionalist thinking. Had Walt Disney not been so passionate about his ideas not one of them would have made it off his drawing board. The surety-conscious board of directors hated his most elegant ideas including Mickey Mouse, Donald Duck, Goofy, and mostly his crazy idea that would become Disneyland. To survive such roadblocks it is necessary for the visionary to not listen, and to do that they must be a driven personality.

Obsessive people not only don't have time for trouble they seldom have time for relaxation. Most disdain vacations and when they succumb take their work with them. Sleep for them is a waste as was the case of Nikola Tesla, the father of alternating current, who slept but two hours a night for most of his long life. Edison refused to leave his lab and napped on his workbench, as did Walt Disney and Bucky Fuller. An associate of Bucky Fuller spoke of his Dymaxion Sleep habit of working six hours followed by 30-minute naps that was aimed at fulfilling his motto, "Progress means mobility." J. Baldwin wrote:

"He never seemed to tire. His lectures would go on for ten hours or more. He seemed to be always scribbling notes, reading, making models, or just prowling around. The ability to keep going in that manner continued undiminished well into his seventies." (Landrum Sybaritic Genius *p. 133)*

Falling Down, Getting Up & Positive Energy

Zealots have a predilection for living life on the precipice. They are always willing to fall down to learn how not to. Do they fall? Often! But that is the way to learn to ski and how to succeed in business. They do not see falls as bad, as do the less driven. You can't have it both ways. You either chase opportunity—which is often risky—and fall down or chase surety and don't have many falls but also will seldom find real success. Surety types seldom find themselves with the brass ring. I often ask students if they want to be rich and famous. The answer is always in the affirmative. I then ask if they are willing to bet everything they have for the opportunity. Most say "No!" If you aren't willing to bet it all you can't have it all. It is also true that those unwilling to violate conventional wisdom can never alter paradigms.

Psychotherapist Valerie Hunt concluded, "The greater the turbulence, the more complex the solution, the greater the jump to a higher order." What does this say about the way we lead our lives? Turbulence is the pathway to a higher order. Risk is the fuel to greater success. The only big regrets for an eighty-year old are those things they didn't dare do when forty. This whole arena is counterintuitive to what most people have been taught: Don't fall off your bike. Don't speak to strangers. Don't drive too fast. Don't lose sleep by staying up late. Eminent visionaries violate every one of these admonitions. Risk is what energizes them and gets them excited. Picasso was a renegade artist who so infuriated his friend Matisse he labeled his monumental work that created Cubism "a horrid mockery." When asked what he though about Picasso's masterpiece *Les Demoiselles d'Avignon* Matisse replied, "Picasso has an all-consuming urge to challenge, shock, to destroy and remake the world." Babe Ruth and Lance Armstrong rose to the top of their sports by doing what their peers feared. Both were obsessive and ferocious and it caused them to be both revered and feared. Positive passion was the catalyst for their success.

Life-threatening experience is paradoxical in that it makes us rather than breaks us. Breakdown does lead us closer to breakthrough. It empowers us by arming us with an inner resolve that was not there prior to the trauma. Without volcanic eruptions we would not have the glorious Hawaiian islands. Had Germany not been totally destroyed in World War II there is no chance that they would today be the most powerful economic force in Europe. Had Walt Disney not been fired as a cartoonist he would never have opened Disney Studios. Students go nuts when failing a test but the ones they fail are the very ones that they don't forget. Why is this? Traumatic experiences leave a more lasting imprint than normal ones. Calamity is the catalyst for growth as well as leaving a permanent mark on our psyche. Most people don't remember where they were on September 5, 2001, but remember trivial detail on where they were on September 11. Those old enough remember precisely where they were when President Kennedy was shot by Lee Harvey Oswald on November 23, 1963, in Dallas, Texas.

Nobel Prize-winning scientist Dr. Ilya Prigogine documented the reason that crisis leads to creativity and that breakdown leads to breakthrough. In an attempt to overcome the nihilistic laws of physics where we all end up burning up in heat death he wrote on what he labeled Dissipative Structures to show how breakdowns lead to breakthroughs. It won him the Nobel Prize in Chemistry. When we break a bone it never breaks there again. Why? It heals stronger where it had been broken. Prigogine showed how the emotions and mind experience similar dichotomies when faced with entropy. "Many systems of breakdown," he wrote, "are actually harbingers of breakthrough." In eloquent terms he told us, "Psychological suffering, anxiety, and collapse lead to new emotional, intellectual, and spiritual strengths." This says that if we haven't been to the bottom it is far tougher to reach the very top.

Mania & Positive Energy

Winning games in business, sports or gambling is not nearly as titillating as just participating in the action. The thrill of the game is why entrepreneur types are willing to bet their jobs and their life savings just to play. They like to win but research has shown it is all about doing it not winning it. And it isn't about the money or the glory but the chance to match their wits against adversaries. Even gamblers admit that they are just as excited about losing as winning. World-class athletes have a similar predilection. Lance Armstrong said of his Tour de France wins, "It's not about the bike. It's about the soul." Former Boston Celtics star Bill Russell said in *Second Wind,* "I literally did not care who had won. If we had lost, I'd still be as free and as high as a sky hawk." Video game guru Nolan Bushnell said, "Being successful is kind of dull." That is why high-rollers play long after there is no longer any reason to play.

Visionaries often exude a frenetic energy that attracts and repels. Many disciples of Mahatma Gandhi and Mother Teresa or even Richard Branson and Donald Trump were drawn to the hyperactive nature and positive vigor of their leaders. Unfortunately, that same kind of fanaticism can be found in the infamous gurus who used their power to destroy rather than build. Adolph Hitler, Jim Jones, and David Koresh used their hyper-energy to mesmerize and cast a spell over their followers. But we can learn from them as well, remembering that this is not about morals but about the question, how did these visionaries incite and excite? Wax enthusiastic and legions of wannabes will be drawn into your sphere of influence. Passion for a cause is an energy conduit like little else. It is but a matter of using it for positive not negative causes.

One of the most positively energized wunderkinds in history was a Croatian inventor named Nikola Tesla. This visionary is responsible for powering our factories and lighting our cities. He was energy incarnate, sleeping but two hours a night and possessing a pre-cognitive ability that mesmerized those who knew him. Tesla wrote in his memoir, "Creation for an inventor makes a man forget food, sleep, friends, love, everything." The intensity and fiery drive permitted him to live five lifetimes in one.

In the words of human potential guru David Hawkins, "Empowerment occurs when you stop blaming and accept responsibility for your actions. It is the capacity for great intensity." Hawkins waxed eloquent when he wrote, "The higher the power of the current running through a wire, the greater the magnetic field that it generates and the magnetic field itself then influences everything in its presence." In other words, man is like a wire. Both have the capacity to attract and repel based on the current flowing through them. The moral here is that we always influence by what we are thinking and tend to get back what we put out. In the words of self-help writer Lyn Grabhorn, "We get what we vibrate." The most insightful work on the influence of positive energy comes from behavioral kinesiologist and psychiatrist John Diamond, who said in *Your Body Doesn't Lie* (1979), "All illness starts as a problem on the energy level. About 95% of the population tests low on Life Energy."

Columbia and UCLA human potential researcher Valerie Hunt offered insight into the power of energy when she said, "Electromagnetic energy nourishes. For all systems to be 'GO', a rich, electromagnetic field (positive energy) must be present" (Hunt, *The Infinite Mind* 1996). Magnetic entertainers have a special ability to energize from the stage. Country singer Naomi Judd said that positive energy saved her life from hepatitis C. Physicians had diagnosed her as terminal but she didn't listen and went to alternative medicine to find a cure. She wrote of the experience, "Energy healing is amazing. It strips everything down to *Qi*
Isaac Asimov wrote an essay about it, "The Relativity of Wrong"—a Chinese energy field—that is a vital life force."

Energy & Power

John Diamond, President of the International Academy for Preventative Medicine, was an expert on human energy potential and the neurological and physiological by-products of energy. Diamond started using tests to trace energy flows and muscular strength based on whether a subject was thinking positively or negatively. After thousands of tests Diamond discovered that pessimists tested weaker than optimists and with less energy flow. In high-stress situations he found that the thymus gland shrinks due to the negative energy flowing through it. When someone dies the thymus actually atrophies. This link between the mind and body, energy and muscularity, becomes the gatekeeper for tracing energy flow. "Muscles are energy pumps," he said. "The thymus monitors and rebalances our Life Energy." In his book *Your Body Doesn't Lie* he wrote, "All illness starts as a problem on the energy level. About 95% of the population tests low on Life Energy." The bottom line is that all powerful people have high energy.

Diamond discovered what most of us have known intuitively: that hanging around with losers makes us more negative and with a higher chance of failing. The converse is also true. Hanging with winners who exude positive energy increases our chances of success. After thousands of tests Diamond found, "If our Life Energy is high, others will benefit from close contact with us; if it is low our relationships with others become part of the problem" (Diamond, *Life Energy*).

In one interesting experiment Diamond tested subjects for high positive energy flow and those who had a highly negative energy flow through their systems. Then he paired off one negative with one positive and asked them to sit in a room and just talk with no given agenda. He had pre-tested them and they agreed to be retested after their time in the room. The high positive energy individual with strong muscularity based on previous tests came out of the hour-long session and tested weaker and with less positive energy. Wow! And the individual who had entered the room with low and negative energy flow came away from the interaction with the positive dude testing far more positive and stronger. In Diamond's words:

"Placing those who tested with a Strong Thymus (positive types) next to those with a Weak Thymus (negative types) caused the positive types to test lower and the negative types to test higher after they had interacted for some time."(Life Energy 1990).

From his extensive research Diamond concluded, "Your thoughts have the power to alter the physiological response of your muscles." Many sages have said that we become as we think and this work seems to validate that theory. A female pundit once said, "If that were true I would have been a boy at age 16." Diamond offered insight and validation into this when he wrote, "The thymus gland is the first organ to be affected at an energy level by an emotional state." He went on to add, "Unfortunately 95 percent of the people I have tested have an underactive thymus gland—too much hate and not enough love, thus low Life Energy." What can we learn from this? Stop hanging with losers. They are draining and actually make us physically weaker. In another far more upsetting set of data medical researchers have found that "Illness soars once the diagnosis is given. Everything we think or feel has a monumental impact on the overall vibration of mass consciousness." Cerebral centering was another outcome of this:

"Life Energy is high when both hemispheres are active and symmetrical— cerebral balance. It is low when in what I call a state of the stress of physiological disequilibrium."

It is not surprising that visionaries know in their gut when things are not working. The father of video games, Nolan Bushnell, was infamous for stalking out of any meeting or environment that flowed negative energy where whiners were complaining. Research shows that he was not unique. Isadora Duncan, the mother of modern dance, spoke at length of this in her memoirs, saying, "I owe the inspiration of the dance I created to childhood freedom. I was never subjected to the continual don'ts of other children." Lynn Grabhorn addressed this relative to health and happiness:

"Every time we think of anything, we're flowing positive or negative energy. The litany never changes; as we think, we feel; as we feel, we vibrate; as we vibrate, we attract. Then we get to live the results." (Grabhorn, Excuse Me Your Life Is Waiting p. 46)

Speed as a Panacea of Success

When Michael Dell quit school at age nineteen few competitors took him seriously. Later when he told his employees, "I'd rather be first than be late in making decisions," he was speaking to the need for mania in such a competitive world. In his book *Direct from Dell*, he wrote, "Being first and wrong is better than 100% perfect but two years late." In Britain another manic entrepreneur named Richard Branson was equally as enamored with speed in the boardroom and barroom. This tenth-grade dropout founded the Virgin Group and ran it in triple time. The hyper adventurer admitted to the press, "I make up my mind about a business proposal or new people I meet within 30 seconds." While other business executives were consulting their legal counsel Branson had already made the deal.

Is such speed dangerous? Of course! But it is not in a Web world where speed is king, queen, and pawn. When all else is equal speed invariably wins out. Branson and Dell were young dynamos willing to bet it all and that is why they were rich and famous by their thirties. They were in such a hurry they frightened associates who often quit working with them for fear of self-destructing. Wannabes want to win but fear erring when living in the fast lane of life. Speed and risk are cousins as when you go fast you are more at risk but that is the path that dynamic people take. That is the nature of competing in a Web world where all things now move at warp speed compared to just a few decades ago.

Even when they are losing, superstars like Tiger Woods play like they are winning. They never throw in the towel until the game is over; they attack, attack, attack. Ferocity is their forte and playing offense is always preferable to playing defense. Even when Tiger is not playing his best golf he is still a threat due to his passionate demeanor, seen by some as controlled aggression. Just watch him putt. He seldom ever leaves a putt short. Even on fifty-foot putts he is not trying to get. He's going for it. On narrow fairways he still pulls out the driver and tries to hit the ball as far as he possibly can. That gets him in trouble but it is also why he is a champion. Also-rans play not to lose. Winners play to win. Billionaire visionary

Michael Dell told us, "Be quick or be dead." The *Saturday Review* described Helena Rubinstein as a "human whirlwind." That is the nature of winners.

Research has shown that proactive people have more positive energy flowing through their systems than reactive or inactive types. And there is a direct correlation between the amount of energy flowing through your wires and your influence on those in your presence. Positive energy has a weird influence that defies the laws of physics. In *Positive Energy* (2004) Judith Orloff wrote, "I believe that the most profound transformations can take place only on an energetic level." This psychiatrist discovered that "The more positive energy we give off, the more we'll magnetize to us—passion attracts passion, rage attracts rage—we are all subtle energy transmitters" (p. 262). The moral is that life is way too short to spend with losers as they will influence us without us even knowing it. Those dark clouds hovering over negative types impact everything they touch and everyone that comes into their sphere of influence. Be careful. They rob others of their energy without them even knowing it.

High-Octane Personalities & the Quest for Power

Pablo Picasso & Helena Rubinstein Personify the Journey

Pablo Picasso and Helena Rubinstein functioned in what associates described as perpetual motion. Even in their eighties and nineties they were maniacs on a mission and refused to slow down. Psychic energy flowed through them like 16-year-olds on Viagra. Rubinstein requested her portrait to be done by Picasso. He refused, saying he didn't paint any woman he hadn't slept with. Not familiar with rejection this woman who was among the richest women in America made him a deal he couldn't refuse. Work was central to both and not even their mates ever deterred them from living life in the fast lane.

Later in life Rubinstein told *Life* magazine, "If I don't keep busy, I'll go mad." Then in her memoirs she admitted, "I drove myself relentlessly for most of my life." This Polish-born woman of the world functioned with both intensity and ferocity. While she was the consummate workaholic, Picasso turned out to be the most prolific artist who ever picked up a brush. Testimony to Helena's nature, she ate, walked, talked, and worked fast. Her manservant Patrick O'Higgins was forewarned about her by a friend who introduced them saying, "Be careful to eat what she eats or she will eat you." Impatience and speed are the characteristics of

Type A personalities, who typically finish before others are halfway through their meals. O'Higgins wrote, "She had finished her meal before I had begun mine." Hyperactivity was the one characteristic O'Higgins commented on in his biography of the woman who would become his boss, mistress, and confidante. "To the very end," he would write, "she continued driving herself and all those around her, unmercifully."

This oldest of eight girls earned the nickname The Eagle by age twelve in her native Poland. Tenacity and honing skills were her forte. An ambitious father saw some potential as a scientist and enrolled her in a technical school. Helena was not thrilled with school and dropped out without her father's knowledge. Incensed, he arranged for her to marry an older man. But the indomitable spirit split rather than become a housewife and mother. The tenacious teen stole away in the middle of the night and boarded a ship for Australia, where she had a distant cousin. With no money or familiarity with English she landed with the same gusto that had led her to run away.

One of the few items Helena had packed in her bags was some bottles of her uncle Dr. Jacob Lykusky's Hungarian skin cream. When she found working for others unfulfilling she started selling the beauty cream and then repackaged it to become an Australian distributor. Helena worked feverishly seven days a week and built a thriving skin care business that evolved into a salon and then a series of them in Melbourne and Sidney. After a few years she was successful enough to open an elegant salon in faraway London. From those meager beginnings she would expand throughout Europe with salons in Paris, Vienna, Berlin, and Rome. Success led her to a Manhattan salon. Enthralled with the cosmopolitan life in New York City she made it her international headquarters.

Picasso was equally as driven as Rubinstein but would not be so inclined to wanderlust. Hypomania was to be his forte as it was Helena's and led to an incredible output that included 50,000 works of art: 1885 paintings, 1228 sculptures, 2880 ceramics, 18,095 engravings, 11,747 drawings, and 9293 lithographs. Biographer Arianna Huffington said of the father of Cubism, "He had an inexhaustible vitality." Intellectual friend and intellectual combatant Gertrude Stein spoke of the Spaniard's limitless energy and indefatigable lifestyle, writing, "He had a relentless, dynamic productivity and anguish. Cosmic rootlessness and destructive rage were the fertilizers of his prolific creativity."

Picasso could draw before he could talk and his first word was "piz" for pencil. He grew up with art and a passion for perverted pontificating. The artist spent his teen years wandering the Pyrenees to commune with nature. As a young adult he decided to cast his lot in Paris, which was an urban existentialist haven just as the Pyrenees had been for him in Spain. Picasso vacillated widely in his art. When he was down everything in his life was negative including his work. Those cathartic scenes of derelicts and the downtrodden were painted during his Blue Period between 1900 and 1904 after his best friend died. It produced *The Tragedy, The Old Guitar Player,* and *Woman and Child by the Sea.* In the Rose Period his personal life came alive with a passionate love affair with Fernande Olivier, whom he painted constantly. Harlequins permeated this gay period that included the famous portrait of Gertrude Stein with a mask. *La Famille de Saltimbanques* was a key work during this period, in which a deep sense of foreboding and destructiveness permeated his colors and imagery. It was during this period of exorcism that he produced the masterpiece *Les Demoiselles d'Avignon* that would become the genesis of Cubism.

In Barcelona he was unable to contain a raging libido. Passion permeated his very soul and he was hard pressed to pass a bordello without sating his boundless sexual energy. The inner compulsion for philandering never waned as he was seldom without a long list of mistresses and kept women until he was in his seventies. At age ninety he told a reporter, "I don't have a single second to spare and can't think of anything else but painting. I am overburdened with work." His explanation for his high energy was:

"I never get tired. That's why painters live so long. While I work I leave my body outside the door, the way Moslems take off their shoes before entering a mosque."

Pablo was an irreverent innovator who became a devout Communist, atheist, and existential free spirit. Love, art, bullfights, and lust preoccupied him. The poet Paul Eluard was his friend to the degree that his actress wife often slept with the womanizing Picasso. Eluard sent one of Picasso's letters to Carl Jung to ask him what he thought of the writer based on the newly founded graphology. Jung wrote back, "He loves intensely and kills what he loves" (Landrum 1995 p. 179). This description was eerily correct for this self-destructive personality. Jung visited a Picasso showing and remarked on the amazing similarity between Picasso's work and the schizophrenic drawings of his patients. Jung wrote, "There is a type of psychological fissures that run through the image that is sick, grotesque and incomprehensible" (Huffington, p. 202). "The work expresses the recurring characteristic motif of the descent into hell."

Much of Picasso's self-absorbed nature can be attributed to having been doted on as the only boy in an all-female household. His mother was the major influence in his life and dotingly told him, "If you become a soldier, you'll become a general. If you become a monk, you'll end up pope." Being reared in a household with a mother, two aunts, grandmother, sister, and housekeeper Picasso was spoiled beyond repair. It left him a lifelong womanizer. Being treated as a little god molded him into an arrogant adult who had to have everything his way. The coup de grace of his feminine nature was when he refused to take the name of his father Ruiz and preferred to be known by his mother's maiden name Picasso.

Mythical Mentoring & Frenetic Energy

Rubinstein & Picasso Personify the Mythological Trek to Success

Feverish energy permeated both Rubinstein and Picasso. One pioneered the beauty movement for women while the other documented the psyche of the twentieth century in art. Both were Promethean personalities with an obsessive need to chase new opportunity and a compulsion to work around the clock. Feminine allure drove Rubinstein while destruction and surrealism preoccupied Pablo Picasso.

Neither paid much attention to conventional wisdom. When her husband passed away Helena refused to return to New York from Europe saying, "He is already gone. What can I do?" The lethal womanizing of Picasso destroyed many who adored him. Dora Marr had a nervous breakdown and his wife Olga was under constant psychiatric care. Mistresses Marie-Theresa and Jacqueline both committed suicide. Picasso told the press, "I'd rather see a woman die any day than see her happy."

Rubinstein was an obsessive workaholic and Picasso painted like a man possessed. Helena left her mark on the world of business and beauty as Picasso did in art but both were eerily alike in their mystical natures. Salvador Dali painted Helena in Promethean garb to illustrate the likeness of a Promethean spirit beyond the pale of ordinary humankind. She was depicted chained to a rock in glimmering emerald robes that emulated a Greek feminine god-like figure. Picasso's self-portraits were similarly eerie with his role as Minotaur and master of his destiny.

Picasso challenged the world with surrealistic metaphors of life on the edge with women portrayed as Madonnas or prostitutes. The radical Cubist wrote, "I have the revelation of the inner voice. I have myself become destiny." To validate such an arrogant self view he painted in opposition with himself as the Minotaur Carries Off a Woman *(1937). His young mistress Marie-Therese was the sacrificial female being carried off to a deathly seduction. Death and annihilation permeated his life and work.*

When Alice B. Toklas questioned him about his portrait of Gertrude Stein that was indiscernible the irascible genius told her, "Don't worry it will." On one diatribe he said:

"Portraits should possess not physical, not spiritual, but psychological likeness. A picture lives only through the one who looks at it—what they see is the legend surrounding the picture."

Picasso's mystic-like nature evolved out of an early influence by existentialist philosopher Frederick Nietzsche. The Nietzschean Superman thesis appealed to the diminutive school dropout who needed to have a reason to be different and to violate traditional conventions. Picasso's approach to art was a type of philosophic existentialism that was beyond the pale of mere mortals. This can be seen in his most famous works of art that were metaphorical treatises on the destructive nature of man and his drives. Les Demoiselles d'Avignon, Guernica, *and* Weeping Woman *were all about the sexual underpinnings of man with his need to use and abuse to be sated.*

Much of the perverted passion of Picasso's art bordered on the delusional and his megalomania. Some had evolved out of his teenage bout with god and the devil when his beloved sister Conchita died a horrid death after Pablo had made a Faustian pact with god to stop painting if he saved her. When she died Pablo was enraged and promised to spend the rest of his life painting in opposition of the church's dogma.

To defy god one must be omnipotent and that is what he became in the Nietzschean sense of a will-to-power. To produce what is potent one must think they are omnipotent and Picasso fit the model. He imagined himself as beyond mere mortals as a poetic philosopher. When he turned fifty he wrote his own epitaph saying, "Here lies a Spanish poet who dabbled in painting, drawing and sculpture."

Rubinstein had a similar penchant for mysticism. She defied her father and started hawking beauty aids during an era when only prostitutes would consider using makeup to look more attractive. To buck the system takes an indomitable spirit who believes in her own destiny. An example is the time a building owner refused to sell her an apartment. When she asked why she couldn't make a deal with the landlord she was told no Jews were permitted to own in that building. The spirited matron bought the building, fired the management, and changed the policy. That is power.

Pure freneticism was the fuel that made Rubinstein great. Each adversary and every debacle was merely another opportunity for this diminutive woman. "The beauty business," she told her husbands and the press, "always came first with me." This was eerily similar to the Picasso statement, "I sacrifice everything to my painting."

Rubinstein was undomesticated and strangely not even romantic, at least with men. She went through husbands like Picasso went through wives. Helena told the press, "I could not enjoy the pleasures of domesticity for which millions of American women yearn." With similar disdain for convention, Picasso told the media, "Taste is the enemy of creativity." In the early '40s Life magazine called Helena, "The world's most successful businesswoman." Picasso in a far more vindictive nature said, "The painter takes whatever it is and destroys it. At the same time he gives it another life. But he must see through what the others see." Their genius was their mystical nature and indomitable natures.

CHAPTER 9

▼

CRISIS INSPIRES CREATIVITY— BREAKDOWN = BREAKTHROUGH

Visiting the bottom is the fuel for the trip to the top

"Our greatness lay not so much in being able to remake the world as in being able to remake ourselves."
Mahatma Gandhi

"Psychological suffering, anxiety and collapse lead to new emotional, intellectual and spiritual strengths. Confusion and death can lead to new scientific ideas."
Dr. Ilya Prigogine, *Order out of Chaos*

"A personality is born of chaos. Resistance to chaos can only beget more chaos and resistance."
Stephen Wolinsky, *The Tao of Chaos* (1994)

Wonder women are impervious to pain. When they visit the bottom they use the experience to fuel their trip to the top. Those that haven't been to the bottom have a tougher journey to the top. Why? Because of the conditioning that takes place when things aren't so good. We learn to deal with adversity better by having deal with it. The kid who never falls off of a bike, seldom ever becomes the best bike rider. There is no gain without pain, as the jocks say. When adversity strikes it is hard to think beyond the horror of a near-death experience or some other calamity. But those who don't let it destroy them come away far stronger for having been there. Few people are aware of this fundamental rule of success. Having been to the bottom wires us for the trip to the top. Why? When an individual hits bottom they are transformed in a way they don't quite recognize at first. They experience an epiphany that imprints them with resolve and tenacity. Once a person has stared mortality in the mirror there are no battles that they fear.

Creativity emanates from a lack of inhibition that can be inspired by dementia. Studies show that when dementia sets in and stops the left brain—the rational side—from functioning effectively the individual becomes far more creative. This right side is the place where divergent thinking is permitted to take place and therefore creativity to spawn. The left side is the rational or convergent thinking place. With the onset of breakdown studies show that many people stop being so rational and permit the flow of ideas.

When most people lose their jobs suddenly they are devastated. Getting fired is the end for them and many crawl unceremoniously into a bottle to drown their sorrows. In fact it is the beginning. When you are no longer tied to a job—one you may even have hated but couldn't leave due to the need to pay the bills—there are no longer any reasons not to chase your real dreams. Suddenly you are free to do your thing, whatever that may be. People can't go there unless tragedy opens those doors. It was because Walt Disney was fired from his idyllic job as a cartoonist at the Kansas City daily newspaper that he opened Disney Studios. Bucky Fuller found himself on the frigid streets of Chicago with a new baby on the way. With no potential for gainful employment he decided to commit suicide but when he saw the error of that he became a world-famous Renaissance man. At age sixty Solomon Price was fired from a retail chain that he was running in San Diego, California. A year later he became the father of the now famous wholesale club industry that is now Costco. Oprah Winfrey was fired as a news anchor in Baltimore. It also led to a near-suicide but then led to her becoming a talk show host. What if these horrible experiences had not taken place? There would not be a Disneyland, domed stadiums, warehouse clubs, or the Oprah show.

Crisis, Creativity & Diversity

During the trauma of a life-threatening event or a career-ending calamity we are devastated but altered in a way we don't really understand. In the midst of the maelstrom we have a tendency to self-destruct but after we reorganize our minds and emotions we are stronger for the experience. Misfortune and adversity are the catalysts to greater opportunity but at the time it isn't always apparent. This principle works both ways. When things are too easy we are not properly molded for adversity. Consider the data on children of the rich and famous who often suffer the ignominy of their past. Few ever experience anything like the success of their parents. Why? Life has been way too easy for them to have learned to cope effectively.

Those not in tune with pain are hard-pressed to truly understand pleasure. People on the beach in south Florida can't appreciate what they have until they get stuck on a mountain in subzero temperatures. The irony that bedevils the healthy is that they have a hard time relating to those with a terminal disease. Those who have never been hungry can't quite relate to those who rarely have a square meal. If there were no marginal people in the world we could hardly appreciate being special. That is the paradox of life. Tragedy grooms us for comedy and vice versa. In this author's research of hundreds of eminent people virtually every one experienced a near-death experience or a major life trauma that transformed them. Empowerment elevated them from the ashes of degradation. Had Edison not been deaf it is unlikely he would have invented the microphone, phonograph, and talking movies. Had Lance Armstrong not been at death's door he admitted he would never have won one Tour de France road race. Adversity takes away but it also gives back.

Diversity can also prove empowering. Without its diversity America would never have become a titanic world power. A look at some of the country's immigrants offers insight into the sacrament of struggle. Jazz, blues, and now hip-hop are the music of such struggle emerging from the black ghettos. The Hispanic work ethic had its roots in the agrarian need to feed their young. Asians came here and showed that education can diffuse bigotry and discrimination. The incredible merchandising skill of Jewish immigrants left its mark on Madison Avenue and in Hollywood. French wines, Japanese sushi, Italian pizza, Middle Eastern couscous, and Thai cuisines have altered the nation's eating habits and have made food a socialization experience as well as sustenance. American music offers testimony to diversity.

Russian immigrants one hundred years ago transformed the burgeoning entertainment industry led by the likes of Al Jolson, Irving Berlin, and George Gershwin. These three titans influenced Broadway more than Shakespeare. Why? When you are from a distant land and culture you see the world through a unique filter and often with far more clarity. It was hardly an accident that Irving Berlin wrote the most memorable American classics: *God Bless America, White Christmas, Easter Parade*, and *There's No Business like Show Business*. Born in Russia and reared in the bowels of Manhattan this son of a rabbi wrote some of the most revered lyrics of America's religious holidays. Only the overt patriotism of a man born elsewhere can put a spin on the true nature of freedom.

Louis Armstrong brought New Orleans blues and jazz north to Chicago. The cool sounds of black music are more about the inner passion from a seething soul than some musical idiom. Few people realize that ragtime music evolved out of black music and then at midcentury took another violent turn into rock and roll. It wasn't long before Elvis, a white man with a black sound, transformed the world with his marriage of movement with rhythm. In a few years the Motown movement came along.

Hitting Bottom Arms Us for the Trek to the Top

As the bumper sticker says, *Shit Happens*. So deal with it head on or you will become a casualty of the curse. It isn't what happens to us on the trek down the highway of life but how we cope with it that makes us or breaks us. Toxicity is far more instructive than non-toxicity. It opens one's eyes to the scourge of reality. Visiting the bottom forces a person to deal with life there and makes the trek up the ladder easier. It gives an edge to those who have been there over those who have had it easier. Encounters with lady misfortune arm them like little else. When forced to face mortality we truly come to grips with the reality that we are not immortal. The warmth of a fireplace can never be fully appreciated until you have been stranded in a blizzard.

John Nash of *A Beautiful Mind* fame offers insight into sanity and objectivity. Until he went insane he was an eccentric unable to break new ground but when he became schizophrenic he finally was able to see without being constrained by conventional thinking. He had to get goofy to find greatness. In 1994 Nash won the Nobel Prize in Economics for his work exploring ideas that were too obtuse to be considered by more rational scientists. Periods of psychosis destroyed Nash's ability to function socially but contributed to his breakthrough on game theory known as The Nash Equilibrium. At Princeton Nash was a social retard but respected for his mind. So-called normal scientists admitted that Nash was able to see opportunities that were way outside their realm of interest. Being out of touch made him more in touch and permitted him to start at the end not the beginning. Biographer Nasar (1998) wrote, "Nash saw the vision first, constructing the laborious proofs long afterward. Nash's genius was of that mysterious variety more often associated with music and art." An MIT mathematician said of his mysterious magic:

"He approached the problem by just transforming the non-linear equations into linear equations (quantifying the vision) and then attacking these by non-linear means. It was a stroke of genius." (Nasar p. 219)

The irony of Nash's insight was that a man who was rational to a fault turned to an emotional solution that would win him a Nobel Prize. This man who was totally out of touch emotionally used his affliction for a breakthrough and did it in a field that was supposed to function rationally. Other scientists used a rational approach to gamesmanship theory but he outdid them by going the opposite way using man's emotional responses to predictable behavior to resolve economic dilemmas. One MIT professor was blown away by his solution to the Riemann Hypothesis, saying, "If a graduate student had proposed such an outlandish idea, I'd have thrown him out of my office. Nash's solution was not just novel, it was mysterious" (Nasar p. 62). Princeton professor of mathematics Peter Sarnak, Ph.D., said, "The way he views things is very different from other people. He comes up with master insights" (Nasar p. 350). Had Nash been more normal he could never have succeeded. Abnormality made him super-normal.

Seldom in the annals of science has hitting the bottom proved more providential than in the life of cycling's wunderkind Lance Armstrong. At the peak of Armstrong's physical powers at age twenty-four he came face to face with his mortality in the form of a terminal diagnosis of testicular cancer. By the time physicians found it the disease had spread to his lungs and brain. The chances of survival were slim and none gave him any chance of ever competing again on his bike. His sponsor looked at the data and cancelled his contract since they saw him as a walking dead man. In his autobiography *It's Not about the Bike* (2001) Armstrong admitted that the death sentence was the catalyst for his trek to the very top. "I could not have won one Tour de France," he wrote, "had I not had cancer. Cancer is the best thing that ever happened to me."

Lance had not finished two of three Tours prior to his diagnosis. In Houston's world-renowned cancer center he had been told that they were sure they could save his life but it would be a surgical procedure that would also ensure he would never ride again and probably never walk again. Lance looked elsewhere for a second opinion. In Indiana a more innovative group were working on alternative solutions and told Lance that they couldn't assure him he would survive their procedures but if successful he might be able to walk and ride. Lance said he didn't want to live if he couldn't walk or ride and opted for the more radical medical care. He survived and the rest is history leading him to say:

"I would not have even won one Tour without my fight because of what it taught me. There's a point in every race when a rider encounters his real opponent and understands that it's himself."

Dissipative Structures in Life & Health

The medical community knows that when a bone is broken it never breaks in that particular place again. Why? It heals stronger where broken. This led to a breakthrough 1983 Nobel Prize for Russian biologist Dr. Ilya Prigogine, who discovered that the emotional system of the mind is much like a bone. His work was on the nature of Dissipative Structures to override the nihilism of the Second Law of Thermodynamics that says all things go through a process of entropy or heat death. In this law all things are in a continual downward trend toward self-destruction and disintegration. Prigogine showed how that is not always the case. Entropy or destruction can lead to negentropy with a reemergence into a higher state of order. In laymen's terms this says that when bad things happen we head downward to a place Prigogine called the bifurcation point. At this point we either reemerge stronger than before or continue down and self-destruct. Prigogine would write of the emotional system reemerging even stronger than prior to the problem, saying, "Many systems of breakdown are actually harbingers of breakthrough."

In similar research psychotherapist Stephen Wolinsky wrote in *The Tao of Chaos* (1994), "It is through allowing chaos that higher order can be revealed. Order is actually born out of chaos rather than chaos out of order. In order to be free one must ride the rapids of chaos." Wolinsky went on to say, "Let chaos be and it will let you be," adding:

"A personality is born of chaos. Resistance to chaos can only beget more chaos and resistance. Chaos is no longer an enemy, but a friend. Trying to get rid of chaos is folly; use it for growth." (Wolinsky p. 4)

An enigma that often plagues mankind is that when faced with adversity most people surrender and crawl into a bottle or worse. They give up. These people become fatalities of their own self-deprecation and live out their days as a victim of the vicissitudes convinced they were the unlucky recipients of being dealt a bad hand. They believe fate meant for them to lose. Such people are merely validating the chaos instead of dealing with it positively or fighting it. They are victims of their own thinking where negativity reigns. Bad luck is their astrological prognosis and they stop trying.

Positive Energy—Antidote for Pain

With enough positive energy there isn't room for negative energy. Valerie Hunt in *Infinite Mind* (1996) wrote, "Entropy can be both evidence of decay as well as the first step in creation…energy introduced into a system causes the substance to be refined and changed—but it does not decay." She went on to speak of the growth when faced with disaster, saying, "The healthy body is a flowing, interactive electro-dynamic energy field. Things that keep flowing are inherently good." On the role of energy she said, "When energy is introduced to matter, the disintegration process (Second Law of Thermodynamics [heat death]) is altered and matter takes on a higher organization." An example is Walt Disney using the loss of his successful cartoon character Oswald to create Mickey Mouse. The trauma caused him to have a nervous breakdown but out of it emerged Mickey. On the train back to California Walt drew to exorcise those inner ghosts and his most famous character resulted. Madame Curie experienced a nervous breakdown just prior to both Nobel Prizes.

All of this intellectual rhetoric is about dealing with problems via altering our attitude. Life's only disability is a bad attitude. It disables and destructs. The type of energy we permit to flow through our systems influences our performance and with that knowledge it is just a matter of forcing ourselves to flow positive energy and as soon as we sense negative energy get rid of it. Even if it is in the form of a family member or sibling, it must be removed or it will bring us down. Negative energy is highly toxic. Positive energy is usually cathartic!

One of life's ironies is that those who need to change the most change the least. This dichotomy has beguiled philosophers for centuries. Why does change scare so many who could most benefit by it? Xenophobia comes into play, the fear of the foreign and strangers carrying strange messages. The ignorant refuse new ideas that for them are frightening. Such individuals resist all change even though resestance can prove lethal. Visionaries have an opposite predisposition. They love change and it piques their interest, allowing them to venture into new arenas that they find inspiring. Those who resist the new often cause their own demise, as is the case in Africa where the AIDS epidemic is out of control. The resistance to using condoms or taking new drugs was found to be a chief cause. Those who took medicine were ten times more likely to beat the disease than those laggards who refused the new. I have often stated:

Most people never learn from their mistakes. Visionaries learn from their errant ways but laggards never learn from anything. That is why there are so few visionaries.

Existentialist philosopher Albert Camus offered insight into this when he said, "Sisyphus is the happiest man alive, because he doesn't know his dilemma." If he doted on his problems he would be emasculated by them. This is why race drivers like Jeff Gordon do well. They put their life on the line every single weekend. If they vexed over potential crashes they would never be able to compete effectively. Anxiety would be the only winner in that contest. The Inventors Paradox offers an interesting look into the mind, taking the opposite tack—trying too hard to succeed leads to more failures than if an individual would just relax and enjoy the engagement. The Inventors Paradox goes: *Inventors Who Solve Problems Succeed; Inventors Who Try to Invent Hit the Wall.*

Fear of Failure Can Fuel Success

Fear can be destructive, as has been shown, but often it can also prove motivational. Some people are paralyzed by fear. Others use fear to push them beyond the norm. Fear of failure is often stronger than the need for success. Most people cannot stand to look bad but aren't nearly as driven to look good. Consequently, the majority avoid failure at all cost. It is scary how many important decisions have their genesis in fear. Anyone who has worked in a bureaucracy understands that the reason nothing worthwhile gets through is that no one has the guts to challenge the system. My conclusion is that *anyone afraid of losing their job probably isn't deserving of it in the first place!*

Research shows that most people spend inordinate amounts of time, energy, and money to stay out of harm's way. After the infamous 9/11 attack on the New York World Trade towers people were paralyzed by fear and altered their lives for many months. Anxiety dominated their behavior. Millions canceled vacations. Executives stopped flying to do business on the West Coast and even to Asia. Many paranoid individuals began stocking up for an apocalypse. They were capitulating to the enemy and permitting their fear to alter their life, just what al Qaeda wanted to happen.

Each year people move from California due to a fear of a major earthquake. The 2004 Florida hurricanes led to thousands of risk-averse leaving their dream homes for colder climes. But the fearless warriors who make a difference are not disarmed by fear. Do you think Donald Trump sold his *Mar a Lago* estate because of the hurricane that hit it in 2004? Did he cancel any trips after 9/11? Not a chance! Think Steve Jobs ever considered moving away from the San Andreas Fault due to a fear of being hurt by an earthquake? No way! The eminent understand that life is a gamble and refuse to permit outside influences to change their life. They have what textbooks call a high Comfort with Ambiguity. Such people never permit the vagaries of life to alter their march to fame or fortune. The also-rans always do. The sad commentary on this is that those who should fear danger never do. Those who shouldn't, usually do. The weak are controlled by outside influences. The eminent try to alter them.

Failure comes with the territory when one aims for success. Babe Ruth learned early that the price for being the Sultan of Swat was strikeouts. The Bambino was willing to suffer the humiliation of striking out for the opportunity to hit a gargantuan blast out of the park. In his era the mantra of baseball was to play conservatively with defense, singles, base stealing as the formula for success. Journeyman players choked up on the bat to ensure they didn't strike out. But not the Babe! He would have rather gone down in flames than choke up on the bat. This is what made him special. You would be shocked how many people, even adventurous athletes, are so afraid of failing they fail. NBA basketball coach Lenny Wilkens won more basketball game than anyone in the history of the sport. He also lost the most, going 1332 and 1155 in his long career.

Astute students learn early that the tests they fail in school are the ones that teach them the most. They forget those they passed but will remember for a long time, maybe forever, those they failed. The revelation here is that we must be willing to fall off that bike to learn to ride it. Fear must be relegated to something we recognize but don't allow to interfere with our success. When Michael Jordan was cut from his high school basketball team he promised himself to never again let that happen. It didn't. And the fanatical intensity that led to him becoming the greatest basketball player that ever laced up his shoes was due to that early failure. Breakdown led to his breakthrough. The axiom in all this is that *those not willing to fail will also never learn to win.*

This admonishes us to chase opportunity and to stop trying not to fail. This demands a positive outlook and the ability to bet on your ideas. Take a look at the millions of wannabe inventors and entrepreneurs who invent and then instead of commercializing it are looking for someone to buy it so they can collect royalties. They have a better chance of hitting the lottery than having someone buy their untested product. Why? Because NIH [not invented here] syndrome gets in the way of any existing firm buying the idea even if it has merit. They will buy it but only after the risk is mitigated or eliminated.

Is failure waiting for you around every bend? You bet it is! But that is why the rich and famous club has so few members. For every super success there are thousands who have bitten the dust. Those who fail but learn from it are the ones who ultimately win. Adversity grooms everyone for success. Consider the greatest jockey that ever mounted a horse, Eddy Arcaro. The maestro lost his first 250 races prior to winning one. Did he stop trying? No! And it led to his eminent success. Erma Bombeck wrote a Broadway play that never saw a stage. Did she stop writing? No! But the experience taught her what worked and led to her becoming a world-renowned syndicated columnist. Surgeons laughed at the eccentric Joseph Lister who insisted on washing his hands before operating. The father of antiseptics was ridiculed by other surgeons. Friends stopped talking to him. It took sixteen years before the British Medical Congress recognized his work in saving lives.

Adversity as the Path to Power

Personified by Ayn Rand & Lance Armstrong

The trek to the top is lined with massive hurdles but few ever scaled such heights as Ayn Rand and Lance Armstrong. Both experienced near-death experiences both physically and emotionally. They each rose above the debacles to become the best in their given field of endeavor—Rand as writer of philosophic epics and Armstrong as the best cyclist in the world.

Publishers scoffed at Rand's intellectualizing that was not in line with mass market books that are bought based more on how many they might sell than what they have to say. They told her *The Fountainhead* and *Atlas Shrugged* were far too intellectual to sell. Editors were aghast at her metaphorical ramblings and radio speech in *Atlas Shrugged* that rambled on with Objectivist dialogue for 35,000 words. The truth was that she had condensed it from 500,000 words. For the uninitiated that is more than almost any published book. William Buckley demeaned the book. Critic Whittaker Chambers called it "A remarkably silly, bumptious and preposterous book." They didn't get it. They confused the railroad metaphors with transportation or business and not a philosophic message. In 2002 a prestigious literary group voted it the #2 book of all-time right behind the Bible.

Lance Armstrong left us a similar legend to emulate. Lance had every reason to stop chasing his dream to be the world's top cyclist when he was given a death sentence of testicular, lung, and brain cancer at age twenty-four. He had yet to win the world's most difficult bicycle race, the Tour de France. In fact he had not even finished two of the three grueling races he had entered. But after he beat cancer the mountains and other riders were a piece of cake. At the low point of his chemotherapy treatments he became enraged at the disease and started screaming at the cancer as if it were a competitor. The disease for him was a personal attack and suddenly he saw it as a matter of kill or be killed. "I told the cancer you picked the wrong guy," he wrote passionately, and then told Dr. Nichols, "You can't kill me. Just dump it all on me. Give me double what you give to other people." In *It Isn't about the Bike* Armstrong (1999 p. 108) spoke of being transformed by the very thing that threatened his life:

"If you asked me to choose between winning the Tour de France and cancer, I would choose cancer, because of what it has done for me as a human being, a man, a husband, a son and a father." (Armstrong p. 259)

Rand's controlled aggression would be an intellectual tirade against the insidious system that had robbed her father of his business and made man a pawn of the system. To get even she created Promethean protagonists—Howard Roark and John Galt—to exalt her Objectivism philosophy that tore at the core of a centralized system known as Communism. Protagonist heroes attacked socialism intellectually with buildings and railroads as metaphors to be destroyed by self-serving socialists. Rand admitted to being an ardent hero-worshipper. The architectural anarchist Frank Lloyd Wright personified her epistemological philosophy of tearing down what you love rather than capitulate to self-serving control freaks. Rand loved the free-spirited renegades who said what they thought and lived rationally whether it was politically correct or not.

In *The Fountainhead* (1943) protagonist Howard Roark was a thinly veiled Frank Lloyd Wright. In *Atlas Shrugged* (1957) hero John Galt was a modern-day Prometheus taking on the socialistic establishment interested in building a welfare state. Both men were heroic philosophers advocating a capitalistic system devoid of socialists who would plunder in the name of ordinary man. For Rand the welfare system was antithetic to all that was right. If man would not work he should starve. If he couldn't work that was what governments were about, but not to tell any man where he could work, where he could live, or what he could strive to become.

When the Communists came to power in Russia Allissa Rosenbaum had just come of age. She had graduated from Petrograd University in 1924 at age twenty with a B.S. in philosophy. The spirited student told her professor, "I learn in reverse," as testimony to her larger sense of the world. The iron-willed girl packed one dress and a typewriter and left for Chicago on the ruse of visiting her cousin. She had defected. Deciding to sound like an American she looked down at her favorite possession, the Remington-Rand typewriter, and said, "I will be Rand from now on."

Rand spent the rest of her volatile life raging virulent invective against the system that had robbed man of his manhood and soul. Those diatribes of vitriolic rhetoric created a whole new philosophy of Objectivism. In her classic *Atlas Shrugged*

Rand has her ideal man John Galt delivering her ideas on the insidious self-serving socialists versus the capitalistic rational man:

"Who do men fear most? The brilliant loner, the beginner, the young man of potential, genius and eminently ruthless integrity, whose only weapons are talent and truth. Today, originality, integrity, independence, have become a road to martyrdom, which only the most dedicated will choose, knowing that the alternative is much worse. A society that sets up these conditions is in deep trouble." Atlas Shrugged (1957 p. 171)

In the famous radio speech Galt philosophizes over the power of the entrepreneurial spirits who deserve the right to be free and to make millions since they are the core of what makes capitalism tick. In the speech he also decries those who espouse self-serving dogma to hold such men down and to take away the spoils of their successes. Rand has Galt pontificating to the world:

"In proportion to the mental energy he spent, the man who creates a new invention receives but a small percentage of his value in terms of material payment, no matter what fortune he makes, no matter what millions he earns." (*Atlas Shrugged* p. 988)

Ayn Rand never backed down from the bastions of bureaucrats who hated her with a passion. Democrats were in power for much of her glory days and they never quite understood her intellectual tirades. The paradox is that Rand was a pacifist and against all weapons but fought violently with words. She was an ardent atheist who created her own dogma of dominance and infuriated the churches when she characterized religion as "mysticism." This consummate feminist was against feminism characterizing man as the reigning master. She insisted that mass education "molded mediocrity," and called Reagan's platform "the moral majority and militant mystics." Despite her refusal to accept a role as matriarch for the Libertarian Party they adopted her ideas of the best government as the least governing.

The Fountainhead was modeled after the rebellious architect Frank Lloyd Wright, who she adored for his refusal to conform to traditional forces. Rand portrays him as the visionary architect Howard Roark who would rather blow up his own building than see it bastardized by the establishment. For her those who would despoil and denigrate are "users" and should be driven out of power without remorse. When Roark ends up before a judge for his act, she has him scream at

the court, "The world is perishing from an orgy of self-sacrifice. The creator originates. The parasite borrows and mutilates. It is a world in which I cannot live."
Free enterprise was the foundation for Rand's work. For her, John Galt was the
ideal man, a quintessential self-actualized superman who would rather die than
live in a centrally managed society:

*"The man who accepts the role of a sacrificial animal, will not achieve the
self-confidence necessary to uphold the validity of his mind—and the man
who doubts the validity of his mind, will not achieve the self-esteem necessary
to uphold the value of his person" (Sciabarra 305)*

Freedom to win or to lose, to gamble and fail and not be a pawn was Rand's mantra of life in the twentieth century. Every word was aimed at showing the
self-serving nature of collectivism that destroyed man as a rational human being.
When she passed in 1983 her casket was adorned with a ten-foot high wreath of
roses in the form of a dollar sign to show her worship of the capitalistic way of
life. Her legacy is that she probably had more to do with tearing down that wall
in Berlin than all the political rhetoric in history.

Like Rand, Lance Armstrong is the quintessential example of a Promethean hero.
He refused to succumb to tragedy and actually used it as the fuel to the top.
When faced with the grim reaper at a very young age he didn't wilt but attacked
with a vengeance. When Houston cancer experts told him they would save him
but the price was walking and riding he said no. How many people would do
that? Not many! For him life was not worth living as a cripple.

The Tour de France is the most grueling sporting event in the world and the holy
grail of cycling. Treacherous mountainous terrain lined with vindictive French
zealots is just one of the hazards. After his bout with cancer the mountains were
not nearly so steep or treacherous. Once one emerges from an ordeal like Lance
had there aren't too many obstacles that make a difference. When told he had less
than a 50 percent chance of living there were no more icy storms that kept him
from training or adversaries who scared him. In comparison to one's mortality
physical torment is a walk in the park. Lance lore was born in those chemo treatment rooms.

Armstrong didn't know he should've died and that is often the difference
between living and dying. Those who don't know they can't often can. After
defeating the biggest adversary of his life, the 80 mph downhill speeds were

child's play. Lance had a very good friend in Dallas whose dad was a physician. When he told his dad about Lance the physician told his son, "Your friend is dead." The only thing was that Lance didn't know it and if he had he wouldn't have bought in.

Armstrong was too stupid to agree with the prognosis of a 10 percent chance for survival. The odds against him didn't matter. Now the battle was a competitive race to beat the disease, since if he lost he didn't care to live anyway. The bet paid off. When all seems lost the edge of the precipice doesn't appear as dangerous. Cancer guru Bernie Segal wrote extensively on terminal remissions saying the first to die when diagnosed are always physicians. Why? They know too much about their chances and mentally and emotionally give up. Not so with men like Armstrong, who refused to accept his death sentence. He envisioned it as an adversary and fought it with the same tenacity as he did on the bike.

After recovering he reflected on what had happened, saying, "We have unrealized capacities that only emerge in crises" (Armstrong p. 267). In 2002 Lance's oncologist Dr. Craig Nichols told the media, "Lance was one of the worst cases. Only one-third in his condition live and only 20% thrive" (*USA Today* July 26, 2002 p. 3C). Lance not only lived, he thrived and spoke of it in his book:

"There's a point in every race when a rider encounters his real opponent and understands that it's himself. He then asks, 'Will I discover my innermost weakness or will I seek out my innermost strength?'" (Armstrong p. 269)

Adversity & the Magic of Mythical Mavens

Ayn Rand & Lance Armstrong Validate the Principle

A mythical magic pervaded the life and work of Rand and Armstrong. Rand admitted to being a hero-worshipper with Aristotle and Victor Hugo at the top of the list. As a kid Armstrong rode off alone on his bike, as it was freedom to interact with the forces of man. In his memoir he wrote, "A bike is liberation and independence—freedom to roam without rules and without adults."

These two free souls had their feet planted firmly in outer space, that ethereal place where the mind and fantasy intersect for creativity. When Rand came home from college pontificating on the power of ideas her sister told her, "All of your bizarre ideas have already been documented by a guy named Nietzsche." She reincarnated her hero

Frank Lloyd Wright as Howard Roark in The Fountainhead. *She documented her philosophy through her protagonists with Howard Roark screaming, "I do not recognize anyone's right to one minute of my life, nor to any part of my energy…I am a man who does not exist for others."*

Atlas Shrugged *is a tale of man's creative life force—with idolization of man's mind as the instrument of his success. Her words were saying that the only one that can beat you is you. Sound like Armstrong? Sure does! In Galt's famous radio speech he says, "An inventor is a man who asks Why? of the universe and lets nothing stand between the answer and his mind."*

There are eerie parallels in the roads traveled by Rand and Armstrong. Rand landed in America without even speaking the language, sans money, job, or any means of remaining in her adopted country. She would marry a young actor and wannabe painter and that permitted her to become an American citizen. Such an indomitable spirit is the same that permitted Lance Armstrong to take on the Big C as the enemy and defeat it.

Mythical mentors permeated both of these success stories. Journalist Robert Lipstye offers insight into such hero-mentoring when he used Armstrong's struggle to motivate him to beat cancer and use a bike to recover. Lipstye was beset by a milder form of testicular cancer than Armstrong, and reading It's Not about the Bike *by Armstrong, he went right out and bought a bike and began entering road races. It worked and led to Lipsyte writing of how he turned depression into passion for competing. During the 2003 Tour de France the feature writer told how Armstrong's fall and recovery in stage eight was inspirational for him. On July 19, 2003, he wrote:*

"When I'm climbing a hill my body wants to stop pedaling and to walk the bike, but my mind has another idea. I shout! Lance Armstrong! Lance Armstrong! The four magic words push me to the top." (*USA Today* p. 11A)

Once obstacles are vanquished new ones always show up and it often takes an outside force to salve our souls. The superstars never lose the intrinsic power to draw on extrinsic powers to heal, even if they are Greek Titans or some comic book hero like Wonder Woman or Spider-Man.

Lance's victory in the Tour de France was an incomprehensible feat for other nations and especially the French press. They began to write that he was on drugs otherwise how could a mere mortal overcome such a death-defying disease and win such a race. They wrote that drugs had helped him climb those mighty hills and the editorials led to chants of "druggie" and "doe-Pay, doe-Pay" by the fans. To Lance's credit he sub-mitted to test after test but the naysayers refused to give up. Those who should have been reveling in such a recovery had to try and show that it was an external force that fueled him. It would have been nice to applaud his courage but they preferred to accuse him of being on drugs. The American media has characterized the French blasts as both anti-cancer bias and ignorance.

CHAPTER 10

▼

OVERACHIEVERS USE
INSECURITY FOR
EMPOWERMENT

The fear of failure inhibits failure via internal motivation

"Whoever can see through fear will always be safe."
Chinese Proverb in the Tao Te Ching

"The visionary allows their subconscious to integrate evidence that not even their conscious minds grasp immediately."
Ayn Rand

"Needing something to change always flows negative energy. You don't have to change anything, just stop thinking about it."
Lynn Grabhorn, *Excuse Me Your Life Is Waiting*

Insecurity is not bad but it can be. Those who use their insecurity, their fear of failing, to make themselves better are the smart ones. Superstars use it instead of permitting it to use them. Instead of being paralyzed by their fears, they use them to overachieve. It isn't the hand dealt but the hand played that differentiates us all. That was seen in the life and success of Lance Armstrong, who could have easily capitulated to cancer. This is also true in all professions: when a door closes another opportunity is suddenly opened. The lives of Ted Turner and Donald Trump show that determination built of a seething inner fear of failing drives them far beyond normal achievement. In Trump's *The Art of the Deal* he shows clearly that characteristic that pervades his every move saying, "The worst thing you can possibly do in a deal is seem desperate to make it. That makes the other guy smell blood and then you're dead."

Berkeley research scientist Fritjof Capra spoke of equilibrium as the solution to success. In his book *Web of Life* (1996), he said, "Any organism in equilibrium is a dead organism." Capra's statement is counterintuitive. It is saying that living a normal, stable, and balanced existence is not the most likely basis for achievement. This is the opposite of what parents tell their children. But that is precisely what occurs in any competitive environment. Abnormality is the panacea of eminence just as insecurity is part of what makes us better if we use it positively not negatively.

Insecurity Motivates like Little Else

Insecurity fortifies the eminent with ardor that makes them special. Conversely, it is the bane of the unsuccessful. Sounds weird, but it is true. Eminent psychotherapist Alfred Adler offered insight into why this is true, saying, "The more intense the inferiority the more violent the superiority." Dostoevsky spent his life struggling against what he called his "mystic terror." In his case it was weird attacks on his ability to write and think. It drove him far beyond that of normal writers and became the fuel behind the fire. It led to his profound words, "purification through suffering." Think of this in context with the shenanigans of the imperious Donald Trump or pompous Frank Sinatra. They were driven to look perfect because they knew deep within they were flawed.

In a similar way Albert Camus was the poster boy for insecurity. All of his works were about those deep-seated fears that frightened him. It led to his existentialist works like *The Fall, The Stranger,* and *The Myth of Sisyphus* where he called on the Greek myth of a man attempting to push a rock up a hill only to see it roll right back down. Camus would write, "Suffering is nothing. What matters is knowing how to suffer." After winning the Nobel Prize in Literature in 1957 he decided he could no longer write and gave up the profession saying, "Writing is not a profession but a vocation of unhappiness." That is not without precedent. The great dramatist and creator of *Pygmalion* (*My Fair Lady*) George Bernard Shaw wrote to Ellen Terry, "I wish I could write a play, but unfortunately I have not the faculty." Nobel-winning poet Sylvia Plath wrote a work of self-deprecation titled *Johnny Panic* to assuage her anguish over not being published.

Frank Sinatra was pathologically insecure but masked it well with his overbearing attitude that bordered on aggression. Inner need for acceptance led to his dressing in sartorial splendor with hundreds of suits, shoes, and matching shirts. Superstar Judy Garland had a similar insecure nature that drove her to overachieve and seek adulation on stage. When such people are unaware of those insecurities they become the slave of them. Their ineptitudes takes on the mask of pomposity. Such a state plagued Charlie Chaplin, an actor with such stage fright he had to be pushed on it to perform. Fans are often unaware of the true inner nature of those they see as blazing stars without fear.

Irving Berlin was such a man. The wealthy man who wrote *White Christmas* and other classics lost millions due to a fear of others using his lyrics. If he were not involved to protect his work he refused to license them to others. Ernest Hemingway had a similar insecurity raging within a tormented soul. It made him into a control freak as it did for Howard Hughes of aviation fame. The external egocentricity of these men was but an external manifestation of internal fears. One Hemingway biographer offered a reason for his problem, saying, "Pseudo masculinity was an over-compensation for being dressed as a girl the first two years of life. He was uncertain to the point of fear" (Gregory p. 10). Hemingway's closest friend's wife Zelda Fitzgerald saw him as an arrogant womanizer, writing, "He's a phony since he has to perpetually prove his manhood with women." Howard Hughes had an identical predilection.

Will Smith told the media that fear was behind his overachieving. In *Parade* (July 11, 2004) he said, "I struggle with fear," and added, "But my fear fuels me. I keep going because I doubt myself. It drives me to be better. My self-confidence is actually my reaction to fear." Smith attacked his fears head on, which is the secret of using the weakness to prevail. Smith admitted to being terrified of water and never had learned to swim. On a vacation in Jamaica he spoke of watching the daring jumping off a cliff into the water below and admitted, "I couldn't leave the place without going off the cliff." His reasoning? "I always have to attack. That's how I deal with seemingly difficult things." Quite insightful for a guy who never studied behavior but knows intuitively how to deal with his fears. Bertrand Russell told us, "Wise people are full of doubts." Occult writer Anne Rice admitted, "I write to explore my worst fears," and billionaire Ted Turner explained to talk show host David Frost, "Insecurity breeds greatness. You won't hardly ever find a super-achiever anywhere who isn't motivated by a sense of insecurity."

Needy People Are Often Desperate People—Especially Salespeople

Desperate people do desperate things and their need is transmitted through energy that no one sees but everyone senses. The need transcends the reality and can prove counterproductive to the purpose. Needy people are uptight people in their personal and professional relationships. The devil-may-care, I-don't-need-you attitude that oozes from the Jack Nicholson persona is the reason myriads of young beauties wanted him. Those chasing don't get chased. And Nicholson seems to have been a master of the psychology of mating. All people are drawn to what is unavailable far more intensely than to what is available. Be a tough prey and you will be preyed upon.

Salespeople who must get an order or make a deal are setting themselves up for failure or worse. They send out mystical signals of need that is part of their very aura. This is precisely why the best salesperson in virtually any large organization is always the best. They don't need to close a deal to keep their jobs and they are not in fear of violating some policy manual or price sheet that is the bane of success to most salespeople. When you don't have to make a deal, that is the best time to make them. That is what makes top dogs like Sam Walton, Bill Gates, or Martha Stewart sales icons. Why? Fear is never a factor in their pitches, and breaking some inane rule is never beyond them. Hired hands always work in some fear of the rules. Entrepreneurs like Henry Ford are never so inclined. No one in any position would have dared price their product below its cost but Henry did and it made the firm. Such men are never found coming out of an important meeting saying, "Let me check with the lawyers or CFO prior to deciding." They decide on the spot as they see the big picture that is lost on or not in the purview of worker bees. Visionaries don't ask for permission, they make deals and if necessary ask for forgiveness. Can you imagine the brash wunderkinds Donald Trump or Richard Branson asking if they should sign, even a multi-million dollar deal? Not in this world! This is why they were so eminently successful. When Virgin head Richard Branson decided to go into the airlines business (Virgin Atlantic) he didn't even discuss it with his partner, who screamed, "You are crazy. You're mad. You're a megalomaniac!"

Libidinal Energy & Deal-Making—Provocative Sells

The paradox of deal-making is that the nonverbal works far better than the verbal. Deals are more perception than reality. This is never truer than when trying to sate our libidinal energy. In his research for *Think & Grow Rich* (1960) Napoleon Hill found to his amazement that America's great industrialists were sexual predators far beyond the norm. The men he studied included America's great industrial giants such as Andrew Carnegie, Thomas Edison, J. P. Morgan, Henry Ford, Andrew Mellon, and Franklin Delano Roosevelt, leading him to conclude:

"Highly sexed men are the most efficient salesmen. Personal magnetism is nothing more nor less than sex energy. People who lack sex energy will never become enthusiastic and enthusiasm is one of the most important requisites of salesmanship."

In *The Art of Seduction* (2001) Robert Greene drew parallels between seduction and success, saying things like, "Being too obvious in your pitch will raise suspicion. Frame what you are selling as part of a new trend and it will become one." One of his suggestions was, "to entice people out of their shell is to become more like them—a mirror image of them," that validates the findings that 80 percent of all sales are made to people who like you. Greene went on to say, "The less you seem to need other people the more likely others will be drawn to you—chase your shadow and it will flee; turn your back on it and it will follow you."

All people tend to be attracted to those like them and are turned off by those who see the world through a whole different filter. But psychologists have said for some time that we are attracted to our opposite. How does that compute? Well, we are attracted to those who are different but then are turned off by their differences and if they are mates attempt to change them. The irony is that we want what is different and then want to change it to what we like. Most people are unaware of this fundamental tenet of mating. The reason for the titillation is that it is the forbidden fruit that we aren't supposed to indulge in and it becomes elevated to a fantasy. This can be seen in the seductions of Presidents John F. Kennedy and Bill Clinton. Did they have to have sex in the White House? Of course not! But it was titillating precisely because it was something that mere mortals would never consider let alone do. Inventors and artisans have the same predilection. This can be seen in the formidable creations by Picasso, Bucky Fuller, and Dr. Seuss. In the world of letters it was the prurient appeal of Balzac, Virginia Woolf, Collette, and Ian Fleming that set them apart from the pack.

The romantic fantasy of dining on a remote island is a once in a lifetime opportunity for most people. Those skilled at such a seduction tend to become the Don Juans of society. They cast a spell of romantic lore with love and romance the win and it works in business and romance. Greene wrote:

> *"Lift people's thoughts into the clouds and they will relax, their defenses will come down, and it will be that much easier to maneuver and lead them astray. Your words become a kind of elevating drug." (Greene2001 p. 260)*

Danielle Steel, the queen of romance novels, took advantage of this in the world of letters. Her novels are little else but romantic escapes from the mundane life in the kitchen. She is a master of taking women to places they have only seen on television or in their dreams—to exotic European spas escorted by some handsome hunk. With minimal literary credentials or skills Steel has sold hundreds of millions of books by giving her audience what they lack. For her it was a cathartic release as she was like them at one time, but had been fortunate enough early in life to have lived in those exotic venues of which she writes. Steel has the personal life of one of her heroines. Marrying a French banker while in her teens but relegated to the role of the trophy wife she was tortured her into writing of it in her first novel. It worked! And after that she went through a horrid husband-picking soiree that included a convicted rapist, drug addict, homosexual, and entrepreneur. None of them worked except for her commercialization of the experience.

Fantasy vs. Reality—Personally & Professionally

Research shows that fantasy always sells better than reality, whether in the game of romance or raising capital for a new business entity. Fantasies are more intriguing and being surreal they don't have to face the reality check. When writing a business plan it is always best to begin with what might be not what is. Make all projections on the basis of the financial infusion of capital that actually will permit new distribution channels, new product improvements, new markets, new target customers. What is tends to be far too grounded to appeal to the greed in those who invest in new firms. Homeruns in the future are far more believable than the singles of the present. What we know is that the upside must be ten times better than the down for funding to be considered. To be ten times better demands a breakthrough technologically or in the market penetration strategy.

Passion by leaders often excites others and can empower them to follow you. Adolph Hitler took over a major nation of the world on the basis of nationalism despite not having a drop of German blood. And he did it through passionate words about how he intended to save them from those who would do them harm. Was it a spurious message? Of course! But it had just enough validity to get him elected to office. This high school dropout used fear delivered passionately to get his way. His appeal was to the people's need for security from the Red Menace from the East and those who had caused inflation and had destroyed the economy. Frightening them with real menaces and then promising to protect them worked.

For centuries gurus and zealots have been frightening people with hell and promising them salvation if they will just follow them. Hitler's incredible psychic energy drove him like a wild man and it proved contagious. Libidinal energy, as Freud reminded us, is the basis of psychic energy. Wilhelm Reich refined this into what he called Orgasmic energy. His thesis has been corroborated by Hitler's experiences while in a state of emotional rapture on the podium screaming to the people to follow him. At the height of his passion physician records tell of his becoming tumescent and experiencing orgasms. At first it alarmed Hitler, who asked the doctors to give him drugs to keep his genitalia normal but the doctors told him that such drugs would not only stop the erections they would stop his emotional appeal.

Insecurity—The Fuel of Overachieving

Poster Boys—Thomas Edison & George Bernard Shaw

Few men overachieved more than Thomas Alva Edison or Irish playwright George Bernard Shaw. Together they never had the equivalent of a middle school education. But Edison made his mark in high-tech as an inventor and Shaw in the world of letters. Shaw has been called the greatest dramatist since Shakespeare. Books fueled both men. Edison brazenly told the media, "I didn't read books. I read the library," beginning at A and not stopping until he had read all the books at the Detroit Public Library. Shaw once spent four years in the British Museum reading everything from the Greek Classics to political philosophers like Karl Marx. Edison said, "Deafness at twelve is probably what drove me to books." It also was a pivotal passion for his invention of the instruments of sound—the microphone, phonograph, and first talking-movie camera. Like

Shaw he was a high-octane personality who attributed all success to work saying, "Success is one percent inspiration and 99 percent perspiration."

Shaw had a similar nature. Like Edison he was influenced by a powerful mother figure that bedeviled him for the rest of his long life. His mother Bessie deserted George for her piano-teacher lover when he was twelve years old. And her lover turned out to be his blood father. Shaw wrote to his soulmate Ellen Terry, "My success is due to my mother's complete neglect during my infancy." Edison's mother took the boy out of school after a few months and home-schooled him rather than permit his contamination by the system. Edison wrote later in life, "My mother was the making of me. She understood me and let me be to follow my bent." Both men escaped into books to seek solace for their personal inadequacies.

When Shaw's mother left him to live with an alcoholic father the teenager lost himself in books. Then while attending a play of Goethe's *Faust* the lonely teen became inspired and wallpapered his room with images of Mephistopheles. The imagery would never leave him and later in life the devil would be center stage in his plays on what he called the Life Force of man versus temptation. In his twenties the shy book-aholic spent four years alone in the British Museum reading voraciously on the lives and works of Karl Marx and Nietzsche. Karl Marx, who ironically had sat in the same building not too many years earlier, became his hero-mentor. "*Das Kapital* was the turning point in my career," Shaw gushed. "Marx was a revelation. He opened my eyes to the facts of history and civilization." The experience proved transformational for Shaw, who in a few years would co-found the British Labor Party. His greatest play *Man & Superman* was rampant with imagery of Mephistopheles—a morality play of good against evil.

The effete intellectual Shaw wrote, "Some men see things the way they are and ask why? I see them as they are not and ask, why not?" For him words were weapons. Humor was a tool to disarm his critics. "Almost all of my greatest ideas," he would write, "have occurred to me first as jokes." His cynicism grew in relation to the rejection rate of his books and plays. Some of his best work was never published. Then he produced *Man & Superman* after his marriage when approaching forty in 1903. It was journey into hell with an intellectual Don Juan—most of his protagonists were cathartic self-characterizations—in an intellectual joust with Mephistopheles. This humorous yet philosophical work brought him recognition as a talented playwright. His most renowned play came ten years later when *Pyg-*

malion hit the London stage. Once again it was a thinly veiled Shaw as the elocu-tionist Professor Higgins transforming a street urchin into a London beauty. This play would be reworked as *My Fair Lady* with flower girl Eliza Doolittle molded into an elegant lady. In his sixties the curmudgeon Shaw was awarded the Nobel Prize in Literature for *Saint Joan*. But the irreverent proved true to his taciturn nature and rejected the highest honor in his field of work.

The radical dissident was an ardent atheist, vegetarian, pacifist, cynic, and faddist. He lived with his mother until his thirties and didn't marry until almost forty and then never bothered to consummate the marriage.

Not unlike Shaw Thomas Alva Edison was an overachieving zealot. For him fail-ure was part of the process of growth. Scholarly pundits were convinced his fail-ures proved he was just an ignorant wannabe but he never capitulated to their insults. Educational institutions continually implied he was a charlatan, with Pro-fessor Silvanus Thompson of the Stevens Institute telling the media, "Anyone trying to invent an incandescent light is doomed to failure and shows the most airy ignorance of the fundamental principles both of electricity and dynamics."

The media spoke of his failures to develop a light bulb. The acerbic told them, "I have gotten a lot of results. I know 50,000 things that won't work." When his dissenters kept up the barrage he screamed, "I have constructed 3000 different theories in connection with the electric light, each of them reasonable and appar-ently likely to be true. I am getting closer to the answer." The tenacious tiger finally developed what he called an Ignoramometer Test for all those who had to see and touch something to understand it. He told them that only 2 percent of mankind could pass his test because only "Only 2% of people think." Later research by Everette Rogers in *The Diffusion of Innovations* (1995) validated Edi-son's assessment, as there are about 2.5 percent that Rogers called Innovators who buy into any original new idea.

The Wizard of Menlo Park became the most prolific inventor in American his-tory. Using heuristic methodology—trial and error methods—he developed 1093 patents, many in voice and sound despite being deaf. In one year, 1880, he applied for 60 patents. In 1882 he applied for an astonishing 141 patents. This workaholic was polyphasic (multi-tasking) with thirty to fifty diverse projects underway at any given time. In 1912 at age sixty-five he averaged 112 hours in his lab. That is equivalent to nearly three times the average work week today that some people find too rigorous.

In 1876 Edison opened the first industrial research laboratory in Menlo Park, New Jersey. By 1877 the microphone emerged from that lab and a year later came the telephone transmitter and phonograph. By 1879 he produced the Edison Dynamo—a device for transmitting electrical current through an electrical distribution system. Then in 1879 his *coup de grace* came with the incandescent light bulb that would transform society like few other inventions. In 1880 came his renowned Electric Railway followed by the first motion picture camera in 1889. A few years later he found a way to project those pictures that paved the way for the first motion pictures.

The indefatigable overachiever waxed philosophical, saying, "I don't care so much about making my fortune as I do for getting ahead of the other fellows. I care more about how to change the world." One of his most redeeming qualities was his openness. He told those who were so secretive about their projects, "Nothing here is private. Everyone is at liberty to see all he can and Edison will tell them the rest." Biographer Josephson (1959) wrote of the Edison mystique:

"Edison could never understand the limitations of the strength of other men because his own mental and physical endurance seemed to be without limit...Edison worked with minimum rest periods of three or four hours a day, his enormous recuperative powers helping to sustain him. He would doze off for a cat nap on a bench, or even under a table."

Edison's friend Henry Ford offered testimony to his greatness saying, "If Thomas A. Edison had confined his energies to only one of the many fields he cultivated, he might perhaps have become the richest man in the world." But money was never high on Edison's priority list. Unbelievable energy and ego drove his success. When he got the original idea of a light bulb the indomitable one called a press conference and announced, "I have a machine to make electricity, a bonanza on electric light. I can produce ten thousand lights from one machine." The truth was he didn't have a clue how to do it. But having said he did motivated him, and also helped raise the capital to see it through.

Mythical Magic of Overachieving Zealots

Thomas Edison & George B. Shaw

Few individuals ever left such a legacy of innovative ideas as inventor Thomas Alva Edison or dramatist George Bernard Shaw. Both made their mark by daring to be different despite having been ridiculed for their ideas. When knocked down, the strong get back up with a renewed sense of "I'll show you." Both Edison and Shaw often turned to fantasy icons to overcome the establishment's rejection of their work. Fantasy heroes supplied solace and inspiration. Protagonists out of books and plays played a huge part.

Both Edison and Shaw escaped derision into the sanctity of heroes out of books. Edison never accepted his lack of formal education as a crutch for not competing with those with such pedigrees. The recalcitrant told the media, "I wouldn't give a penny for the ordinary college graduate except for those from institutions of technology. Do you think I would have amounted to anything if I went to school? University trained scientists only see that which they were taught to look for and thus miss the great secrets of nature."

Edison was infamous for his tour de force projects held in what was spoken of as a Faustian laboratory. When in a state of rapture he would often refuse to leave for days at a time. The eccentric inventor lived a mythic-like existence, often working in a kind of trance-like state. "It takes a deaf man to hear," he liked to tell the media who asked how a man who couldn't hear could invent a microphone and phonograph. When the financial moguls in New York refused to finance his light bulb he became upset and told the media:

"If there are no factories to make my inventions, I will build the factories myself. Since capital is timid, I will raise and supply the products myself. The issue is factories or death."

Edison supplied 90 percent of the capital to build those first General Electric plants. When asked why he took such a risk at his advancing age he responded, "You take the risk to build your product or you do not survive to see the product flourish" (Landrum 1993 p. 17).

Biographer Jacobsen wrote, "Edison could never understand the limitations of other men because his own mental and physical endurance seemed to be without limit." The source of such drive is often fueled by an inner passion that appears magical. Testimony to his unabated passion is the time he locked his employees and himself in the lab for sixty hours without food or water to resolve a difficult problem.

Like Edison, Shaw was self-taught. Books were his friends and tutors. After his teens when he had become mesmerized by Goethe's Faust *he became an iconoclast of mystic proportions. Shaw saw himself in the image of the devil or anti-hero dedicated to fighting for the rights of the underdog.*

This Nietzsche-influenced Superman was enthralled with the Greek titans Androcles, Prometheus, and Pygmalion. Thus Spake Zarathustra *left an indelible mark on Shaw that can be seen in* Man & Superman *and* Pygmalion. *It is a strange twist of fate in recent years that Zarathustra, a mythical figure out of Muslim lore, embodied the premise that power emanates from within the soul of a driven man. Shaw pontificated on same with profound insights like, "The reasonable man adapts to the world, the unreasonable man attempts to adapt the world to him, therefore all progress depends on the unreasonable man."*

When Shaw's first six novels and seven of eight plays were rejected the indomitable spirit took a job as a literary critic to gain insight into what it takes to succeed. Despite being an introvert he went out and made thousands of speeches to show that he was an expert so "publish me." This self-proclaimed failure until age fifty would become an international authority on the literary arts. American author George Orwell would write, "Shaw's best works were early novels that were never published." Biographer Holroyd wrote of the self-made man:

"Shaw's greatest creation was himself, setting himself up in London as a man of genius. He did not wait until he was famous to behave like a great man."

The ability to relegate insecurity and rejection to the garbage cans of history is the thing that make men like Edison and Shaw superstars. It permitted them to go where others feared and that is the strength of all innovative progress. These two visionaries tattooed images of Superman on their psyches and used the empowerment to take them to the Promised Land.

▼

SUPERMEN ARE NONCONFORMISTS & ECCENTRIC

Be Different or Be Average

"The poet has no invention in him until he has been inspired and is out of his senses."
Socrates

"Whoever wants to be the creator of good and evil must first be an annihilator and break values. Thus, the greatest evil belongs to the greatest goodness; but that is being creative."
Nietzsche, *Zarathustra*

"Consciousness starts as an act of disobedience."
Carl Jung, psychotherapist

The world's superstars are never found conforming to the pack or throwing away their imaginary capes. They relish the fact they are different whereas conformists are frightened by the thought of being seen as eccentric. Conformists are predictable but non-creative. In contrast, the world's nonconformists alter paradigms and create magical new things by daring to live outside the box of mediocrity. Proactive rebels are seen as eccentrics by those steeped in rules. They are ridiculed when not bowing to budgetary constraints even if they excel. The textbook definition of innovation is creative destruction—breaking budgets and drawing outside the lines—and the reason Mark Twain and Dr. Seuss made a difference in the world of letters. Both operated on the fringe where all great breakthroughs take place. The pack is unwilling to tread in the murky waters of make-believe.

Visionaries thrive in the white-rapids where you live or die by your ability to cope.

It is evident from studying life's superstars that conventional wisdom is inversely related to creativity. Originality is the trademark of eccentrics. Status-quo is the trademark of traditionalists and that is why the two clash. Normal is never a word used in describing the innovative. Think anyone ever described Walt Disney or Howard Hughes as normal? Never! Mother Teresa or Einstein? No chance! Dr. Seuss? Not even close! Dr. Seuss challenged the way children's books were written, to the chagrin of traditional teachers. *Dick & Jane* reigned supreme until Seuss's off-the-wall *Cat in the Hat*. A Cat with a Hat would have been accepted by children but not teachers. It took a man-child to understand the mentality of a child. In the same way, Picasso used Cubism to violate traditional art—to destroy what is to create the new. Coco Chanel did the same with her phenomenally successful Chanel No. 5. The androgynous *femme fatale* legitimized black for other than mourning. Traditional maestros of couture were not so inclined.

Conformists are invited to church socials. Eccentrics don't get such invites until they make their mark in the world. Why? They frighten those steeped in conventional ways. When young inventor Philo Farnsworth showed up at the Motorola offices with his radio-picture machine the executives refused to see him and sent a secretary to the lobby to get rid of the kook. She was told to watch out for knives. The inventor of television was not to be denied; his mistress was his passion. It was frightening to the establishment. Until the creative learn that 95%—99% won't accept radically new concepts, they are destined to die by rejection.

Destruction of traditional ways is the only path to new ones. Find the pack and go elsewhere is the mantra of visionaries. In other words, if you want a new house where the old one sits it is imperative that the old one gets torn down. If you want a new breakthrough product you must be prepared to obsolete the existing product. Few people are willing to do that. They protect what they have until forced to change and by that time it is too late. AT&T protected their copper-wire communications for long distance calls until it was too late and VOIP—Voice Over Internet Protocol—ate their lunch. To alter paradigms the innovative must be willing to destroy what they have to get what they don't. That is virtually impossible for the majority of the population. It is especially repugnant to hired hands that run Fortune 1000 firms. Consequently most true innovators travel alone. The establishment protects the status quo while they are determined to destroy it. Traditionalists never dare fix what isn't broke while innovators are infamous for breaking what isn't broke. The vast majority of people have been conditioned not to dance with dame chance. Consequently, they never alter paradigms or leave any lasting mark on the world.

Because of social conditioning one must be eccentric—a little bit goofy—and highly self-confident in order to overcome the forces of traditionalism. This was true of Mother Teresa. She had to rock the boat of the Roman Catholic hierarchy to create her Pontifical Congregation known as the Sisters of Charity. Had she not resigned her order and appealed to the Pope she would never have succeeded or won the Nobel Peace Prize. Had Maria Montessori capitulated to the system and just practiced medicine, life would have been far easier. But she rebelled to become the Prophet of Pedagogy. It was no accident that Sir Isaac Newton, Frederick Nietzsche, Nikola Tesla, and Carl Jung were in the state of mental breakdown when they arrived at their breakthrough ideas. Why did the breakdowns lead to breakthroughs? It permitted them to lose touch with normality to become abnormally creative. Without their psychosis they would not have been able to defy authority.

Divergence—The Innovator's Mantra

History has given us a myriad of examples of why the greater the divergence the greater the win. In a Web world change is rampant and those who resist it are not being safe but setting themselves up for a schizophrenic experience. Change conjures up fear for most people. It excites the visionary. What paralyzes the ordinary empowers the extraordinary. In *The Paradox of Innovation* (2002) Farson and Keyes validated what most of us already knew, "School related evaluations are poor predictors of economic success." Had Thomas Edison, Bill Gates, and Michael Dell remained in school it would have been highly unlikely they would have become so successful. They would have been hired in some larger institution instead of establishing their own. The story of young Michael Dell is interesting. The refusal to listen to his well-meaning parents who had enrolled him in pre-med at the University of Texas is what made him the multibillionaire head of Dell Computers. What if he had conformed to his parents' wishes and become a physician?

It is amazing how educators—sages on stages—buy into the BS of textbook theories. The concept of the past being prologue no longer works in the Internet Age.

Two Yale professors were guilty of the myopia of believing they knew what was right for their students, when the truth is they didn't have a clue. Then-Yale Junior Fred Smith was given an inglorious C for his paper on Overnight Package Delivery. Why? The professor told him it was not a viable concept and if it were the airlines would have done it. And if they didn't the U.S. Post Office would. What? Maya Ying Lin was given a B on her research project for a Vietnam Memorial in Washington, DC. Miss Lin was told it was "unorthodox architecture." Fortunate for history both students ignored the sages' advice. Smith launched the now-successful Federal Express. Lin submitted her project to the Veterans Committee in Washington, DC, as one of 1500 entries and it is her polished black marble memorial edifice that adorns the Mall in Washington, DC, that has been called, "one of the most powerful monuments ever built."

Traditionalists are prone to pan the ideas of Innovators. Ironically, the reason they are ridiculed is precisely why they are viable. This suggests that drawing within the lines will earn you kudos and good grades in school but is diametrically opposed to success on the street. Paradigm-shift ideas are ridiculed in the beginning and then bought into later when others see the insight or vision. Virtually every concept developed by Walt Disney including Mickey Mouse, Donald Duck, Snow White, and Disneyland was ridiculed by Hollywood experts and even the Disney Board of Directors. Had Walt not been resilient and ignored their opinions these wonderful projects would all have died on the drawing board.

Crop Circles—Myth or Man-Made

Those mysterious geometric circles, shapes, and symmetrical patterns found in the middle of cornfields have baffled scientists and attracted mystics since the mid-twentieth century. These inexplicable symbols proliferated between 1980 and the turn of the century. Scientists liken them to the mysterious formations in Stonehenge that cropped up in southern England more than 1000 years ago. Today the consensus is that genuine *crop circles* are created by magnetic fields or some other mysterious energy field. During the 1990s Prince Charles found these inexplicable circles on his land in England. Visiting scientists offered insight into them with some suggesting a Viagra Effect since women walking on them became impassioned. Men experienced sudden erections thus the name. But the circles have remained a mystery despite some men's need to try and baffle the scientific community by toying with the facts.

In the mid-eighties Circle Mania and Croppy Art proliferated until two Brits, Doug Bower and Dave Chocky, admitted to creating crop circles as a hoax. But research scientist Colin Andrews says that only 80 percent of circles are created by Hoaxers leaving 20 percent as mysterious phenomenons of nature—weather-related, alien-related (UFOs), electromagnetism, or some other mysterious event. The Andrew's logic was based on a 1975 circle in Minnesota that left a calf dead and 47 circles randomly situated in remote areas that would be difficult or impossible for any human to have created. Canadian crop circles were also outside the potential of human intervention with nature.

Live on the Edge for a Utopian Life Experience

Change masters live in a fantasy land known as *Newville*. Myopics and Laggards languish in a land called *Sameville*. In Newville *Yes* and *Can Do* are the mantras of choice. In *Sameville* the lexicon of choice is *No* and *Can't*. Think of what causes this type of thinking. Bruno was burned at the stake for saying the earth moved during the Renaissance. A modern physician transported back in time 100 years would see bloodletting used as a cure. Suggesting that doctors wash their hands prior to surgery was scoffed at in the time of Joseph Lister. Having a woman performing the surgery would have been heresy. It took 150 years for scurvy to be eradicated after the cure was proven by Dr. James Lind. The pioneering research on speed of adoption was the lifelong work of Everett Rogers, who found those in power resisted all change until it was prudent for them to accept it. Picasso painted outside conventional lines and drew the ire of friend Henri Matisse, who called his masterpiece "grotesque and nihilistic." Picasso placed the *Le Desmoilles d'Avignon* in a closet for almost ten years before the world caught up with his vision.

Philosophy plays a primal role in the lives and work of creative types. Leonardo was as much philosopher as painter and engineer. A holistic vision permeated his majestic works. Napoleon and Picasso were of a similar bent. Picasso envisioned himself more philosopher than artist and said so in his epitaph written when he turned fifty. Paintings were a vehicle to depict his sense of what was happening in the world, which is why his most notable paintings bristle with nihilism. "Art," he said, "is used to destroy conventional stereotypes." Did this win him patrons? Not many! But Picasso, like most visionaries, was able to remove himself from mass opinion. Not to do so would would have kept him from becoming the father of Cubism and Surrealism in art. Creative destruction was the foundation of most of his work, as shown by his quote, "The painter takes whatever it is and destroys it, giving it another life. He must destroy. Art is a lie that makes us realize truth."

Screw Up & Become Special— It's Okay to Be Manic!

Tom Peters said, "Nothing is more important or beneficial for individuals or organizations than screwing up." Touché! What he was trying to show is that those who play it safe and refuse to push the limits get surety but not necessarily success. They reap what they sew and if it is only through fear of failure they become a failure. Refusal to change in a web world only guarantees that you will fail. Visionaries seldom get caught up in the acceptance syndrome and that is why they are often highly creative. Babe Ruth was walking out of Wrigley Field after his famous called shot in the 1932 World Series and was asked by a reporter, "Babe, what if you had struck out?" In his unflappable style the Babe shrugged his shoulders and replied, "Never thought about that."

In *Touched with Fire* (1993) Kay Jamison offered insight into those who live life on the edge—those highly creative types beset by wild swings of temperament labeled bipolar disease. Jamison wrote extensively on the renegade nature of such types, "There is agreement that artistic creativity and inspiration involve, indeed require, a dipping into pre-rational, or irrational sources while maintaining ongoing contact with reality—life at the surface." Such divergence is both a blessing and a curse. It leads a person like Walt Disney to be haunted by the constant rejections but it seldom deters them from their objective. An example is Walt not listening to the Stanford Research Institutes market research that said Disneyland was not viable. Walt was bipolar, as was his friend Howard Hughes, and Mark Twain before them. So were Balzac, Edgar Alan Poe, Charles Dickens, Virginia Woolf, Ernest Hemingway, and Sylvia Plath. Notable leaders like Alexander the Great, Julius Caesar, Napoleon, Stalin, and Hitler were all manic-depressive. When up they were invincible! When down they were incompetent.

Psychotherapist Carl Jung wrote, "To be normal is the ideal of the unsuccessful." The Swiss psychotherapist knew that normal people achieve normally but it would take an abnormal person to achieve abnormally. Not abnormal in terms of deviance, abnormal in terms of drive, work ethic, vision, perseverance, risk-propensity, and competitive zeal. An example can be seen in the behavioral characteristics of some of the world's wunderkinds studied by this author. Forty percent of individuals like Nikola Tesla, Mark Twain, Walt Disney, Howard Hughes, Sylvia Plath, and Ted Turner were obsessive-compulsive and/or bipolar. Entrepreneurial geniuses like Coco Chanel and Thomas Edison were off the chart when it came to irreverence and a renegade nature. These wunderkinds were found to be: 90 percent hypomanic and right-brain dominant, 98 percent high risk-takers, 92 percent Type A's, 80 percent with a propensity for Machiavellian behavior, and 96 percent with a predilection for being a different.

This data offers insight into the eccentric nature of the innovative personality. Being weird and unconventional for them was an asset even though it is considered to be sociopathic by the establishment. The afternoon-tea set is disinclined to accept such people. It is why many of them had horrid personal relationships. Edgar Allan Poe offered an elegant aphorism on this principle when he wrote, "Men have called me mad but the question is not yet settled whether madness is or is not the loftiest intelligence." The manic-depressive Kay Jamison of Johns Hopkins University offered insight into the vagaries of it:

"Who would not want an illness that has among its symptoms elevated and expansive mood, inflated self-esteem, abundance of energy, less need for sleep, sharpened and unusually creative thinking, and increased productivity?"
(Touched with Fire 1993)

Those who live on the precipice are seldom invited to tea with the Joneses. The establishment does not just forget to invite them for cocktails, it fears them as dangerous for having such radical ideas. Well-meaning family and friends see innovators as ticking time bombs and are waiting for the flakes to self-destruct. Normal relationships are difficult at best for innovator types. Chester Carlson invented the first plain paper copier—the Xerox 914 that revolutionized office work—and paid dearly for his passion. His wife left him, as did his partner, and he went broke in the process until Xerox materialized out of his ardor. Educator Warren Bennis wrote in *Managing the Unknowable* (1992), "The current mental management model focuses on stable equilibrium as the hallmark of success but innovation is bounded instability, also called chaos. That is the true state of a successful business." *Business 2.0* in May 2001 offered insight into this in an article on the often ludicrousness mentality of the establishment:

"New companies are all passion and little rationality. Any rational person wouldn't have done it. Traditional firms focus on operational excellence) and

becoming very good at efficient execution. Such convergent thinking is essential to operating a company. But for high performance it's not enough. Executives must be divergent."

Find the Pack Then Split for Utopian Horizons

There are no big wins where the herd lives. Find out where they are and go someplace else. There are no big wins if everyone is already there. Most people are blown away by such comments. They fear ambiguity and tend to remain in safe havens. That is why the overprotective parent tends to be the bane of the creative child by trying to protect them. Their need to keep them safe actually harms them because the only way to learn to deal with adversity is to deal with it. Visionaries like Leonardo were never so protected and it shows in their work. Those without a protetive veil when young are able to cope better as adults. There is a long litany of individuals who almost died in their youth and it armed them to become better than their peers.

Most people faced with not making a payroll start a regimen of tranquilizers. Not the visionaries. They get turned on when things get tough. When faced with some great dilemma they feel a rush to test their mettle. When Larry Ellison, founder of Oracle and one of the world's richest men, was queried about his flirtation with bankruptcy in 1990 he very cavalierly told the reporter, "It's exciting. It's a rush man" (Wilson p. 228). When the mother of modern dance Isadora Duncan was queried about what made her tick she said, "I am a revolutionist. All geniuses worthy of the name are; in order to make their mark in the world." Touché! One of the great philosophers John Stuart Mill validated this with his profound insight, "That so few dare to be eccentric marks the chief danger of our time." Thoreau was equally profound when he wrote, "If a man cannot keep pace with his companions, perhaps it is because he hears a different drummer. Let him step to the music he hears however measured or faraway." Virginia Woolf was another rebel who wrote, "Madness is terrific I can assure you." What motivated such a statement? She knew when mad she could escape into creative work. Edgar Allen Poe was introspective enough to seem himself candidly and wrote, "Men have called me mad but the question is not yet settled whether madness is or is not the loftiest intelligence."

British psychiatrist Anthony Storr said, "The majority of gurus are madmen." In *Strange Brains & Genius* (1998) Clifford Pickover wrote:

"Almost all mad geniuses have had irreverence toward authority. Many scientists experienced both social and professional resistance to their ideas. Alexander Fleming's revolutionary discoveries on antibiotics were met with apathy, Niels Bohr's doctoral thesis on the structure of the atom was turned down—it later won him a Nobel Prize. Joseph Lister's advocacy of antisepsis was resisted by surgeons."

Studies have shown that visionaries tend to go where the timid fear. Such bizarre behavior drives their mates crazy. The grounded see such people as having a death wish. But they just want to be free to pursue their dreams. This dichotomy was best described by educator-author Jacques Barzun, who wrote in *The Paradoxes of Creativity* (1990), "Mad passion or passionate madness is the reason why psychopathic personalities are often creators and why their productions are perfectly sane."

The term *paradigm shift* was coined by Thomas Kuhn in his landmark work *The Structure of Scientific Revolutions* (1962). Kuhn used the term to define what happens when a creative act alters whole systems. He concluded that new ideas would be rejected until the old supporters of existing ideas died off, noting that new shifts didn't occur until the old power elite no longer could defuse them. An example was Edison's refusal to accept alternating current. Here was a brilliant innovator who went to his grave disclaiming the alternating current system devised by his adversary Nikola Tesla.

Establishment types view radically new breakthrough products as dangerous because they are threatened by them. When the first handheld calculators hit the market in the early '70s at an affordable price educators went berserk and had them banned from the classroom. Teachers feared becoming obsolete, which was even more ludicrous than their hate campaign against a marvelous breakthrough product. Had the educators had their way the product that is now required for a calculus course would have gone the way of the buggy whip. Fortunately for the world the truly innovative seldom listen to the naysayers. They creatively destroy—the textbook definition of innovation—in order to make their mark in the world. Isadora Duncan "didn't sleep while in one of her manic periods," according to friend and biographer Mary Desti who wrote, "She acted like a person demented." And that is what made her great.

Divergence—the Panacea of Power

Nikola Tesla & Isadora Duncan Personify the Concept

Few people in history were as divergent as Nikola Tesla, father of alternating current, and Isadora Duncan, mother of modern dance. Both were castigated for operating well outside the mainstream and neither cared. Tesla's nemesis Thomas Edison told the press that people would die if they powered their homes with the Westinghouse power distribution system developed by Tesla. To diffuse such statements the intrepid Tesla stood on a stage at the 1883 World's Fair in Chicago and with a light bulb in one hand and a power line of 1 million volts in the other used his body as the conduit to light the bulb. His body was ablaze and it would lead to his nickname of "electrical sorcerer" by the *New York Times*.

Marconi got the credit for radio transmission but it was Tesla who first transmitted sound across space. It took half a century for the U.S. patent office to finally admit it was Tesla who should be granted those patents. This Renaissance man not only held the patents for alternating current and the inductive motor (1884), he also developed radio transmission (1893), the first electric clock (1895), fluorescent light (1897), solar engines (1898), the Tesla coil (1898), VTOL (1915), and remote-controlled cars (1899).

This Serbian-turned-American was brilliant, attractive, athletic, and articulate beyond belief. But he never married for fear women would drain him of his creative energies. The loner was obsessive-compulsive, hyperactive, manic-depressive, precognitive, and spoke eight languages fluently. Testimony to his obsessional nature he was unable to stay in any hotel room not divisible by three. In addition he could not partake of any meal prior to computing its cubic contents. In 1916 he correctly predicted the coming of cable television some fifteen years prior to the first television transmission.

Tesla was a perfectionist who did all things in excess. While attending the University of Prague in engineering the headmaster wrote to his parents saying, "Your son is a star of the first rank but should not return for fear he will kill himself with his obsessive work ethic." If he began a book he could not stop until it was finished even if he had to read for two days without sleep. During school he read a book by Voltaire and almost killed himself due to having to finish all 100 volumes. He admitted, "I have a veritable mania for finishing whatever I begin."

Biographer John O'Neill spoke of him in Herculean terms saying, "Tesla's greatest invention was himself as Superman." Every nuance of his dress and actions were perfection personified; he wore impeccable clothes befitting a dandy. Living and dining nightly at the regal Waldorf Astoria made him an attractive catch for women of the period but he never had a date as he was bewitched by women's hair and earrings. The mania that made him so great caused him to sleep but two hours a night for much of his long and productive life. From the perspective of intellectual precocity Edison could not carry his briefcase. When Tesla first came to America the first man he called on was Edison and the Wizard of Menlo Park offered him $50,000 to fix his Manhattan DC generators. The manic-man worked around the clock for 90 days to the total bewilderment of Edison who could not believe any man could be so driven. When he asked to be paid Edison told him, "You don't understand American humor," and Tesla never spoke to him again. Twenty years later when they were to be awarded a joint Nobel Prize in Physics Tesla declined rather than stand on the stage with Edison.

The development of alternating current and the induction motor were inspirations during a period when Tesla was in a state of emotional breakdown. Walking in a park he was reciting poetic words from Goethe's *Faust* when he saw the solution in his head. In his memoirs he wrote, "The idea came like a flash of lightning and in an instant the truth of A/C was revealed." In America George Westinghouse heard the charismatic Tesla speak at a technology conference and was mesmerized and made a deal to buy the rights to the Polyphase inventions, saying they were "the greatest invention in the field of electricity." The Serb received $1 million plus $1 per horsepower from Westinghouse, who built the first power stations anywhere in the world. Within four years the royalties due Tesla were $12 million and growing exponentially. Fate intervened or Tesla would have become the wealthiest man in history. By 1897 Westinghouse was insolvent and visited bank tycoon J.P. Morgan for funding. Morgan refused to help Westinghouse unless the Tesla contract was cancelled. Westinghouse went to Tesla, who for another $216,000 canceled the agreement. It was to be the most costly decision of his life. Tesla would die a pauper and many of his incredible inventions went without commercialization due to the Westinghouse deal. Some of Tesla's most notable inventions included:

☼Invented alternating current and induction motors in 1879
☼Built first power distribution plant for Westinghouse in the 1890s

☼Transmitted radio signals in the 1890s and granted patent in the 1940s for radio

☼Invented the first electric clock in 1895 but had no interest in commercializing it

☼Demonstrated the first remote-controlled toys in 1899 in Madison Square Garden

☼ In 1891, patent approved as the precursor of the electron microscope

☼Pioneered work that was precursor of x-rays and cosmic rays

✧In 1896 developed a solar engine

☼Used fluorescent lights to light his Manhattan lab from 1895—not commercialized until 1943

Mysticism pervaded the life and work of Isadora Duncan as it did Tesla. Testimony to her powerful persona was being described by no less than the sculptor Rodin as "the greatest female who ever lived." Those are pretty strong words for a woman who only made it through the fifth grade. But like Tesla the diva of the theater was mesmerizing to fans and lovers.

The free-flowing surrealism that surrounded her every move was captivating. An example of her charisma was her teenage trek from New York City to Europe. With no money, clothes, or a job in London she talked her gullible mother and brother into joining her on a cattle ship to cross the Atlantic. The vagrants landed in London with no place to stay or money for food. They were sleeping in a park when Isadora had enough and marched boldly into the majestic Dorchester Hotel on Hyde Park. Isadora took charge and announced to the desk clerk that their baggage was delayed and in it was their money and credentials. She assured the management that as soon as it arrived they would be paid but in the meantime they needed a suite and food. After two days of elegant feasts and first class accommodations they were discovered as urchins and found themselves back on the street. Such was the moxie and flamboyant nature of the great Isadora.

This indomitable spirit was energy incarnate. Her passion and appeal led to socialites inviting her into the living rooms where she performed. Her hatred for religion, marriage, and the established traditions like ballet caused traditionalists to be wary of her. Her mother had sent her for ballet lessons as a young teen and when told to stand on her toes she asked why because it hurt. The ballet teacher told her, "Because it is beautiful." The recalcitrant screamed, "It's ugly," and ran out, never to return. In her climb to dance immortality the renegade came to believe in her mystical destiny. In her memoirs she would write, "Terpsichore taught me to dance." In her teens she tried out for the Broadway impresario Augustin Daly and told him, "I have discovered the dance, the art that has been lost for two thousand years. I bring you the idea that will revolutionize our entire epoch." This was from a teen that had never had a lesson and never performed except on the streets of San Francisco.

Hero-worship permeated the life and work of Isadora. Prometheus and Aphrodite were titans that had infiltrated her body. She would say, "I was so into my work I would go into a state of static ecstasy." A voracious reader, she was a fan of the Greek Classics and of Nietzsche's *Zarathustra*. When depressed the mystical one said, "The seduction of Nietzsche's philosophy ravished my being." When asked about her wild and uninhibited lifestyle she responded, "I fell in love with males at eleven and I have never ceased to be madly in love." Duncan was a rebel with a cause who bore three children by three different men, none of whom she married. In that Victorian era such behavior made her a radical of the first order. Traditionalists in America never understood her passions and that made her work mostly in Europe.

Mythical Magic of the Divergent Personality

The Titans—Tesla & Isadora

Few visionaries have ever been as wild and surreal as the Serb Nikola Tesla and the San Francisco wild child Isadora Duncan. Tesla lit the cities of the world and powered their factories. Duncan danced with the seductive nature of a woman possessed. Each was empowered like few others in history. Both were adored by brilliant disciples and feared by those with less understanding of such genius. Mark Twain was enthralled by Tesla's incredible intuitive powers and Duncan by the power elite from Paris to Berlin.

Interestingly, Tesla, the purported virgin who never went on a date, would hold women in very high esteem. In his memoir he wrote, "The struggle of the human female towards sex equality will end up in a new sex order with the female as superior. Women will ignore precedent and startle civilization with their progress."

Tesla was an enigma beyond the pale of the establishment, as was Isadora. Both could mesmerize both sexes by their words and deeds, especially the well-read and well-bred.

The early life and actions of Tesla were almost eerie. He spoke of living through flashes of light that appear to have been some kind of seizures or epileptic in nature. These flashes of light often preceded some great insight according to Tesla, who didn't fear them like Dostoevsky did, but they did take him way out of the mainstream. Biographical data on Van Gogh and Mohammad offer striking similarities.

Even when functioning in a state of normalcy Tesla was a man with extraordinary mental powers dwarfing those of mere mortals. In school a professor would put a differential equation on the board and ask for a solution. Tesla had committed the logarithmic tables to memory and would walk up to the blackboard and write down the answer and walk back to his seat. Other students were busy with pencil and paper attempting to solve the problem and were dumbfounded by the mystic-like virtuosity of Tesla.

Like other technological geniuses, Tesla saw problems and their solution in his mind prior to solving them. That says that if you can't see it you can't solve it. Tesla offered validation when he said, "I could visualize with such facility. I needed no models, drawings or experiments." He went on to show how this worked, saying, "When I get an idea, I start at once building it up in my imagination. It is absolutely immaterial whether I run my turbine in my thought or test it in my shop. Before I put a sketch on paper, the whole idea is worked out mentally."

A mystical hypersensitivity pervaded Tesla that was implausible to associates including Mark Twain and the son of Nathaniel Hawthorne, Julian, who wrote for the New York Times. *John O'Neill, his biographer, said he had a "cosmic vision." Hawthorne wrote in the* New York Times, *"His psychic energy was awesome." Tesla said, "I had the sense of a bat and could detect the presence of an object at a distance of 12 feet by a peculiar creepy sensation on my forehead. I could hear a ticking clock three rooms away." His mysterious flashes of light and flame-like protuberances led people to characterize him as a mad scientist that was exacerbated by an oscillator in his Manhattan lab that shook the city. The wild visionary often brought on his own problems by telling the media, "I could drop the Empire State Building in a matter of hours." This pacifist didn't have a destructive bone in his body despite his own self-destructive nature. Tesla would activate the oscillator and shake buildings blocks away, causing the police to say, "it's that weird scientist again."*

Tesla was used as a mad scientist character in the first Superman comic book in 1934 by Jerry Siegal and Joe Shuster, and in the first comic book in 1939. It came about due to his wild statements to the press on having a death ray that could destroy 10,000 planes 250 miles away. He scared residents in Colorado to death by light up the sky with his experiments. Needless to say reporters were mesmerized by this self-proclaimed Prometheus with supernatural powers.In many ways Isadora Duncan cast a similar spell over her entourage and the media. She came across as a sensuous woman possessed of mystic powers. Duncan could elevate into a trance-like state when on stage that mesmerized the audience. In her memoir Isadora wrote:

"When dancing I feel the presence of a mighty power within me which listens to the music and reaches out through all my body, trying to find an outlet, this power grows furious, sometimes it raged and shook me until my heart nearly burst from passion." (Landrum 1999 p. 224)

Isadora wrote one of the most objective and erudite autobiographies ever written. The woman with little formal education had self-educated herself in the arts and Greek classics. In her memoir she spoke of herself as a "Promethean puritan, a daughter of Aphrodite." When visiting a new city like Berlin, Rome, Athens, or Madrid she went first to the museums and the libraries to gain insight into their cultural heritage. In her memoirs she wrote, "I'm a revolutionist. All geniuses worthy of the name are in order to make their mark in the world." Excellent self-insight!

Freedom of movement in life and the dance personified her life and romantic soirees. It permeated the dance she is credited with having created. Her on-stage moves were free-floating expressions of inner feelings performed in elegant flowing gowns. Restraint for her was verboten. But it was freedom that made her and that would destroy her, as is so often the case for such free spirits. In her late forties she was vacationing on the Mediterranean and had met a new potential love mate. She had told friend Mary Desti, "I'm off to the moon, so don't be surprised if you don't see me again." The new beau picked her up in his sleek new sports car and on getting in waved at on-lookers shouting, "Adieu, mes amis. Je vais a gloire" [Farewell my friends. I go to glory]. The beau hit the accelerator and the Bughatti leaped forward and the free-flowing scarf around her neck caught in the axle of the car and snapped her neck. She died instantly as she had lived.

CHAPTER 12

POSITIVE ENERGY IMBUES OMNIPOTENCE

Progress *Comes in Can's;* Problems *Come in Cannot's!*

"Pessimism is rampant in cultures on their way out!"
Frederick Nietzsche, *Zaruthustra*

"Once you label me you negate me."
Philosopher Soren Kierkegaard

"Confidence is the sweet spot between arrogance and despair."
Rosabeth Kanter, *Confidence*

Omnipotence is born within a seething soul that refuses to allow the negatives to live anywhere in its presence. Supermen like Alexander the Great refuse to permit pessimists to get in the way of the ascent to power. Why? They know intuitively that whiners and losers take their toll on even the most positive of personalities. And the one thing we know from modern psychology is that positive energy is the penultimate antidepressant drug. Even the deluded, those optimistic zealots who believe in the Easter Bunny of life, tend to be healthier and more successful than others according to recent medical research.

Positive energy pervades every cell and every facet of a wannabe Superman. History is abundant with examples of individuals who were positively driven nothing could keep them from incredible success. Positive energy in many ways can be the catalyst to an invincible persona. Alexander's mother preached to her son that he was truly the son of Zeus. The very idea inspired him take off for the ancient city of Delphi to consult with the all-knowing Oracle to validate his mother's words. Alexander was told, "Yes my son" and he went on to fulfill that destiny. Frank

Lloyd Wright had a mother with a similar penchant for the arcane. She reared him t believe that he was the reincarnation of the mythical god Taliesin. Were these mothers a little off base? Sure! But it bequeathed in their sons the magic of mythical omnipotence that would not be denied.

The positive energy that raged through Napoleon was awe-inspiring and led to his erroneous belief that he was pre-destined to rule the world. This positive energy flowing through them is part and parcel of their positive thinking. When a person thinks positive thoughts serotonin is released in the brain. The endorphins send messages to the central nervous system in the body and every cell that makes it strong. Peace and productivity are the payoff. The serotonin elevates the immune system leading to greater power, health, and positive energy. Optimism becomes pervasive and the whole system is in overdrive. People call this getting into Flow or the Zone but it is the direct consequence of looking at life positively not negatively.

Positive thinking is the fuel for optimistic actions. Victims are beset by negative energy flowing through them just as positive actions are the external manifestations of inner optimism. Many optimists are irrational about their lot in life, but their delusions actually enhance their ability to succeed. This is true in the game of business, sports, or life. Those poor souls who flagellate themselves are only setting themselves up to fail. Those who delude themselves into thinking all is good actually influence what transpires in their life. Those who think positive thoughts actually influence their health and how others treat them. Sounds weird but those who expect to win tend to win more often than their talent would otherwise predict. Conversely, negative types lose more often than their talent says they should. This makes attitude the key variable and winning and losing a self-fulfilling prophecy.

In her book *Confidence* (2004) Rosabeth Kanter wrote of the pervasive influence of winning on future wins. "Growth cycles produce optimism," she wrote, "and declines produce pessimism." She speaks of an aura surrounding those who win and lose, one positive, the other negative:

> *"Winning creates a positive aura around everything—a halo effect that encourages positive team behavior that makes further wins more likely…Those who have self-efficacy are likely to try harder and to persist longer when they face obstacles."* (*Confidence* 2004 p. 39)

The mind is the traffic cop that makes us an optimist or a pessimist. Those happy dudes walking down the street with a bright smile are merely reflecting their inner sense of self. Such people see the upside in every challenge and their positive demeanor leads to success. Conversely, those victims walking around with a grimace are perpetuating their next lost deal. In other words both positive and negative energy are the panacea of peace and productivity, with one successful and the other a failure.

Research into energy flow offers insight into why internal energy affects external behaviors. What is manifested externally has been nurtured internally and we live with how we think. Shakespeare's line about the eyes being the windows of the soul was right on. Optimism can be a façade but in the long run actions scream out how you really think. Dostoevsky offered prescient insight into us not being able to fool ourselves even when we can fool others in his magnificent psychological novel *Crime & Punishment*. The Russian author depicted protagonist Raskolnikov as a cold-blooded killer who got away with the crime. In the work he spoke of the cool Raskolnikov as a culprit endowed with "ideological self-intoxication." The brilliance of the work lay in the fact that he duped the Chief of Police and others but was incapable of duping himself. At the end of the book he walked into the police station and confessed.

The Contagion of Positive Energy

Energy permeates every single cell and results in positive or negative behavior. Each person has the ultimate control of their actions by the way they think. Something as inane as hanging with winners instead of losers programs us for positive or negative energy. This sounds far too simple to be effective but it works. Try it! Lance Armstrong had every reason to capitulate to cancer and let the doctors cut it out so he could just remain alive. He refused! What sets him apart was his refusal to become a martyr when he took on the disease as if a combatant and took the tough road that led to his superstardom.

The next time you are faced with a life-and-death decision refuse to think of the downside and only consider an upside alternative. You will be shocked at the result of an optimistic attack on the problem. Victims crawl into patterns of self-pity and it engulfs every neurological particle of their being. Optimists refuse to consider losing so seldom lose. When integrity and truth are armed with positive energy an indomitable force is released around you. Abraham Maslow described this state as self-actualization—being all you can be. In such a state peace, health, and happiness pervade the environment. People who pervade themselves with pathology get pathology.

All progress depends on giving not taking. The world's givers tend to get because they have set themselves up for positive outcomes and that is what they reap. Users expend vast amounts of energy trying to get and end up losing. Those who are content with what they get create positive energy flows within that ensure that they keep getting positive results. Those who fail create a failure syndrome that permeates all they do, and they tend to keep on failing. If what you are doing is working then keep it up. If it is bad then go look into a mirror at the one responsible. Pretty simple stuff! To be happy be positive! Most people are not introspective enough to get this fundamental principle. We get the behavior we desire and until we come to grips with the hard reality that we are the father's of our own destiny we cannot grow beyond our inner conditioning. Growth is all about changing what you are to be what you are not. To become an adult one must stop being an adolescent. Hear that Michael Jackson? To have a better future one must let go of the past and rewrite those inner tapes to say, "I am master of my destiny."

Positives Often Lead Inextricably to Negatives

One of life's political ironies is that the more democratic a society the more it is prone to crime and terrorism. Only because America is so free does it lead the world in violent pedestrian crimes. Only because America is so open is it open to terrorist attacks that would not be as possible in harsh nations such as China or Israel. Tolerance is the backbone of freedom but can become its Achilles heel. September 11, 2001, could not have happened in planes operated by the Israelis or the Chinese where freedom of the passenger is far less pronounced than for American airline firms. In places like Shangai China or Singapore one is never fearful of walking alone down a street at 2 a.m. Try that in Manhattan, Detroit or LA. Muggings are not tolerated in Tehran or New Delhi as they are in America. The reason is that in those nations muggers are dealt with swiftly and without remorse. Do the crime and do the time. The time for stealing in the Middle East countries is the loss of a hand. Is there much stealing? No! Freedom in America is pervasive and so is its crime.

The Paradox of Gambling—Fear & Greed Mess Up Decision-Making

The ultimate paradox in gambling shows us that most people risk when they should be playing it safe and play it safe when they should be risking. They opt for the wrong strategy when faced with odds. Why? Fear! Psychologists studying gambling found that an offer of a sure thing versus a better thing with reasonable odds leads people astray. Fear rears its ugly head and people place the wrong bet based on the odds. The most prudent decision would be to take the odds of a big win. The majority cannot do it. When faced with the choice of losses they behave in the opposite manner. The best bet is to go with the sure thing and in this case the majority opts for the odds.

People become risk-takers when they should not and risk-averse when they should take risks. Business people are guilty of the same behavior. They dance with dame risk to get to the top but once they arrive change their strategy and start dancing with dame surety. Football coaches do the same. They stop playing the game with abandon when the end is near and change to a conservative strategy and often lose because they stop trying to win. They stop dancing with dame chance that got them there. This can be seen on any given weekend in sports when one team gets a big lead. Prevent defense replaces positive energy with negative energy. That is a strategy for disaster because it changes the mentality of the combatants. Napoleon is considered the greatest military man who ever lived. Why? Because he took the offensive every time! Studies have repeatedly shown that positive begets positive and negative begets negative. So if you are on a roll keep doing it until someone stops you from doing it.

Kids who improve the *most* are those that are *most challenged*. When life is too easy, as is often the case for kids of the rich and famous, success is far tougher to achieve. Making life too safe is not the best way to motivate people. Challenge them and you'll keep them motivated. Yet most business executives do the exact opposite. When life is too easy it does not provide an opportunity to grow and learn. By protecting personnel you are grooming wimps to run the ship. By overprotecting children you are grooming them for life in Sameville, where mediocrity reigns supreme. Since they haven't had to overcome adversity it is virtually impossible for them to deal with it effectively later in life. Throwing children and personnel into whitewater rapids grooms them for a changing world.

A Wonder Woman Psyche Removes Limits

Greatness is born of a driven person with a dream. Fantasies permit them to operate outside those venues of the ordinary. To be extraordinary it is imperative to
function as if you are not ordinary. Ordinary people achieve normally. It takes an
extraordinary individual to achieve eminence. For most people fantasies are too
surreal to consider real. That is not true of visionaries. Great leaders like Alexander the Great are far more inclined to live life above the pack and that is why
they excel far beyond the ordinary. An example is Irving Berlin, who wrote songs
that the musical world demeaned as being out of touch with normal. Berlin
refused to listen to those musical mavens who told him *God Bless America, White
Christmas, Easter Parade,* and *There's No Business like Show Business* were totally
without merit. By chasing his own dreams of the ultimate American lyric he created American classics.

Why do fantasies lift people up and make them more productive? They permit
people to defy tradition and to operate outside of consensus. Existentialist
Jean-Paul Sartre said, "Genius is not a gift, but the way a person invents in desperate circumstances." So be desperate and you can invent your pathway instead
of following in the footsteps of the ordinary. Be ethereal and you can go beyond
real. The reason this always works is that the establishment can be found worshipping at the altar of safety and that leaves open those roads to the Emerald
City. Psychiatrist David Hawkins says, "The source of power and creation is in
the invisible nonlinear domain."

This tells us to get out of the rat race of the norm and permit the imagination to
take us down that yellow brick road to success. Joseph Campbell told us, "Images
of myths are reflections of the inner being. A myth is a life-shaping image."

In his book *Consciousness Physics,* Evan Walker offered further validation when he
wrote, "We do not see images created by our brain, we see our consciousness—
enlightenment lies within."

Fantasies not permitted to ferment are repressed and killed by the establishment.
Roy Disney, Walt's brother, constantly castigated him for permitting his fantasies
to take form. When Walt presented his plan to build a theme park that would
one-day become Disneyland his brother Roy told him he had finally crossed the
line to insanity. The Disney Board of Directors refused to invest one cent in the

venture. Not to be denied Walt, the consummate innovator who saw the ironical stupidity in the horde sold his Palm Springs home and cashed in his life insurance to buy the land in Anaheim. Frightened that Walt would proceed on his own and be gone from Disney Studios Roy suddenly hired the Stanford Research Center to analyze Walt's fantasy park plan. SRC is the second-largest market research firm in the world. They agreed with Roy, not Walt, and recommended to the Disney Board not to invest one cent as the idea as it had no merit. Walt was at wits end and prepared to destroy the company to get his park and negotiated a deal with the firm's mortal enemy—ABC TV for the Walt Disney presents show in return for the $15 million he need to build his park since the Board refused to build it. Walt had done the unpardonable but it worked as the Board had no choice but to go along with the deal. What if Walt had capitulated to the no-risk board?

Magic is what makes the innovator great but it is lost on those too grounded in reality. They see magic as too bizarre for business. The rejection of fantasy has far more to do with anthropology than technology. To enjoy innovative rainbows one must deal with the storms and those who don't care for rainbows should find a desk in some bureaucratic office. The 3M Company is infamous for permitting their employees to spend 20 percent of their time on non-funded ideas and are satisfied if 60 percent of their ventures go belly-up. That would be intolerable for most firms. It is what makes 3M a great firm. There can be no sacred cows in seeking eminence. IBM creator Thomas Watson, Jr. offered this sage advice, "The fastest way to succeed is to double your failure rate." Research shows that most firms protect what they have but in so doing are sacrificing what they don't have. Innovators like Walt Disney do the exact opposite. They use what they have to ensure they are in the forefront of what they don't yet have.

Innovation & Positive Passion

Positive passion and self-confidence are integrated in an innovative person. It is what it takes to deal with a dynamic world. Those who believe tend to be enthusiastic and positive and that permits them to knock down barriers. Self-confidence destroys obstacles and disarms adversaries. And passion moves mountains. An example of such a demeanor can be seen in the life and success of Napoleon, who wrote, "I had confidence in my power and enjoyed my superiority." Frank Lloyd Wright was confident to the point of arrogance and said, "Early in life I had to choose between hypocritical humility and honest arrogance. I chose arrogance." Oscar Wilde was so confident that when he arrived in the United States and was asked by customs what he had to declare he responded, "Nothing, but my genius."

Success takes time. Until one has enough self-efficacy—belief in one's ability—to change paradigms little progress is made. What self-esteem does is trump fear. Fear of the unknown—xenophobia—is rampant in those who lack confidence. They represent the majority of people and why Innovator types make the money and progress. They represent less than three percent of the population. Their strong sense of self lets them rely on their own counsel. Most people need proof. Not so with visionaries. What is scary when looking closely at the research on who accepts new concepts and who rejects them is the timeline for acceptance. Laggards take between ten and one hundred times longer to accept new ideas than Innovators. That includes products that could save their lives. This is why the adoption time for new concepts has such a long incubation period, as shown in the chart below. It took forty-six years for 25 percent of the population to start using electricity in their homes. The telephone was quicker at thirty-five years. The automobile took over half a century, and the airplane had been around sixty-four years prior to being adopted by one-quarter of the population. Even the personal computer took 16 years to penetrate one-fourth of the homes. As we move forward notice that the time for adoption is speeding up.

Timeline from Start to One-Quarter Adoption in the United States *

Product	Year Invented	Years to 25% Adoption
ELECTRICITY	1873	46 YEARS
TELEPHONE	1876	35 YEARS
CAR	1886	55 YEARS
AIRPLANE	1903	64 YEARS
RADIO	1906	22 YEARS
TELEVISION	1926	26 YEARS
VCR	1952	34 YEARS

Timeline from Start to One-Quarter Adoption in the United States (Continued)[*]

MICROWAVE OVEN	1953	30 YEARS
PERSONAL COMPUTER	1975	16 YEARS
CELLULAR PHONES	1983	13 YEARS
INTERNET	1991	7 YEARS
BROADBAND (BROOKINGS INST.)	MID-'90S	15–25 YEARS

[*]   Source: IBD JULY 17, 2001 PRADO P. A8 "HIGH SPEED ACCESS TO NET"

Conformity—Innovators vs. Laggards

In every society since the Stone Age the power elite have created dogmatic rules in order to maintain order and control their constituency. Those who didn't abide by the rules were punished. Those who conformed were protected and some were given special privileges. Nonconformists like Socrates and Galileo were punished for daring to challenge the dogma of the top dogs. Such a system programs the pack for mediocrity. It is still rampant today and is why the *New York Times* referred to Frank Lloyd Wright as the "anarchist architect" and why the FTC prosecuted Bill Gates. These men refused to be programmed for mediocrity but pay for their insurgence. Walt Disney lasted one week working as a cartoonist and Martha Stewart was put in jail for failing to capitulate.

Not everyone can be an innovator or special and that is why there need to be rules for the followers to adhere to. Visionaries are not inclined to follow the policy manual and that is precisely why Sam Walton was able to build the largest corporation in the world while his competitors were struggling to survive. This is also why highly creative inventors like Howard Head of metal ski and oversized tennis racket fame was repeatedly fired after graduating from Harvard with honors. Head finally quit his job as an aerospace engineer and built the first metal ski and the first oversized tennis racket. Baffled over his real-life failures he saw the light and became a renowned entrepreneur where policy manuals are not in vogue.

"If it ain't broke don't try to fix it" was popular in the twentieth century but like all things is going the way of the typewriter. Inventor Charles Kettering created the electric self-starter that revolutionized the auto industry but was shocked over the rigor and myopia of those who had too much formal education and told the press, "Overly educated people are least likely to make new discoveries." Psychologist David Kirton also saw this emerging pattern and studied two categories of managers with Innovators—those who prefer operating differently and Adapters—those who prefer doing things excellently. There is a dire need for both but they must place themselves where they function most effectively.

The following chart shows the timeline and probability for acceptance of truly original ideas. Creative types operate on the left and as you can see will have 98 percent of the world telling them they are nuts. The establishment is way to the right, as they don't accept the new until it has been proven. In the interim they will be the ones ridiculing those who are creating. By the time they get it all opportunity ceases but it takes a long time. Early Adopters get it quick but Laggards sometimes never get it. They are the ones still with black and white televisions sets, without cell phones, who think a DVD player is something from outer space. This vast divide between those who see the possibilities in new ideas and products and those frightened by them is what causes friction in the world of commerce. The majority sees the Innovators as eccentric radicals who could be dangerous and the Late Majority and Laggards are seen as myopic imbeciles by the world's visionaries.

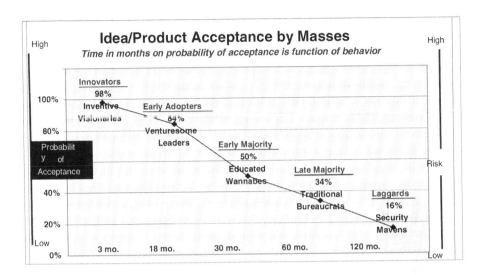

Be Stupid to Be Innovative

In 2004 the Olympic Gold Medal winner Laura Wilkinson told the press the reason for her success: "I dive stupid." The bewildered journalist asked why and the diver responded, "I must turn off my brain." Without other insight except how she functions Wilkinson had hit on the breakthrough success. When riding a bike or dancing the body has stored the information in muscle memory. The body knows what to do. Engaging the mind is counterproductive to the process and thinking interferes with optimum performance. Sports psychologists encounter this every day. Questioning the ability to make a free throw with no time remaining or to hit a golf ball over a water hazard is contra to success. Medical researcher Robert Ornstein in *The Evolution of Consciousness* (p. 140) wrote, "Virtuoso (performances) in all arenas is when another mind takes over. A spontaneous act begins before we are aware we have decided to act." Therefore thinking or questioning your ability actually interferes with performance.

Crunch time in sports, business, or life is when you should just stop thinking and go with the flow. Weekend warriors are often guilty of thinking way too much. Their minds are actually interfering with their body's ability to perform. Amateur golfers alter their game to avoid sand traps. Pros often aim at sand traps since they are a known adversary. Writer Lynn Grabhorn in her book *Excuse Me Your Life Is Waiting* (2000) offered insight into the power of this inner energy. Negative energy for her was the adversary, not the opponent. She says, "Needing something to change always flows negative energy. Blame is the culprit since it focuses on pessimism. Changing focus on problems changes the energy. You don't have to change anything, just stop thinking about it."

Empowerment Hierarchy—Positive vs. Negative Energy

Eminent psychiatrist David Hawkins offered insight into empowerment through positive energy flow. In his book *Eye of the Needle* (2001) Hawkins shows the correlation between positive energy and enlightenment. At the bottom of his hierarchy is total negativity and where people get lost in their anger, fear, and shame. When people are afraid they can't leap tall buildings or even cope with adversity. At the opposite end of such a hierarchy (see below) is the top where positive energy dominates all things and people become empowered. Those who walk in this enchanted land are special people like Jesus, Gandhi, and Mother Teresa. Just below this elevated place are the approximately 4 percent who are enlightened due to high positive energy. In the middle we find those with Self-Efficacy who believe they can but are also often disarmed by the negative types below them. The sad commentary is that 85 percent of any given distribution tends to be engulfed by negatives. They are engulfed with a no-hope syndrome with fear dominating everything they do and everyone they touch.

Hierarchy of Evolution from Fear to Empowerment

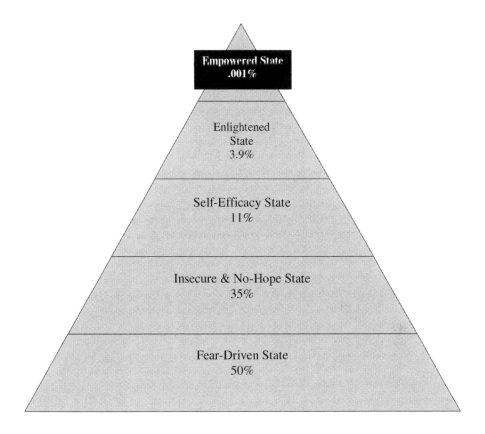

Recent research offers validation to Hawkins' work. "Nobel Prize winners who did exceptionally creative work," one article said, "attribute their great break-throughs to their detachment from what other people in their fields were doing. They didn't know how things were done in the past, how things ought to be done, and what was believed to be impossible or absurd. So they did what they thought was logical." This indicates that Nobel winners tend to be self-motivated and empowered by an ethereal presence.

Hawkins found in his research that "Muscles strengthen and weaken from posi-tive or negative stimuli." How? Through the release of toxins and endorphins that come from a smile (positive thoughts) or frown (negative thoughts) an individual tests either weak or strong. Endorphins released into the bloodstream from a smile lead to "physiological strengthening of the muscles and positive energy flow." The converse was true when a frown was shown to the subjects. Their immune systems were weakened by the negative energy flow. This would suggest that eminent people are positive thinkers causing them to be stronger than their adversaries. More energy flows through their systems, making them less vulnerable to illness and disease due to an elevated immune system. Hawkins' findings validate my finding on the rich and famous who tend to be less ill despite a frenetic work ethic and live-on-the-edge lifestyle and when ill they always recovered faster than the normal population.

Positive Energy & Performance

The impact of positive energy on performance is remarkable. Berkeley researcher Mark Rosenzweig found, "Positive experience alters brain size, IQ, and learning ability." The renowned psychologist Erik Erickson found a similar response in children and wrote, "Study after study has shown that children with superior intelligence but low self-esteem do poorly in school while children of average intelligence but high self-esteem can be unusually successful." Winston Churchill was more profound saying, "A pessimist sees the difficulty in every opportunity. An optimist sees the opportunity in every difficulty."

In *Quantum Psychology* (1990) New Age writer Anton Wilson found, "Patients fed on a high dose of optimism statistically fare somewhat better than those fed only on grim pessimism. If a doctor expects the patient to get well, this has some effect on the patient, if the doctor expects the patient to die, this also has an effect." We know that peak performers tend or have a high Internal Locus of Control, a measure of whether one thinks one is in charge of one's destiny or that some other entity has control. Internal types are less conforming and far more capable of rebounding from adversity. It turns out that those who say success is all in the head are correct.

After years of research behavioral kinesiologist John Diamond found positive energy to be the secret for success. His subjects who tested with higher positive energy were stronger and healthier than the average person. Diamond tested thousands and the results were always the same—optimists tested strong and pessimists tested weak. Once he was sure of who was positive and who was negative he paired them off and tested what happened when they interfaced with each other. The result is what most people intuitively sense. The pessimist came out of the room after an hour with the optimist and tested stronger and more positive than when he went in. The optimist emerged weaker and with less positive energy then when he went it. What does this tell us? Don't ever associate with losers. Diamond wrote:

"The optimists with a strong thymus tested weaker while the pessimists with a weak thymus tested stronger. If our Life Energy is high, others will benefit from close contact with us; if it is low our relationships with others become part of the problem."

Time & Speed Are Precious Commodities

George Gilder wrote the history of the Web in a book titled *Telecosm* (2000) in which he said, "In the *Telecosm* speed is king, and time and lifespan are the ultimate scarcity. The future is the Internet over fiber optics. The net will be central and the CPU will be peripheral." In the words of one Silicon Valley cyber-head, "No other thing in our lifetimes has produced this kind of change. It will represent the biggest business change in 100 years. By getting to real-time enterprise we'll achieve 30% lower costs automatically." Touché! But we had better use it positively and refrain from using it negatively. In today's world there is voice mail to field our calls. Voice mail is a great benefit for those wanting to receive calls from important clients while they are at lunch or in a meeting. But we tend to abuse what is helpful. Ever try to reach the IRS or Social Security offices? Not a prayer! Many bureaucrats have learned to hide behind voice mail just as many introverts avoid confrontations and conflict by e-mailing negative information to their staff. We must be careful to use technology not abuse it.

Change is the order of the day, with speed and time key to coping. Sound bites are dropping precipitously. Suddenly we don't have time to read or write whole sentences as can be seen in the cyberspeak of e-mail messages. E-mails are often written in phrases and acronyms. Attention spans are narrowing due to the proliferation of information. There are now 250 megabytes of new information created daily for every human on the planet. Researchers believe the totality of information in the world is doubling about every 2.5 years. Between 1965 and 1995 TV news sound bites dropped from 42 seconds to 8 seconds, an 81 percent drop in just thirty years. *Time* magazine cover stories in 1979 averaged 4500 words. By 2000 they were averaging 2800 words—a 40 percent drop—and they're headed downward as more info deluges our media and life.

Think what has happened since Bill Gates launched Microsoft in the mid-seventies. In his book *Success* (1977) Michael Korda spoke of the nerd Gates walking around with a "Loser's Jacket Pocket holding three pens and his glasses." By the millennium those nerds had become multibillionaires. What we thought is no longer viable. And what we are doing may not be viable for very long. "Change or be changed" is the mantra of today. Things that were once stupid, like techie toys, are now the symbols of being in tune with the Web world we live in. That is the paradox of progress especially in a world driven by innovative technologists who have never been keen on social conventions.

Speed of communications is growing geometrically making it important to make decisions without the help of legions of staff. A leader in the twenty-first century must have the confidence to make decisions without a bevy of legal-beagles and CPAs. For self-efficacy to work a leader must be bold and intuitive and have a higher comfort with ambiguity than his predecessor. The irony of this need is that bureaucrats have moved further in the wrong direction. They continue to number-crunch to justify their roles and validate their decisions. In the World-Com trial in early 2005 David Myers told the jurors, "Accountants made false entries repeatedly until they satisfied CFO Scott Sullivan's need to make the numbers work."

There is a paradox of living written some twenty-six centuries ago by Lao-Tzu that goes:

> *The human spirit is fond of purity*
> *But the mind disturbs it,*
> *The human mind is fond of tranquility,*
> *But desires meddle with it.*

Never has this ancient wisdom been more pertinent than today. Life at warp speed is not easy and must be dealt with positively or frustration will dominate. The world, contrary to many, is not black or white. It is grey. Reality and truth are amorphous and ephemeral. Speed is king. To get a handle on where you are it is important to find where you are not. To really appreciate your health, get sick! To truly understand ignorance work on getting smart! To be brave face fear down! To remove negative energy do not permit energy vampires to invade your turf. To experience a fantasy remove yourself from reality. Immersion is what athletes call going into the Zone. When in that special place life is surreal. Gamblers know this truth. They will tell you the next best thing to winning is losing. Titillation comes from playing the game far more than winning the game.

Myth & Positive Energy in the Path to Power

Frank Lloyd Wright & Amelia Earhart Exemplify the Process

Architect Frank Lloyd Wright and aviatrix Amelia Earhart believed in themselves when no one else did. Both were Midwestern vagabonds who chose the world as their playground. Wright lived in ten states before he was ten years old and it made him a man who could cope with adversity. Amelia attended three high schools in three different states. It led her to want to "go where no man has."

Frank Lloyd Wright was an architect who married form with function like few others. His work was called "organic architecture" since it was a mystical "life force of nature." Traditionalists saw Wright as a scary man lost in his own reverie. Others saw his genius and became disciples. This modern-day Promethean married buildings with their environment no matter the cost in time, money, or energy. Such thinking led to incredible edifices, the most famous of which are *Fallingwater* and Manhattan's Guggenheim Museum.

An example of Wright's brilliance was the home he designed for multimillionaire Edgar Kaufmann. The department store monarch commissioned Wright to build a vacation home overlooking Bear Creek waterfall on his remote Pennsylvania property. In Wright's inimitable fashion he disagreed with his client's wishes— Kaufmann wanted a home looking at the mountain stream. Wright saw the home perched precariously over the water and didn't work on it for months due to the difference of opinion. Wright was always preaching to his protégés, "Never attempt to resolve a design until the idea has taken a clear shape in your imagination" (Seacrest p. 419).

Wright kept procrastinating on the initial design for Kaufmann and when he called told him not to worry. One day Kaufmann called from the O'Hare airport while on business and told Wright he was renting a car and driving up to Wisconsin. Wright had not even drawn the first line for his client and he would be there in a couple hours. Students watching Wright that day were blown away by the tour de force of a man in his late sixties working feverishly on a plan that should take weeks but was finished in two hours complete with furniture, fixtures, and accoutrements. Wright had even designed the seats in which the Kaufmanns could view the waterfall running beneath their deck. Kaufmann showed up expecting a home design looking at the water to find a design of a home over the water. The maverick Wright had pulled off a miracle; Kaufman was bedazzled and told him, "Don't change a thing."

"Destroy the box" was the mantra preached by the ever-defiant Wright. Positive energy raged through his system like a man possessed. His doting mother had reared him with the belief that he was the reincarnation of the Welsh mythical god Taliesin. Gods are not held to the same standards as mere mortals and Wright raced through life with the deluded belief he was god and acted the part. The buildings he designed were equal to his own self-image. When asked by the media about his flaunting of tradition he responded, "Ordinary men follow rules. I am not an ordinary man. I am the world's greatest architect." One time in court, and he was there often, he responded to a cross-examination calling himself a genius. When he walked out of the courthouse a reporter stopped him and asked, "Mr. Wright how could you have had the audacity to refer to yourself as a genius on the stand?" Without hesitating the insurgent said, "I was under oath, wasn't I?" That is positive energy beyond the pale of normality.

Like Wright, aviatrix Amelia Earhart was an indomitable spirit who was her own worst enemy on that ill-fated plane trip in 1937. Prudence never had been a high priority for Amelia. But on that trip she pushed the window of rationality in order to break a world record. To reduce the weight Amelia elected to leave off the most fundamental communications equipment of the era. In a business where safety is of primal importance this intrepid spirit was fearless. Had she listened to aeronautics experts she would have been able to radio for help during the last days in the South Pacific. In an even more brazen move she hired the card-carrying alcoholic Fred Noonan as navigator. When she turned up missing the *New York Times* wrote, "Amelia was in rebellion against a world which had been for women too safe, too unexciting." Her close relationship with Eleanor Roosevelt had led to a huge Navy fleet in the South Pacific to watch out for her but they were unable to help due to the lack of communications. What price glory?

During her early flights Amelia wrote poetry to calm her. Just before her first transatlantic flight that would make her famous she wrote, "Courage is the price that life exacts for granting peace." That courage was legend ever since that eventful day when her dad bought her a ticket to go up in a bi-plane while on a college break. "As soon as we left the ground I knew myself I had to fly, knowing full well I'd die if I didn't." She left Columbia University and moved to Southern California to be near her father and for the chance to fly. Flight instructor Cora Skinner said, "She used to scare me to death. She would have flown between two high-tension power lines eight feet apart if I didn't watch her all the time." To earn the money for the lessons the girl went into business and then to get the money to buy her own plane she bought a truck and began hauling gravel.

On December 15, 1921, Amelia earned her pilot's license. Within a year the daring girl set her first flying record in an open cockpit biplane painted yellow named *The Canary*. Testimony to her mystical nature, she used color as motivation—yellow has been found to be the color for energy. In concert with her energetic nature she named her dazzling yellow car *Yellow Peril*. Within a year of earning her license she began trying to set records. On October 22, 1922, she took off from Rogers Field in Southern California and with no oxygen. The fearless female climbed straight up to 14,000 feet through fog and sleet. Fearing a stall she purposely put the plane into a tailspin after having set the altitude record and went into a steep dive straight toward the ground. She had no idea how low the fog and clouds were to the ground and once through pulled the plane out of its dive. On landing a veteran pilot asked her what would have happened had the clouds been 100 feet lower. She shrugged and admitted it hadn't crossed her mind.

On Earhart's record-breaking flight across the Atlantic in 1932 she was perilously close to blacking out due to the nauseous fumes in the cockpit. She refused to become a victim of the elements and persevered. The brave female would be nicknamed Lady Lindy by the press and was awarded the Legion of Honor and became an international superstar for having crossed the Atlantic alone. Later the daredevil decided to break the speed record from Mexico City to New Orleans. Famed aviator Wiley Post told her, "Don't do it. It's too dangerous." Such words from a male ensured that the woman dedicated to going where no man had gone would take on the challenge.

Fast cars and sleek planes were the fuel that drove Amelia. If it wasn't dangerous she wasn't interested. Such things energized her and took her to places most women of her era could only imagine existed. By her mid-thirties Amelia was being queried about settling down and having a family like most other women of the time. The indomitable spirit told the press, "I don't want anything all the time. I've had 28 different jobs in my life and hope I'll have 228 more." On the eve of her marriage to publishing baron George Putnam she told reporters, "I'm unsold on marriage." When asked what her husband thought of her lifestyle she offered an answer with a double-entendre, "My husband does not interfere with my flying and I don't interfere with his affairs."

The coup de grace of Amelia's life on the edge came in 1937 with her attempt to circumnavigate the globe some 27,000 miles in distance. Experts repeatedly warned her of the slim odds of hitting a small island in the middle of the South Pacific for refueling. World-class pilot and close friend Jacqueline Cochrane said, "I hope you don't go. There are too many risks." When Cochrane came to Miami to see her off, Amelia was emotional and gave her a lucky silk American flag to hold. Cochrane told her, "No! You keep it and I'll relish it on your return." With emotion Amelia said, "No, you'd better take it now."

When Earhart was lost the *New York Times* wrote a eulogy saying, "She was in rebellion against a world which had been too safe for women, too unexciting" (Landrum 1995 p. 197). Fear was always nonexistent in her life while overheated energy was her forte. When she ran out of fuel in the South Pacific not far from her destination of Howland Island she had fulfilled her desire to "go where no man has ever gone."

Mythical Mentoring & Energy Incarnate

Frank Lloyd Wright & Amelia Earhart Went Where Others Feared to Go!

These two neophytes who had virtually no formal training in their fields, no pedigrees, and were never considered one of the best in either architecture or flying by their peers altered the world through pure energy. Wright never made it through high school. But his lack of being told what he couldn't do worked to his advantage. In a similar manner Earhart never felt that she couldn't achieve because of her gender or go where no one else had gone before her. She did the improbable because such words as "can't" were antithetic for everything she stood for. Earhart told the press she knew she was never the best female pilot but tenacity was her forte.

Both ignored all conventional advice and played by the rules they saw as exciting and rational. Listening to their own counsel is what made them great. Wright was called an anarchist by the media for his refusal to design like traditionalists but it never bothered him in the least and certainly never caused him to change his approach to design. His mother's influence made him arrogant but the arrogance made him reach the pinnacle of his field.

This wunderkind was a passionate free spirit that fueled her success. She always spoke of being proud to have been the sixteenth female in the world with a pilot's license. Few women had a driver's license in the early 20th century but this indomitable spirit drove trucks to earn the money to buy her plane. The same moxie led to her record-breaking flights as well as seven crashes. The last offered validation to her poetic rhetoric on what it takes to be great, "Courage is the price that life exacts for granting peace." And peace was her objective, as can be seen from her last words to the ground crew, "When I go, I'd like to go in my plane. Quickly!"

Wright's mother told her son that he was a little god. That prophecy was a bit deluded but left an indelible mark on his soul that helped him rise to the very top of the world of architecture. He had been molded with a success imprint that left him with an omnipotent sense of self, leading to a motto: "Early in life I had to decide between hypocritical humility and honest arrogance. I chose arrogance." In another diatribe on what made him special he told the press without qualms, "Ordinary men follow rules. But I am not ordinary."

Wright sauntered through life as if on a mythical adventure. He wrote, "Architecture receives its power from the life force." Such an ethereal sense allowed him to create edifices like Fallingwater and the Guggenheim Museum. As with other visionaries there strengths are often their greatest weakness. In Wright's case his majestic buildings like Fallingwater had leaky roofs and ineffective plumbing due to his inability to sweat the details. His refusal to license his designs to developers kept him from profiting from the replication of his work. The stream of royalties from developers would have given him the money to create even more magnificent edifices but he wanted no part of it. The same was the crucible for Nikola Tesla.

Both Wright and Earhart had an androgynous nature. Wright dressed elegantly with style and grace and has been described as feminine by many biographers. When the sartorially attired architect showed up for a bid adorned in top hat, flowing cape, and magnificent cane he was unforgettable. Dressing in opposition was also found in Amelia who disdained makeup and feminine attire. She always had her hair short and wore pants rather than dresses. She had the stride of an athlete and the boldness of a business tycoon. Amelia was independent in an era when women were trophies for powerful husbands. Not Amelia! She dominated her marriage to publisher George Putnam refusing the role of wife or housekeeper.

CHAPTER 13

▼

THE PARADOX OF POWER—TRYING IS COUNTER TO GETTING

Power Emanates from a Driven Person with a Passion for a Dream

"As soon as you give it all up you can have it all; as long as you want power, you can't have it. The minute you don't want power you'll have more than you ever dreamed possible."
Ram Dass, *Be Here & Now*

"Power accedes to he who takes it."
Frederick Nietzsche, *Zarathustra*

"Empowerment occurs when you stop blaming and accept responsibility for your actions."
David Hawkins, MD, PhD

Mental mysticism is the crack cocaine of transformations. Those who experience an epiphany have paid a big price in terms of ridicule by the establishment or a near-death experience that contributes to their moving from a grounded state into a higher-order state. Mid-century kids tripped out on a newsboy screaming "Shazam" to become Captain Marvel. This comic book stuff sounds mystical but many boys have transformed themselves by daring to be something they were not to become more than may have otherwise been possible. Don't feel it is an accident *Shazam*—an ancient Egyptian wizard spouting heroic words of wisdom on Hercules strength, Atlas-like stamina, Zeus' power, Achilles courage and Mercury's speed. The comic book mavens endowed Captain Marvel with these qualities and those capable of mimicking these qualities—even if deluded—are far better prepared to cope than their peers. Those kids wandering into their own rendition of a Batcave leave armed with more resilience than those steeped in fear and conformity. Mental transitory escapes are laden with psychological benefits. *To optimize mind, body and soul tattoo Superman on your psyche and life will be a piece of cake.*

Mental mysticism is in many respects the crack cocaine of transformations and the fuel for life's wannabe's. The path to power is paved with epiphanies of "I can" that require inner transformations from programmed fears into positive reveries of reprogrammed "Get out of my way." Utopian fantasy images actually do make us better than we could otherwise hope to be. Escaping into a netherland of make-believe is a metamorphosis of the mind. Why? Because creativity is spawned in the imagination and that is the fuel of all men. Talent can only take us so far. It takes a seething will to elevate us above the horde. Paradoxically, all virtuosity is a by-product of entering the un-real or surreal.

Despite what the conventional wisdom says, success comes from maniacs on a mission that is more surreal than real. Those who are too grounded in the rational become victims of their rationality. Those who can give rein to their imagination and listen to mythical magicians have a significantly greater chance to become a superstar than life's conformists. Elevation into that ethereal land of make-believe is where most visionaries tend to live. Had Walt Disney been an even-keeled conformist we would never have had Disneyland and certainly not Epcot. Mind guru from Stanford Robert Ornstein told us in *Evolution of Consciousness*, "Virtuoso performance is when another mind takes over and doesn't ask questions, doesn't require any conscious direction" (p. 140).

Power Is Paradoxical

Fear is the enemy of any trip to the pinnacle no matter the discipline. And optimistic arrogance with a touch of mysticism lurks behind all eminent work such as Frank Lloyd Wright's world-renowned home *Fallingwater*. By permitting fantasies to lead us in our trek through life we are better able to go down paths that would otherwise not be possible. The power of paradox was rampant in the life of most eminent individuals with none quite as profound as in the life of Mahatma Gandhi. This man was a paradox. He was spiritual to a fault but detested all dogmas. Gandhi was a timid gentleman, but with the soul of a fearless tiger who fought the British like a man possessed. The ardent pacifist refused to allow his allies to use any form of weaponry on his behalf. The ascetic leader abstained from sexual relations with his long-suffering wife after his mid-thirties but fought for the right of others to bear as many children as they desired. This frail man was like the Rock of Gibraltar. He preached nonviolence but had a hot temper scolding his wife unmercifully.

Power as Unconscious Insight

Michelangelo looked at a piece of raw marble and saw the figure of David in it and thus his only problem was removing the excess marble to give David freedom. The consummate rational thinking scientist Bertrand Russell saw this and said, "The sense of certainty and revelation comes before any definite belief." Ornstein found in his research that we are governed by unconscious forces far more than our conscious ones. That is why I ask my students, "How old would you be if you didn't know how old you were?" The message here is to stop being constrained by too much knowledge. Act like you are ten years younger and it permits you to perform at that chronological age. That magical power from within is far greater than the cognitive one; as Ornstein said, "We cannot consciously control our actions and still function at peak. Virtuoso performances and quick reactions are below consciousness."

Power is an anomaly. Great scientists all over the world have found that their great insights have been far more mystical than rational. And that is the scientific community. When looking at the musical, artistic, and philosophic worlds the need to go beyond logic is far greater. Virtually all great jazz musicians are far more creative when into spontaneous improvisations than when reading musical notes. In fact, Irving Berlin, Frank Sinatra, Judy Garland, and Elvis Presley were unable to read a note of music but altered the discipline like few others. The power of penultimate performances cannot be pursued or will be found wanting. Power emanates only from those in tune with their inner sensitivity. Consider the enormous power wielded by a newborn baby. It cries and macho men jump. Conversely a bully only has the power given to him by his victims. Bullies only pick on the weak who allow it to happen. Stop being a victim of those who would have you march to their drum beat and write your own tunes.

Mahatma Gandhi is a classic example of getting power by not trying to have power. This ascetic man with no visible vestiges of what most people consider the bastions of power was able to topple the mighty British Empire. Gandhi's power was ethereal. He could not be bribed by money or position, or threatened by imprisonment or physical harm. The Brits were puzzled as to how to deal with a man who was beyond sexual intrigues, financial inducements, or threats on his life. Gandhi was empowered from within and all these offerings were external bribes. The British hierarchy had never encountered such a man. The enigma of Gandhi was spawned by his faith in *Satyagraha*—passive resistance through positive nonviolence—a power beyond the reach of ordinary men. When the British imprisoned him he went on a hunger strike. Fearing he would die and become more of a threat as a martyr, they capitulated and set him free. The power from within was a far greater force than could have been found had Gandhi capitulated.

Such men have a philosophic nature, viewing most things from an epistemological perspective. Most visionaries have a holistic sense not unlike a Grand Master who plays the game at least seven moves ahead—and aware of multiple permutations along the way. They seldom confuse the map with the territory since the map is but an image and the territory is often much more than what appears in the details of that map. "There will be no end to the trouble of states," Plato told his students in Athens, "until philosophers become kings." This was prophetic for a man who saw the power of ideas as more important than political agendas. Other greats functioned above the game of life. Napoleon went into all battles with a clear picture of the essence of what was taking place. It permitted him to attack the adversary's weakest link to ensure victory. Similarly, Picasso painted with a philosophic and poetic voice infiltrating his images and colors. Like philosophers, poets have a similar bent relative to going beyond the obvious and looking deeply within the nature of what is transpiring. The Poet's Lament—**write drunk and revise sober**—has a message suggesting us to get surreal and outside conventional bounds when creating and then use a realistic filter to make it palatable for the masses. This is only possible by starting at the end and working back to what is plausible. This works since those too grounded in what is happening are unable to make new things happen. The realities stifle their ability to chase life's possibilities. The world's concrete-sequential types are all from Missouri—the Show Me State—and have trouble operating in foreign vistas that are the province of the visionary.

Einstein was a visionary. His mental map permitted him to do what other scientists could not see until proven. His prescient insights into the interrelationships between time, space, and energy were not due to his mental brilliance but a function of his intuitive powers. Nikola Tesla had a similar ability and was actually precognitive. Nobel Prize winner John Nash, featured in the film *A Beautiful Mind,* had a similar disposition. High school instructors were baffled when he walked to the board and wrote down answers to differential equations that the other students were struggling over with pencil and paper. Frank Lloyd Wright had a similar predilection for design that he described as "organic Architecture." The man who has been eulogized for having documented the psyche of the twentieth century in art spoke of his work beyond the pale of the ordinary. He boldly told the press, "I have the revelation of the inner voice." These brilliant visionaries had a prescient power of seeing beyond the data to resolve the dilemma. Making the complex simple was their path to fame and fortune. This fundamental truth is often lost on traditionalists.

The Crazy Part of Power

A powerful leader is often weak in many ways. Aristotle wrote, "No great genius is without some mixture of insanity." Research has shown the Greek philosopher to be more than a little correct. Newton was brought to his knees by schizophrenia. Dostoevsky was plagued with epileptic fits that he called his "mystic terrors," the "fiend" within. Napoleon had to cope with debilitating manic-depression and Catherine the Great had to deal with what she called "uterine frenzies" that led to spending the equivalent of $1.5 billion on paramours. Nietzsche was institutionalized when *Thus Spake Zarathustra* was released as the cornerstone of existential thinking. Both Freud and Jung were in a state of mental collapse when they made their great breakthroughs in psychology.

Leaders cannot come across as weak or they will lose their power. The minute the Roman power elite saw the Caesar's weakness for his mistress Cleopatra they decided he wasn't strong enough to lead Rome. It wasn't the indulgence they feared. It was his weakness for her womankind and refusal to dump her or just set her up as a mistress that was disturbing to the power elite. That was not true in the cases of either John F. Kennedy or Bill Clinton, who had blatant affairs but dumped the damsels to remain in power. It is never the sexual liaison that irritates the pundits but the leader's inability to limit it to a one-night stand that they fear. Charm has its place but when it runs amuck those that made you will often attempt to destroy you.

Servant leadership is a great example of power gravitating to those not trying to get it. Never was this more apparent than when the 90-pound ascetic leader Mahatma Gandhi brought down the powerful British Empire. Had Gandhi resorted to traditional power sources such as taking over the army or creating a political machine to dump the Brits it would all have come to naught. Gandhi's power came from a deep commitment to a cause larger than life, a power that cannot be dealt with by soldiers or guns. His power was ethereal and that transcended weaponry. Psychiatrist David Hawkins preached the incredible force of positive energy. It makes us strong and makes us invincible.

Academic Francis Bacon told us, "Knowledge is power." Politician Mao Tse Tung preached, "Power comes out of the end of a gun." Psychotherapist Alfred Adler felt, "Power is the ability to manipulate or control the activities of others." But it appears that current thinking is more aligned with that of David Hawkins, who wrote, "The source of power and creation is in the invisible, nonlinear domains."

Innovation Hierarchy

Empowered people have a positive persona. Their opposite types are those who can find something wrong with baseball, apple pie, and a fun day at the beach. Fear is their god and they see the world as either black or white. They exude negative energy and consequently tend to be powerless. In contrast the movers and shakers of the world elevate optimism to the top of their agenda and only do things with a positive nature. They refuse to hang with losers. These proactive overachievers tend to represent a very small percentage of any organization or group. The bottom dominates about 85 percent of any organization and that is the reason for policy manuals, budgets, and things to constrain the pessimists from running amuck.

Psychic Energy as Power Source

Psychic energy can break down barriers like no other thing including money, muscles, or brilliance. The paradox of empowerment reaches its zenith in the political world where three major nations of the world became the pawns of three people with positive energy incarnate. Catherine the Great was not Russian but led that nation as if she were possessed. Napoleon was not French and Hitler was not German but they exuded passionate zeal to make their adopted nations the best in the world. What is strange is that each of these indomitable leaders used the ploy of nationalism as their mantra.

Catherine said it was "poison or prison" that motivated her to wrest control from her husband Peter. She told biographers she wanted to be the incarnation of the Russian move into the future. It would be only a few years later that the power-mad Napoleon showed up from his Corsican home to take over a nation that was still suffering from a revolution that had brought her to her knees. The irony of his platform was in making all of Europe into French colonies. Napoleon's fantasy-hero was Alexander, who he attempted to emulate. Adolph Hitler thought he was the reincarnation of a Nietzschean Superman when he convinced a nation wallowing in self-pity to put him in power. The mad Austrian did take on the Red Menace from the East and through a military buildup stopped unemployment and ended the recession and inflation. These psychic energy gurus used the fear at the bottom to reach the top. It offers testimony that the negative energy and fear at the very bottom can be used as a catalyst for empowerment.

These political power brokers lived in a state of mythical transcendence beyond the pale of normality. All were voracious readers who escaped into the dreams of their protagonists and used them to break down doors and to gain power. Like Catherine, Napoleon was hyper beyond comprehension. Both dictated to six secretaries at once in a torrid flood of exuberance. These two mesmerized disciples, and passion dominated their lives and loves. Catherine wrote, "Plutarch and Voltaire fortified my soul." She admitted to having "uterine frenzies" that dominated her lifestyle. As we know libidinal energy is aligned with physical energy and that is what made her so powerful. The Little Corsican took books to the front and read poetry prior to battle mimicking his mythical hero Alexander. Napoleon's foolish engagement in Egypt was only because his hero Alexander had done so. The Little General wrote, "God gave me the will and the force to overcome all obstacles," a comment not unlike Hitler's messianic diatribe, "I am more godlike than human." Both succumbed due to their self-described messianic arrogance.

Hitler carried Schopenhauer books to the front in World War I and became enthralled with will as the master of man. As a teen Hitler became so enthralled with Wagner's operas he went into a wild reverie. Teen friend August Kubizek spoke of their attending a *Rienzi* opera, "Hitler entered a state of ecstasy and rapture with visionary powers as though a demon had possessed him." Later when Hitler became the Fuhrer he admitted that it was in those days that the dream became a reality as he wrote in *Mein Kampf*, "I will lead Germany out of servitude and to heights of freedom. It was at that moment that it all began."

Power Pendulums Never Return to Equilibrium

One paradox of power is the fact that it defies the law of homeostasis that says all things tend to equilibrium. Two five-foot parents tend to have children grow taller than they are, just as two seven-footers have smaller children. This is also true in other disparate arenas like wages around the world. In the '60s wages in Taiwan were a fraction of those in America. They are almost equal now. Parity reigns supreme in most venues but it does not seem to in power struggles. At one time females were taken advantage of in the workplace then inane laws were enacted that could cause a man to be fired for complimenting a woman on her attire. The twentieth century depicted magical potions like Spanish Fly to offset lethargy in ladies. One hundred years later we find romantic profundity flip-flopping with Viagra the elixir used by those fair maidens to enhance the sexual proclivity of the male partners.

During the Cold War era paranoia permeated the minds of the masses over the threat of nuclear war. But no one thought a thing about the proliferation of handguns and Uzis that were being used to rob and maim. The AK-46/47 has been responsible for more deaths than all the nuclear weapons combined. Even more paradoxical is the security in America. Prior to 9/11 security was pretty loose due to America's underlying nature of freedom. But after the World Trade Tower attack security was more prevalent than in a communist country or Israel. For awhile airport agents were confiscating nail files that couldn't harm a fly. Another pendulum swing took place with desegregation. First there was rampant abuse and kids in poor schools could not attend better schools. Then the Brown vs. Board of Education legislation led to the busing of kids to places they didn't even want to be.

From a more personal perspective those one-time boozers who never hit the bed sober become crazed evangelists once off the booze. They often become intolerant of anyone having a glass of wine with dinner. Born-again Christians have a similar predilection. They see salvation and can't stand those who don't see what they see. In 1919 the teetotalers got enough power to pass a constitutional amendment called Prohibition aimed at saving the nations innocent women from the insidious booze hounds. The intent was to return husbands home at night from the local pubs and to ensure the welfare of women. The amendment did exactly what it was intended to stop. It became the death knell for legitimate brewers and their legitimate distributors and created a criminal underground that took over the business of supplying alcohol. Then the unspeakable occurred. The law led to a proliferation of speakeasies frequented by both young men and young women who would never have been found dead in a corner pub with the old-timers. The titillating experience of a soiree underground launched one of America's most lurid periods during the roaring '20s. The world seems to see a problem and then over-corrects to a fault.

The above would suggest that every time we pass a law we lose a freedom. Do we need some laws? Of course we do! But the more laws the less freedom. In Communist China a person can never live anywhere the government decides is not in their best interest. Who has the right to decide where you can live or work? No one! Laws are needed to protect society from terrorists and criminals. But when looked at closely most laws are based on political agendas deemed right for the majority by some minority interest. Such laws end up destroying freedom from the inside.

Myth as the Panacea of Power for Wannabes

Catherine the Great & Napoleon Bonaparte Were Mystical Mavens

Catherine the Great had a mythical sense of her destiny that conjures up images of the Amazon princess Wonder Woman of TV lore. The German teen was sent to Russia to marry the grandson of Peter the Great. She did bear an heir to the throne as expected but the child was taken from her and she was of no further need for either Peter or his mother Elizabeth. Catherine escaped into the fantasyland of books to survive. An occasional lover assuaged her distress but when Empress Elizabeth died Catherine was told that her husband Peter would place his mistress on the throne. Rather than end up in a convent or worse Catherine tattooed Wonder Woman on her psyche and rose up and crushed Peter.

In her memoir Catherine wrote, "I lived a life for 18 years from which ten others would have gone crazy and twenty in my place would have died of melancholy."

The fantasy imagery from years of introspection rescued her. When told she was about to be destroyed, the indomitable woman walked boldly into the barracks of her guard and donned a Captain's uniform replete with sword. She mounted her white stallion Brilliant full-straddle, not the thing any self-respecting female could do in that era. That was the province of men not women, for many psycho-sexual reasons. Catherine addressed the guard saying, "Any man who wants to shoot your empress now is your time." No one raised a hand and she boldly led them into a confrontation with Peter, defeated him, and returned to take over the throne of all Mother Russia that at the time represented one-seventh of the globe. Had Catherine capitulated to the role of a submissive female she would never have become the longest-reigning female head of state in history.

Catherine wrote in her memoir, "I have the most reckless audacity." Never before or since has a woman dared lead a nation the size of Mother Russia. Knowing she was operating in a unique arena she very astutely maneuvered the various factions to ensure her future. She astutely knew that a woman could not lead if she didn't come across with similar qualities and traits of a male leader. Ambassador Harris validates her approach when he wrote, "Catherine has a masculine force of mind and wants the more manly virtues." Catherine reigned with an iron-fisted style, executing those that were in her way and sleeping with those who could be of help.

In his memoirs written in St. Helena, Napoleon spoke of his allegiance to taking charge when in charge with comments like, "Keep acquiring more and more power. All the rest is chimerical." For such a diabolical leader to gain power they must go beyond the bounds of reality and see themselves as mythical. Napoleon actually became a bit deluded about his mortality. In one crazed moment he screamed, "If I lose my throne I will bury the world beneath my ruins." Mania was Napoleon's friend and fiend. Testimony to his maniacal need for speed at any cost was his words, "I will lose a man but never a moment." Biographers spoke of him cheating at cards rather than face the ignominy of losing.

Napoleon rose quickly to power in France in the absence of many talented military leaders who had been wiped out in the French Revolution and the Reign of Terror. But when in charge he hastily crowned himself emperor. Convinced of his invincibility in battle he went on a messianic rampage throughout Europe. "I can divine everything in the future," were words said more for effect than to be believed. Such a deluded sense of power is often born of the insecurity that they aren't quite sure of their success. Once a dream comes to fruition it must be authenticated. The way to do that is through the exercise of power. Early in his career he would write of his imaginative fantasies, "I was full of dreams. I saw myself founding a religion then marching into Asia."

Napoleon's mounting mania and insatiable need for speed were born of his battle with manic-depression. Studies have shown a high correlation between those with bipolar disease, elevated sexuality, and insatiable need for power. They tend to be intensely driven, but success in such a hyperactive state doesn't come without a price. Such people are bedeviled by extreme swings in mood with exhilaration soon turning to depression. One day they are on cloud nine and invincible and the next they are debilitated by despondency. They vacillate between the indestructible warrior and loathsome loser. While up they are grandiose with a decreased need for sleep and armed with a racing mental and physical persona. When down they suffer from severe melancholy, apprehension, and depressed feelings that sabotage everything they do. In her book *Touched with Fire* (1993) Kay Jamison wrote:

"Hypomanics have increased energy, intensified sexuality, increased risk-taking, persuasiveness, self-confidence and heightened productivity all linked with increased achievement and accomplishment."

Napoleon rose to power in a kind of euphoric state. When in a manic mood he was mesmerizing and oozed energy that affected everyone in his presence. Associates saw him as superhuman. On his memorable march across Europe he pulverized the Austrians, Prussians, and Russians. But on arriving in Moscow he confronted a city that had been burned and pillaged by the Russians. The conquering hero had been idolized when he arrived in Cairo and put on a carriage and eulogized as a conquering king. In Moscow he became lost in his megalomania and depression set in and he retired to his tent unable to function. With the onset of winter he lost half a million men of his Grande Army. Without a leader capable of leading they were sitting ducks for the Russians. Psychiatrists Hermann & Lief wrote, "The very mania that gave him such advantages in battle doomed him to waste his victories and destroy his empire." Speed was Napoleon's forte. When up he was like an energized bunny and would dictate to four secretaries at a time. On one manic four-day ride across Europe he killed four horses. He never slept or rested and even changed clothes. Such behavior led his valet Constant to say, "I never comprehended how his body could endure such fatigue during his endless trek across Europe, yet he enjoyed almost continuously the most perfect health." At Elba one of his captors, a British Colonel, told the press:

"I have never seen a man in any situation of life with so much personal activity. He appears to take much pleasure in perpetual movement and in seeing those who accompany him sink under fatigue."
(Hermann & Lieb 1994 p. 145)

The Power of Mythical Mentoring

Catherine the Great & Napoleon Exemplify the Process

Both Catherine the Great and Napoleon Bonaparte were indomitable spirits who used an inner fire to burn their way into history books. Neither of these powerbrokers had a childhood that would have suggested such monumental success. Such power transcends things like luck and education or even talent. Some deep inner force is at work to elevate such people above the pack. They were certainly different than the norm but were different in eerily similar ways. Both had a kind of messianic mania that was imprinted by mythical heroes out of books they read early in life. Catherine wrote, "Voltaire and Plutarch fortified my soul." Napoleon actually wrote an apocryphal response to Goethe's classic Faust with a soliloquy on his own mania for success saying, "What fury drives me to my own destruction."

Like European male leaders of the time Catherine had a long list of concubines and courtesans to sate her passions. Her audacious courage and ability to take risks were legend. In many respects Catherine seduced men the way men traditionally seduce women. She wrote, "There is no woman bolder than I. And I am sustained by ambition alone." She was also quite philosophic and a bit precognitive, predicting the coming French Revolution in 1788 and the coming of a great man to save the nation. She wrote in her diary these prophetic words:

"When will this Caesar come? Oh! Come he will, make no doubt about it, there will be another Ghengis. That will be Europe's fate. You can depend on it. If France survives, she will be stronger than she has ever been. All she needs is a superior man, greater than his contemporaries, greater perhaps than an entire age. Has he already been born? Will he come? Everything depends on that."

Catherine's superior man had already been born in Corsica in 1760. Who was he? Napoleon Bonaparte! The Little Corsican was a huge force that came to fulfill Catherine's prediction. And ironically it would be in Russia that he would suffer his most devastating setback. Napoleon turned out to be a leader with similar egalitarian values as Catherine as shown by his Napoleonic Code. Catherine had freed the serfs and enacted the first general education in Russia. Each had a Utopian sense of protecting the masses but were tyrants when it came to dealing with those who didn't accept their policies. The Little General wrote, "Combine absolute power, constant supervision and fear." A lesser ego would not have been so inclined. Napoleon had an omnipotent sense that emanated from an indomitable will shown by his statement, "I am destined to change the face of the world. God gave me the will and the force to overcome all obstacles."

One biographer wrote that "Napoleon's only friend were books." In his teens Napoleon wrote a poem titled Young Werther to counter Goethe's The Sorrows of Young Werther *that offers insight into his raging fear of failure with words validating his inner torment:*

"What fury drives me to my own destruction?…Life is a burden to me because I taste no pleasure and all is pain to me, because the men with whom I live, and probably always shall live, have ways so different from mine as the moon from the sun."

Both of these power brokers kept journals and both were loners. Each was highly enamored of larger-than-life ideas that led them to see life through a mythical filter. When Peter's mother passed Catherine was thirty-three. When told that Peter had issued orders to take her prisoner she went beyond reason and took over Mother Russia as a fearless female to be reckoned with. Napoleon experienced a similar epiphany at age twenty-four in the Battle of Lodi. The Little General was assigned the task of fighting a combined force of Italians and Austrians twice the size of his fledgling army. The power elite, not enamored with his arrogance, saw this opportunity to teach the upstart a lesson in humility. The decisive battle took place in April of 1796 with his 30,000 French troops engaging combined forces of 70,000 Austrians and Italians. Napoleon concentrated fire on one area and when that was breached the equilibrium was broken and he moved in for the kill. Against insurmountable odds the Little Corsican won a battle no one expected him to win and made him believe in his destiny. He retired to his tent and wrote in his journal, "I am a superior being."

In St. Helena he wrote of the transformation that took place that day in Lodi. The wannabe military genius wrote of his omnipotent attitude in what Joseph Campbell defined as, "The symbolic way a man will discover his true identity." Napoleon said, "It was only after Lodi that I realized I was a superior being and conceived the ambition of performing great things which hitherto had filled my thoughts only as a fantastic dream." (Landrum 1995 p. 127)

The Napoleon Complex is about the insecure being motivated to be more than would otherwise be possible. The little man with the big soul! A man who didn't like Napoleon, Prince Tallyrand, gave him the ultimate tribute, saying, "His career is the most extraordinary that has occurred in one thousand years. He was clearly the most extraordinary man I ever saw." His mortal enemy at Waterloo, the Duke of Wellington, offered further testimony, writing, "Napoleon was not a personality, but a principle. The Corsican's presence on the field of battle was equivalent of 40,000 soldiers." Madame Germaine de Stael despised Napoleon but still said of him, "That intrepid warrior is the most profound thinker and the most extraordinary genius in history."

The charismatic power of Napoleon was never more apparent than that memorable afternoon on the fields near Grenoble after he had escaped from his exile on the island of Elba. With a small band of men the fearless one jumped on a ship and landed on the shores of France on March 1, 1815. When King Louis XVIII heard of his escape he sent Napoleon's archenemy, General Ney, to take him prisoner or kill him. Ney was fortified with one thousand skilled soldiers to combat the small band of vigilantes. In what historians describe as Napoleon's finest moment the charismatic leader saw the situation and made a move so characteristic of his rise to power. When engaged he dropped his weapons and walked toward Ney's small army. Ney ordered him to stop or be shot. Refusing the order Napoleon kept walking and screaming to the men, "Kill your emperor if you wish." Ney ordered the men to fire. No one fired. The soldiers were in awe of the brave little man who had captivated a nation. They dropped their weapons and yelled back at the mesmerizing leader, "Vive l' Empereur."

Napoleon's band now included one thousand men as he marched to regain his throne. The king heard of the event and fled Paris capitulating power to the inscrutable Corsican. At St. Helena Napoleon wrote, "Before Grenoble I was an adventurer; at Grenoble I was a reigning prince" (Landrum 1995 p. 132). Such was the awesome power of personality. Balzac became enamored of Napoleon and wrote, "Before him did ever a man gain an empire simply by showing his hat?" A lieutenant once said, "That devil of a man exercises a fascination on me that I cannot explain. When I am in his presence I am ready to tremble like a child. He could make me go through the

eye of a needle and throw myself into the fire." Napoleon's wife Josephine was bedazzled at first, then, in shock of the hyper-energy permeating Napoleon's actions, wrote,
"I am alarmed at the energy which animates all his doings."

Empowerment Self-Assessment

SOURCE: Landrum's Research especially book: *Profiles of Power & Success* **(1996)**

Being able to influence others is critical to gaining respect and power. To find if you are empowered or need to be answer the questions: 1 = seldom, 2 = not often, 3 = middle ground, 4 = often, 5 = always

		DISAGREE	?	AGREE

1.	OTHERS TEND TO BE INFLUENCED BY MY SUGGESTIONS	1	2	3	4	5
2.	I USE ALL THE SYMBOLS AT MY COMMAND TO GET THINGS DONE	1	2	3	4	5
3.	I AM HIGHLY SELF-SUFFICIENT & SELF-MOTIVATED	1	2	3	4	5
4.	I FIND THAT THREATS & PUNITIVE ACTION ARE THE ONLY THINGS THAT WORK FOR MANY PEOPLE	1	2	3	4	5
5.	IF I WIN A TROPHY I PROUDLY DISPLAY IT FOR ALL TO SEE	1	2	3	4	5
6.	I REALLY FEEL THE ENDS DO JUSTIFY THE MEANS IN MOST THINGS	1	2	3	4	5
7.	I TEND TO REWARD THOSE WHO DO WELL & PUNISH THOSE WHO DON'T	1	2	3	4	5
8.	I BELIEVE IT IS ESSENTIAL TO HAVE GOOD INTERPERSONAL RELATIONS WITH SUBORDINATES AND IT IS MY DUTY TO MAKE THEM BETTER	1	2	3	4	5
9.	INDEPENDENCE IS MY FORTE	1	2	3	4	5
10.	I HAVE BEEN CRITICIZED FOR HAVING A PHILOSOPHIC WORLD VIEW	1	2	3	4	5
11.	I TRULY BELIEVE THAT HE WHO HAS THE GOLD MAKES THE RULES	1	2	3	4	5
12.	I AM ENERGIZED BY LIFE'S POSSIBILITIES, NOT BY WHAT IS EXPECTED	1	2	3	4	5
13.	I BELIEVE IN THE ADAGE, "AN EYE FOR AN EYE, A TOOTH FOR A TOOTH"	1	2	3	4	5
14.	I TRY TO GET THE BEST TITLE SINCE IT IS WHAT HELPS ME BE EFFECTIVE	1	2	3	4	5
15.	I FIND THAT AUTHORITY IS CRITICAL TO MY ABILITY TO LEAD	1	2	3	4	5
16.	MANY FRIENDS LOOK TO ME FOR LEADERSHIP ON CRUCIAL ISSUES	1	2	3	4	5
17.	FRIENDS TELL ME I HAVE SUPERIOR SALESMANSHIP ABILITY	1	2	3	4	5
18.	THERE ARE TIMES WHEN THE TRUTH MUST BE MODIFIED TO FIT THE SITUATON OR THINGS JUST DON'T GET DONE	1	2	3	4	5
19.	TAPPING INTO PERSONNEL TALENTS IS KEY TO ACHIEVING SUCCESS	1	2	3	4	5
20.	FRIENDS OFTEN SEE ME AS AMBITIOUS & FEARLESS	1	2	3	4	5

ADD UP YOUR SCORES AND TOTAL HERE:_____

Your score will range between 20 & 100 with the highest scores representing the most empowered:

100–80   **EMPOWERED.** LOOK OUT WORLD I'M ON THE MOVE—YOU WITH ME?

79–60   **POWER MODIFIED BY REASON.** LEADERSHIP POTENTIAL WITH RATIONALE

59–40   **MODERATE POWER.** MANAGEMENT SKILLS WITH LEADERSHIP ABILITY

39–20   **POWERLESS.** SHOULD WORK AS A FOLLOWER WITH EMPOWERED LEADER

"Invincibility is in oneself, vulnerability is in the opponent."—
Sun Tsu, *The Art of War*

Zone Propensity—Zone-Food for Wannabes

Based on Landrum's research on eminent athletes, entrepreneurs, leaders, artists, and scientists

DIRECTIONS: Rank yourself at #1 if you are not like the statement or #5 if you fit the statement perfectly. One mark should be made for each question and each section should be totaled for insight into that particular dimension of placing yourself in the best position for the Zone. Total each dimension and evaluate your propensity for the Flow Zone.

A. COMPLETE RELAXED EUPHORIA

1-2-3-4- 5

1. I am able to relax even at crunch time _____
2. I am able to psych-up without getting psyched out—throwing clubs _____
3. A quiet intensity pervades me; I feel I am in charge of my destiny _____
4. I can compete aggressively while having fun at competing _____
5. I know when I am aroused but can sublimate it into my play _____

_____

B. FOCUSED BEYOND DISTRACTION

1. I am able to become so absorbed in the moment that I block hecklers _____
2. Friends tell me I'm oblivious of what is happening around me _____
3. I tend to get lost in space when playing; time is of no consequence _____
4. I have been called a big kid with a giggly demeanor when competing _____
5. I can be totally oblivious of the environment—a true space cadet _____

_____

C. FLOW STATE OF AN ETHEREAL NATURE

1. I'm often lost in just doing without being distracted by life's clutter _____
2. Friends tell me that harmony through escape is my forte _____
3. I am able to get lost in the reverie of play and lose track of time _____
4. I have the ability to remain totally confident in the face of adversity _____
5. Even when upset I am able to refocus on the task at hand _____

_____

D. PHILOSOPHICAL ATTITUDE & LIFESTYLE

1. I often see the world through a unique filter that others don't see _____
2. I have been told that I have a poetic sense of life _____
3. I believe that money is nothing more than the way we keep score _____
4. I am far more interested in the essence of things than what is happening _____
5. I am able to suspend belief to escape into the wonders of stories _____

_____

E. **SELF-CONFIDENCE OR SELF-EFFICACY)**

1. I have unquestioning belief in my ability even if I haven't tried it before   _____
2. Friends say that I'm far more optimistic than the situation calls for   _____
3. If faced with a unique situation I seldom find myself without options   _____
4. I trust my instincts even when coaches or teammates disagree   _____
5. I am willing to make a move or shot without engaging the mind   _____

F. INTERNAL LOCUS OF CONTROL (CONTROL OF DESTINY)

1. I believe that I control my destiny—not some other being or dogma   _____
2. I tend to be in charge of my emotions in almost all situations   _____
3. I happily accept the responsibility for my moves and actions   _____
4. I tend to rebound well from adversity and injury   _____
5. I am willing to take charge even when I'm not in charge   _____

TOTALS   _____

ZONE PROPENSITY: Getting into that Zone arena where all things work like magic is not easy. There is no absolute as it demands the marriage of the mind, body, heart, and soul to be in complete harmony at any given time. A low score is guaranteed to keep you out of the Zone and a high one merely sets you up for the chance to enter that ethereal state that most athletes and others have visited and really want to return to. A low score on one of the above dimensions like Self-Confidence offers insight into the weakness that keeps you out of the Zone.

SCORE	ZONE POTENTIAL	PROGNOSIS
135–150	An Ethereal Presence	A special mental magic for escaping into Netherland
120–134	The Surreal Persona	Ability to get into the Zone more often than majority
100–119	Good Chance with Work	Meditation or other visualization techniques will help
85–99	Slim Chance without Change	Self-inhibiting due to cognitive interference
70–84	Not Much Chance	Mind is your opponent and emotions your foe
< 69	Little Chance	Cut off your head to find harmony

ON EACH INDIVIDUAL DIMENSION A SCORE OF 20–25 IS CONDUCIVE TO THAT TRAIT

*   A STRONG *INTERNAL LOCUS OF CONTROL* ENHANCES CONTROLLING DESTINY

*   *SELF-CONFIDENCE* OPENS VAST VISTAS FOR MAGICAL EXECUTION

*   A *PHILOSOPHICAL ATTITUDE* HELPS WITH SEEING THE ESSENCE AND OPTIMIZES PERFORMANCE

*   ESCAPE INTO AN *ETHEREAL ARENA* LETS THE MIND, BODY & SOUL SYNERGIZE

*   *FOCUS* WITHOUT REGARD TO DISTRACTION IS THE PATHWAY INTO THE ZONE

*   *RELAXED CONCENTRATION* IS THE FUEL TO OPTIMAL BEHAVIOR (see Empowerment Book 2006)

About the Author—Gene N. Landrum, PhD

Gene Landrum is a high-tech start-up executive turned educator and writer. He originated the Chuck E. Cheese concept of family entertainment among other entrepreneurial ventures and now lectures extensively on the genesis of genius—what makes great people tick. Landrum is a full time professor at International College in Naples, Florida and instructs in various doctoral programs around the United States when not on the tennis courts or golf courses of Naples and Lake Tahoe. His books in print are as follows:

Empowerment—The Edge in Sport, Business & Life (2006)

Entrepreneurial Genius—The Power of Passion (2004)

Sybaritic Genius—Sex Drive & Success (2001)

Literary Genius—The Power of the Written Word (2000)

Eight Keys to Greatness—Unlocking Your Hidden Potential (1999)

Prometheus 2000: Truth—Vision—Power (1997)

Profiles of Black Success—13 Creative Geniuses (1997)

Profiles of Power & Success—14 Geniuses Who Broke the Rules (1996)

Profiles of Female Genius—13 Women Who Changed the World (1994)

Profiles of Male Genius—13 Males Who Changed the World (1993)

> **"When it comes to geniuses, Gene Landrum wrote the book"**
> *Naples Daily News May 5, 1996*

REFERENCES FOR THE
SUPERMAN SYNDROME

Baumeister, Roy & Smart, Laura. (1996) <u>American Psychological Association, Psychological Review</u> Vol. 103 The Dark Side of High Self-Esteem.

Bygrave, William. (1997). <u>The Portable MBA of Entrepreneurship</u>, John Wiley & Sons, New York, N.Y.

Collins, James & Porras, Jerry (1999). <u>Built to Last</u>, Harper, New York, N.Y.

Drucker, Peter. (1985). <u>Innovation & Entrepreneurship</u> Harper & Row, N.Y.

Farley, Frank. (May 1986). <u>Psychology Today,</u> "Type T Personality" pg. 46–52

Franzini, Louis & Grossberg, John. (1995). <u>Eccentric & Bizarre Behaviors</u> John Wiley & Sons, N.Y.,N.Y.

Garber, Michael. (1995). <u>The E-Myth</u>. Harper Business, N. Y., N. Y.

Gardner, Howsard (1983). <u>Framing Minds</u>, Basic Books, N. Y.

Gilder, George. (1984). <u>The Spirit of Enterprise</u>. Simon & Schuster, N. Y., N. Y.

Hill, Napoleon. (1960). <u>Think & Grow Rich</u>. Fawcett Crest, N. Y.

Homer-Dixon, Thomas. (2000). <u>The Ingenuity Gap</u>, Knopf, N.Y.

Hutchison, Michael. (1990). <u>The Anatomy of Sex & Power</u>. Morrow, N.Y.

Jamison, Kay. (1994). <u>Touched with Fire</u>. The Free Press, N.Y., N.Y.

Kanter, Rosabeth. (2004). <u>CONFIDENCE—How Winning Streaks and Losing Streaks Begin & End</u>. Crown Business, New York, NY

Kraft, Ullrich. (May 2005). The Schientific American Mind, p. 16

Martens, Rainer, Vealey, Robin, & Burton, Damon. (1990). <u>Competitive Anxiety in Sport</u>. Human Kinetics Books, Champaigne, Ilinois

Peterson, Karen S. (9-14-98 pg. 6D). <u>USA Today</u> "Power, Sex, Risk"

Pickover, Clifford (1998). <u>Strange Brains and Genius</u>, William Morrow, N.Y.

Saxon, A. H. (1989). <u>P. T. Barnum—The Legend & the Man</u>, Columbia University Press, N. Y., N. Y.

Sciaberra, Chris Mathew. (1995). <u>Ayn Rand—The Russian Radical</u>, Penn State Univeristy Press,

Storr, Anthony. (1996). <u>A Study of Gurus: Saints, Sinners & Madmen Feet ofClay</u>. Free Press, N. Y., N. Y.

Szegedy-Maszak, Marianne. (Fe.b 28, 2005). <u>Mysteries of the Mind</u>, U.S. News & World Report p. 53–58

<u>Time—Collector's Edition</u>. (July 2001). "American Legends"— Builders & Titans Section, Ford, Walton, et al

Zubov, V. P. (1968). <u>Leonardo da Vinci</u>, Barnes & Noble, N.Y.

GENERAL REFERENCES

Adler, Alfred. (1979). <u>Superiority and Social Interest</u>. Norton & Co. N.Y.

Boorstin, Daniel. (1992). <u>The Creators</u>. Random House, N.Y., N.Y.

Branden, Nathaniel. (1994). <u>Six Pillars of Self Esteem</u>. Bantam, NY

Buckingham, Marcus & Coffman, Curt. (1999). <u>Rirst, Break All the Rules</u>, Simon Schuster, N. Y., N. Y.

Campbell, Joseph. (1971). <u>The Portable Jung</u>. Pneguin Books, N. Y.

Collins, James & Porras, Jerry. (1997). <u>Built to Last</u>, HarperBusiness, N.Y.

Clark, Barbara. (1988). <u>Growing Up Gifted</u>. Merrill Publishing, Columbus, Ohio

Conger, Jay. (1989). <u>The Charismatic Leader</u>, Jossey-Bass San Francisco, CA.

Csikszentmihalyi, Mihaly. (1996). <u>Creativity—Flow and the Psychology ofDiscovery & Invention</u>. Harper-Collins, N.Y.

Frankl, Victor. (1959). <u>In Search of Meaning</u>. Pockey Books, N.Y.

Gardner, Howard. (1997). <u>Extraordinary Minds</u>. Basic Books, N.Y.

Gardner, Howard. (1983). <u>Framing Minds—The Theory of Multiple Intelligences</u>. Basic Books— Harper, N.Y., N.Y.

Gardner, Howard. (1993) <u>Creating MInds</u>. Basic Books—Harper, N.Y.

Ghislin, Brewster. (1952). <u>The Creative Process</u>. Berkeley Press, Berkeley, Ca.

Gilder, George. (1984). <u>Spirit of Enterprise</u>, Simon & Schuster, N. Y.

Goleman, Daniel. (1995). <u>Emotional Intelligence,</u> Bantam, N.Y., N.Y.

Heatherton & Weinberger. (1993). <u>Can Personality Change?</u>. American Psychological Ass., Washington, D.C.

Hershmann, D. & Lieb, J. (1988). <u>The Key to Genius—Manic Depression and the Creative Life.</u> Prometheus, Buffalo, N.Y.

Hirsh, Sandra & Kummerow, Jean. (1989). <u>Life Types</u>. Warner, N.Y.

Hopkins, Jim. (Dec. 18, 2001 p. B-1), <u>USA Today</u>, "Bad Times spawn great Start-ups—Entrepreneurs Flourish when recession strikes"

Jung, Carl. (1976). <u>The Portable Jung</u>. "The Stages of Life" Penguin, N.Y.

Keirsey, David. (1987). <u>Portraits of Temperament</u>. Prometheus, Del Mar, Ca.

Keirsey, D. & Bates, M. (1984). Please Understand Me. Prometheus, Del Mar, Ca.

Klein, Burton. (1977). Dynamic Economics, Boston, Ma.

Landrum, Gene. (2004). Competitive Success in Sports & Life, Brendan Kelly Publishing, Toronto, Canada

Landrum, Gene. (2004). Entrepreneurial Genius—Power of Passion, Brendan Kelly Publishing, Toronto, Canada

Landrum, Gene. (2001) Sybaritic Genius, Genie-Vision Books, Naples, FL

Landrum, Gene. (2000). Literary Genius. Genie-Vision Books, Naples, Fl

Landrum, Gene. (1999). Eight Keys to Greatness, Prometheus Books, Buffalo

Landrum, Gene. (1997). Profiles of Black Success. Prometheus Books, Buffalo, N.Y.,

Landrum, Gene. (1996). Profiles of Power & Success. Prometheus, Buffalo, NY

Landrum, Gene. (1994). Profiles of Female Genius. Prometheus Books, Buffalo

Landrum, Gene. (1993). Profiles of Genius. Prometheus Books, Buffalo, N.Y.

Landrum, Gene. (1991). The Innovator Personality UMI Dissertation Service, Ann Arbor, Michigan

Leman, Kenneth. (1985). The Birth Order Book. Dell Publishing, N.Y.

Ludwig, Arnold. (1995). The Price of Greatness, Guilford Press, N. Y.

Ornstein, Robert. (1972). The Psychology of Consciousness. Penguin. N.Y.

Ouchi, William. (1981). Theory Z, Avon, N. Y., N. Y.

Prigogine, Ilya. (1984). Order Out of Chaos, Bantam Books, N.Y.

Rosenzweig, Mark. (1971). Biopsychology of Development, Academic Press, NY

Silver, A. David. (1985). Entrepreneurial Megabucks, Wiley, N.Y.,

Simonton, Dean Keith. (1994). Greatness. The Guilford Press, N. Y.

Sternberg. Robert. (1996). Successful Intelligence. Simon & Schuster, N.Y.,

Storr, Anthony. (1996). Feet of Clay—A Study of Gurus. Free Press, N. Y.,

Storr, Anthony. (1993). The Dynamics of Creation. Ballantine, N.Y.

Sulloway, Frank. (1996). Born to Rebel—Birth Order, Family Dynamics, & Creative Lives. Pantheon Books, N.Y., N. Y.

Walker, Harris. (2000). The Physics of Consciousness. Perseus Books, NY

Weeks, David & James, Jamie. (1995). Eccentrics: A Study of Sanity & Strangeness, Villards, N. Y., N. Y.

Wilson, Anton. (1990). Quantum Psychology, Falcon Press, Phoenix, AR

Wolinsky, Stephen. (1994). The Tao of Chaos, Bramble Books, CN

978-0-595-34697-4
0-595-34697-9

70754688R00151

Made in the USA
San Bernardino, CA
06 March 2018